KING'S COLLEGE LONDON

MEDIEVAL STUDIES

V

King's College London

Centre for Late Antique and Medieval Studies

King's College London
Centre for Late Antique and Medieval Studies

Director: Roy Wisbey

KING'S COLLEGE LONDON MEDIEVAL STUDIES

CHAUCER AND FIFTEENTH-CENTURY POETRY

edited by

JULIA BOFFEY

and

JANET COWEN

King's College London

Centre for Late Antique and Medieval Studies

1991

ISSN 0953-217X

ISBN 0 9513085 4 8

British Library Cataloguing in Publication Data

Chaucer and fifteenth-century poetry. - (King's College London
Medieval Studies; 0953-217X, 5).
1. English poetry
I. Boffey, Julia II. Cowen, Janet III. Series
821.1

ISBN 0-9513085-4-8

Printed on

Acid-free long life paper

by

Short Run Press

Exeter

1991

LIST OF CONTENTS

PREFACE

This volume of essays originated in a series of Intercollegiate Lectures given in the University of London in 1989. We would like to thank the contributors for their cheerful co-operation at all stages of the work.

We are greatly indebted to members of the King's College London Computing Centre staff, especially to Susan Kruse, without whose patient advice and assistance this book could not have been produced. We would also like to thank the two readers who read the book on behalf of the Editorial Board of King's College London Medieval Studies for their helpful comments and suggestions.

J. B.
J. C.

LIST OF EDITIONS CITED

Unless otherwise specified in individual essays, references to medieval texts are to the editions below (not all editorial diacritics have been reproduced in quotations); references to classical texts are to the relevant volumes of the Loeb Classical Library.

[Ashby] *George Ashby's Poems*, ed. by Mary Bateson, EETS ES 76 (London, 1899)

Benoit de Sainte-Maure, *Le Roman de Troie*, ed. by Léopold Constans, SATF, 6 vols (Paris, 1904-12)

Boccaccio, Giovanni, *Concerning Famous Women*, trans. by Guido A. Guarino (London, 1964)

Boccaccio, Giovanni, *De Casibus Virorum Illustrium*, ed. by Pier Giorgio Ricci and Vittorio Zaccaria, *Tutte le opere di Giovanni Boccaccio*, ed. by Vittore Branca, IX (Milan, 1983)

Bokenham, Osbern, *Legendys of Hooly Wummen*, ed. by Mary S. Sergeantson, EETS OS 206 (London, 1938)

Capgrave, John, *The Life of St. Katharine of Alexandria*, ed. by Carl Horstmann, EETS OS 100 (London, 1893)

[Charles of Orleans] *The English Poems of Charles of Orleans*, ed. by R. Steele and Mabel Day, EETS OS 215, 220 (London 1941, 1946; reprinted as one volume with bibliographical supplement 1970)

[Chaucer] *The Riverside Chaucer*, third edition, general editor Larry D. Benson (Boston, 1987)

Christine de Pisan, *Oeuvres Poétiques*, ed. by Maurice Roy, SATF, 3 vols (Paris, 1886-96)

Christine de Pizan, *The Book of the City of Ladies*, trans. by Earl Jeffrey Richards (London, 1983)

[Clanvowe] *The Works of Sir John Clanvowe*, ed. by V. J. Scattergood (Cambridge, 1975)

Colonne, Guido delle, *Historia Destructionis Troiae*, trans. by Mary Elizabeth Meek (Bloomington and London, 1974)

Court of Sapience, The, ed. by E. Ruth Harvey (Toronto, 1984)

[Dunbar] *The Poems of William Dunbar*, ed. by James Kinsley (Oxford, 1979)

[Henryson] *The Poems of Robert Henryson*, ed. by Denton Fox (Oxford, 1981)

[Hoccleve] *Hoccleve's Works*, Volume I, *The Minor Poems*, ed. by Frederick J. Furnivall, Volume II, *The Minor Poems*, ed. by I. Gollancz, EETS ES 61, 73 (London, 1892, 1925; reprinted as one volume and revised by A. I. Doyle and J. Mitchell, 1970); Volume III, *The Regement of Princes*, ed. by Frederick J. Furnivall, EETS, ES 72 (London, 1897)

Holland, Richard, *The Buke of the Howlat*, in *Longer Scottish Poems*, Volume I, *1375-1650*, ed. by P. Bawcutt and F. Riddy (Edinburgh, 1987)

James I of Scotland, *The Kingis Quair*, ed. by John Norton-Smith (Oxford, 1971)

[Lydgate] *Lydgate's Fall of Princes*, ed. by Henry Bergen, EETS ES 121-24 (London, 1918-27)

Lydgate's Minor Poems: The Two Nightingale Poems, ed. by O. Glauning, EETS ES 80 (London, 1900)

Lydgate's Reson and Sensuallyte, ed. by Ernst Sieper, EETS ES 84, 89 (London 1901, 1903)

Lydgate's Siege of Thebes, ed. by Axel Erdmann and Eilert Ekwall, EETS ES 108, 125 (London, 1911, 1930)

Lydgate's Temple of Glas, ed. by J. Schick, EETS ES 60 (London, 1891)

Lydgate's Troy Book, ed. by Henry Bergen, EETS ES 97, 103, 106, 126 (London, 1906, 1908, 1910, 1935)

The Minor Poems of John Lydgate, ed. by Henry Noble MacCracken, Part I, Religious Poems; Part II, Secular Poems, EETS ES 107, OS 192 (London, 1911, 1934)

The Pilgrimage of the Life of Man, ed. by F. J. Furnivall and Katharine B. Locock, EETS ES 77, 83, 92 (London 1899, 1901, 1904)

Lydgate, John, *The Life of Our Lady*, ed. by J. Lauritis, R. Klinefelter and V. Gallagher, Duquesne Studies, Philological Series, 2 (Pittsburgh, 1961)

Plowman's Tale, The, in *Chaucerian and Other Pieces*, ed. by Walter W. Skeat (Oxford, 1897; A Supplement, Volume 7, to *The Complete Works of Geoffrey Chaucer*, ed. by Walter W. Skeat, 6 vols, Oxford, 1894)

Skelton, John, *The Complete English Poems*, ed. by John Scattergood (Harmondsworth, 1983)

Usk, Thomas, *The Testament of Love*, in *Chaucerian and Other Pieces* (see under *Plowman's Tale* above)

CHAUCER, CHAUCERIANS AND THE THEME OF POETRY

Pamela M. King

As late as the 1960s, conceits which rendered the processes of artistic creation deliberately visible were somehow seen as crimes against sustained realism. The critical prejudices of which René Wellek (1937, 376) accused Leavis in the 1930s die hard:

> Allow me to sketch your ideal of poetry, your 'norm' with which you measure every poet: your poetry must be in serious relation to actuality, it must have a firm grasp of the actual, of the object, it must be in relation to life, it must not be cut off from direct vulgar living . . . the only question I would ask you is to defend this position more abstractly and to become conscious that large ethical, philosophical, and of course ultimately also aesthetic *choices* are involved.

As issues of artistic legitimacy have come to be questioned in the post-modern period, however, it has become commoner, particularly in novels, to force the reader to acknowledge the artifice of what he is reading, even to participate as its co-creator. Such strategy, termed metafictional (by e.g. Waugh 1984), is no longer seen as a sign of the decadent exhaustion of literary forms.

Critical discussion in this area still focuses chiefly on the modern novel, although parallel tendencies can be found which pre-date even Cervantes and Sterne in the verse narratives of Chaucer and his fifteenth-century self-styled disciples. For them too, artistic legitimacy, particularly the legitimacy of using vernacular verse forms to impart verities to their audiences, led to an aesthetic introspection far removed from the frank dramatic realism which thankfully we have, by and large, stopped finding to be the pervasive quality of their work.

Robert Payne (1963, 63) demonstrated some time ago that, although Chaucer neither inherited nor wrote an English *Ars Poetica*, there are, scattered throughout his work, evidences of his consciousness of the nature and problems of the artistic process:

> In nearly every one of his major poems there appears some variant of the 'old fields — new corn' metaphor . . . usually employed as part of the machinery introducing some acknowledged plagiarism through which we are to be conducted to the heart of the poem.

Many of the sections of Chaucer's poems which Payne quotes in support of his argument concern Chaucer's anxiety both about the validity of the artistic process itself, and about the adequacy of his medium for conveying meaning, as, for example, in *The Legend of Good Women*:

> For wel I wot that folk han here-beforn
> Of makyng ropen, and lad awey the corn;
> [And] I come after, glenynge here and there . . . (G 61-63)

Chaucer's self-consciousness is not restricted to narrative asides, however, but can assume the status of a sustained theme within an entire work. In *Troilus and Criseyde*, the narrator's voice constantly questions the validity of judgements made on characters drawn from another book which does not supply him with all the details he might wish. Most memorably, the narrator's voice remarks upon Diomede's success with Criseyde:

> And after this the storie telleth us
> That she hym yaf the faire baye stede
> The which he ones wan of Troilus;
> And ek a broche — and that was litel nede —
> That Troilus was, she yaf this Diomede.
> And ek, the bet from sorwe hym to releve,
> She made hym were a pencel of hire sleve.
>
> I fynde ek in stories elleswhere,
> Whan thorugh the body hurt was Diomede
> Of Troilus, tho wep she many a teere
> Whan that she saugh his wyde wowndes blede,
> And that she took, to kepen hym, good hede;
> And for to helen hym of his sorwes smerte,
> Men seyn — I not — that she yaf hym hire herte. (Tr 5.1037-50)

Behind these stanzas there lies the dramatic fiction of the narrator searching through accounts of the legendary infidelity looking for the truth about its nature and extent. He fails to find the information he wants in any one authority, but has to go 'elleswhere', and ultimately offers his own opinion as to the veracity of what 'men seyn'. He also expresses one opinion of his own, 'and that was litel nede', as nothing more than an incitement to emotion. By Book V, the audience of the poem has become accustomed to his asides in any case, and has learned of his unreliability: in Books I, II and III he is to be heard lauding the benefits of sexual love, in Book

IV he falls silent, only to return in Book V, increasingly converted to another view. Through his voice Chaucer has abstained from presenting a closed text, forcing the completion of the creative process, that is judgement, back upon the reader. From this arises the immensely rich critical response to a poem which resists a single reading.

In so far as the narrative voice functions in *Troilus and Criseyde* specifically to draw attention to the ethical problems of the very mechanics of composition, it exhibits metafictional tendencies. In two other of Chaucer's poems, *The House of Fame* and The Nun's Priest's Tale, the creative process itself is the major theme. Both poems apparently exist purely to examine their own processes. They are more fundamentally metatextual, exploring their own fictionality along with other aspects of the processes of their creation.

The House of Fame reflects structurally upon three conventions (Delaney 1972). Firstly it uses the dream vision in a way which casts doubts on its reliability as meaningful discourse. The dream allows for transitions between and simultaneity of different levels of consciousness, conveying the poet's matter by a variety of figural means. Dream visions by the time that Chaucer was writing depended heavily on their own enclosed system of creating meaning by the ordering of certain *topoi*. *The House of Fame* deliberately distorts, manipulates and parodies those *topoi* in order to raise questions about the dream vision as creative process. It opens with an extended *dubitatio* which questions the reliability of dreams while forcing the attendant stylistic conventions beyond all naturally acceptable limits. This excessively long and self-contradicting first sentence carries a covert level of intertextuality by parodying the opening of *Le Roman de la Rose*. The gross inflation of the passage coupled with the off-centre seasonal setting of the dream itself, the tenth of December, call into question the value of all that follows. Chaucer has thus created immediately a self-reflexive framework for his narrative, bringing the *langue* of the dream vision into conflict with his *parole*, that is, he contrivedly sets the rules against this individual example of their application.

The dream gives way to the second conventional element which is significantly relocated in the poem, the book. The book in *The House of Fame* is not a device by which the dreamer makes his transition from waking to sleeping state, but lies within the dream itself, as the dream landscape is made up of the matter of old books. The poem's logic moves from questioning the reliability of dreams to, within a dream, questioning the reliability of another vehicle of truths, books or authorities. The two are then combined within two parallel questions concerning the usefulness of a dream for the dreamer, or a book for the audience. The text is thus engaged not only in the search for its own form, but in questioning the whole nature of literary tradition, as Winthrop Wetherbee has suggested (1984, 17). He draws parallels with the narrator of *Troilus and Criseyde*, for both appear to be seeking to place their love stories in proper relation to the achievements of other poets.

The problem of authority is demonstrated in Part I of *The House of Fame*, as the dreamer-narrator unsuccessfully attempts to fuse two equally authoritative but contrary sources for the

story of Dido and Aeneas: Virgil's account, with Aeneas as hero, and Ovid's with Dido as
wronged heroine. It presents first the heroic duty which bound Aeneas ethically to leave his
lover, then shifts to a sentimental focus upon Dido the abandoned lover and Aeneas the traitor.
Of course the whole of the ensuing journey to the House of Fame serves to illustrate directly
the unreliability both of earthly fame and, vicariously, of authoritative matter; but the anxieties
so plainly exposed there have already been illustrated by the setting up of countertechniques
within the poem's process in order to undermine the premise that there can be a definitive
interpretation. At this point the poem grinds to a halt and the dream landscape becomes a
desert:

> Then sawgh I but a large feld,
> As fer as that I myghte see,
> Withouten toun, or hous, or tree,
> Or bush, or grass, or eryd lond;
> For al the feld nas but of sond
> As smal as man may se yet lye
> In the desert of Lybye. (482-88)

That 'feld . . . of sond' is the correlative of the poem's position at this point, the wasteland of a
poem robbed of its confidence in tradition. All its processes have been systematically undercut,
it is forced into a new beginning.

In that new beginning the poem must redefine itself. It does this first by moving literally
up and away from the tradition of *Le Roman de la Rose*, into a flight which is suggestive of
Dantean visionary literature. It also attempts to introduce in this new allusive context rational
scientific matter, explaining the nature of poetry as emissions of sound subject to physical
laws, as a new test of its own validity. But this material is presented as a monologue whose
rationality is entirely spurious. Its speaker, a talking bird, challenges the reader to enter into
debate with him:

> And whoso seyth of trouthe I vary
> Bid him proven the contrarye. (807-08)

The foregoing disquisition is, however, based upon a tautological premise, impossible to
refute. It is also wrapped in an impenetrable blanket of high style, parodying and thereby
exposing the authenticating effects of rhetoric. The narrator's giddiness at the height
demonstrates as great an uneasiness with this type of matter as with the first. But if discrete
discourses are exposed as limited or unreliable matter for the artistic process, the alternative,
vividly objectified in the House of Rumour, remains unmanageable:

> And somtyme saugh I thoo at ones
> A lesyng and a sad sothe sawe. (2088-89)

Not only are discrete discourses exposed as unreliable matter for the artistic process, but *The House of Fame* proposes the unreliability of all utterances, whether ordered or not. The creative process becomes, therefore, something with which the narrator constantly seeks divine assistance (Delaney 1972, ch. 6):

> 'O Crist,' thoughte I, 'that art in blysse,
> Fro fantome and illusion
> Me save!' (492-94)

The poet-narrator is self-dramatized as unequal to holding responsibility for his poem, which finally and abruptly ends at a point which is another frustrated new departure:

> Atte laste y saugh a man,
> Which that y [nevene] nat ne kan;
> But he semed for to be
> A man of gret auctorite . . . (2155-58)

Without going so far as to assume that *The House of Fame* is contrivedly unfinished, one is assailed by the impression that it has nowhere left to go, having systematically dismantled all its own structures.

Troilus and Criseyde and *The House of Fame* both reflect a deep anxiety about the validity of the poetic process. The Nun's Priest's Tale is in tone quite different, parodying the variety of discourses available to the poet in a more assertive manner which directly questions them from an ethical point of view. It presages the retraction at the end of *The Canterbury Tales* where 'translacions and enditynges of worldly vanitees' (Retr 1083-84) are rejected. The Nun's Priest's Tale extends the *moralitas* of Aesop's fable of the cock and the fox, the exposure of worldly vanity, into the very discourses employed in the telling of the tale. One critic (Aers 1986, 9) has read this as an exposure of the 'self-congratulatory way jargon of a social group works against those outside it to keep them outside'.

The problem of turning self-reflexiveness into self-emasculation experienced in *The House of Fame* is avoided in The Nun's Priest's Tale by the proposing of an alternative form of discourse. Within the Tale, Pertelot's homely wisdom performs this function without establishing for itself any serious alternative authority, but, within the frame, the discourse of the narrator seems to be proposed as a serious and ethically acceptable alternative. As the widow has no need of 'poynaunt sauce' for her meat, he needs no rhetorical colours, as the self-consciously plain style of the Tale's opening demonstrates. What follows, however, is what Stephen Knight has aptly described as 'a genial front for a cultural holocaust' (1986, 144). The cock is a parodic romantic hero: his relationship with his ladies is much more the stuff of fabliau. The matter of dream is again subject to scrutiny and debate. It is seriously deflated by the hen's suggestion that, far from being prophetic, it could simply be the product of a digestive disorder, but it then receives a much more crushing blow from its initial proponent, the dreamer, Chanticleer himself, who apparently tires of his philosophical posturing and ignores his dream altogether. In the process of the intervening debate, he heaps authority upon authority, digressing to a comic and intolerable degree, thereby devaluing the matter further. The Boethian debate about fortune, theories of music, rhetoric and the classics are all dismantled. As all the vanities of the human intellect, all attempts to systematize knowledge of the world, are rejected, so too are the rhetorical processes by which they are commonly expressed. As an exercise in metatextuality, nothing could be more orderly or more ruthless.

That Chaucer was clearly fascinated by the problem of the validity of creative writing has been identified by a number of recent critical studies. It is evident from the devices he employed to demonstrate the limitations inherent in his own vernacular fictions from within, using the modes and discourses available to him as a means of exploring and possibly of rejecting them. That the limitations and the artifice of writing had, for Chaucer, attendant ethical and philosophical connotations impels his readers to address problems of epistemology which are fundamental to many of his works. Accordingly, the very process of writing poetry is not only a recurrent and fundamental theme in Chaucer's art, but is also an important legacy which was taken up by fifteenth-century poets who felt themselves indebted to him. Ironically, for the succeeding generation of English poets, such was the status of Chaucer that the very same discourses were unassailable precisely because he had made possible 'a vision of the possibilities of his newly established literary vernacular' (Ebin 1988, 18). Hence, when the writings of fifteenth-century Chaucerians become self-reflexive, it is a much less purgative process, much more a celebratory one. Chaucer represented the inception of a new tradition all his own, a tradition which had recognizably built into it as one of its fundamental postures the mechanics of aesthetic self-examination. For those who elected to write within the Chaucerian tradition of the fifteenth century, therefore, art and artifice were quite centrally self-conscious.

> Quha wait gif all that Chauceir wrait was trew?
> Nor I wait nocht gif this narratioun
> Be authoreist, or fenȝeit of the new
> Be sum poeit, throw his inuentioun . . . (64-67)

wrote Henryson in his *Testament of Cresseid*. For him, Chaucer's value was not only as the source of inspiration for the creation of a specific new fiction, but also as a liberator who had conferred status on vernacular fictional writing. Henryson's clear testimonial to the possible veracity of fictions is available in the prologue to *The Fables*:

> Thocht feinʒeit fabils of ald poetre
> Be not al grunded vpon truth, ʒit than,
> Thair polite termes of sweit rhetore
> Richt plesand ar vnto the eir of man;
> And als the caus quhy thay first began
> Wes to repreif the of thi misleuing,
> O man, be figure of ane vther thing. (1-7)

When Henryson came to retell the story of Chanticleer and the Fox, he reversed the logical force of The Nun's Priest's Tale, using rhetoric to expose the worldly vanities of the birds. The result is a more conservative reading of the fable, but one executed in a way which makes plain its debt to the intermediary Canterbury Tale. The false premise of the three hens, that God has chosen to take their husband from them, leads them each to articulate a manner of coming to terms with their loss. Pertok approaches the problem from an ambitious stylistic height:

> 'Quha sall our lemman be? Quha sall vs leid?
> Quhen we ar sad, quha sall vnto vs sing?
> With his sweit bill he wald brek vs the breid;
> In all this warld wes thair ane kynder thing?' (*Fables* 502-05)

Sprutok, on the other hand, takes more homely comfort:

> 'Ceis, sister, off ʒour sorrow.
> ʒe be to mad, for him sic murning mais.
> We sall fair weill, I find Sanct Iohne to borrow;
> The prouerb sayis, "Als gude lufe cummis as gais." ' (*Fables* 509-12)

The timing of the joke, that the attitude-striking of the three hens is somewhat premature, is part of the plot of the fable. It is nonetheless an in-joke, for the delicious creation of the dramatic voices of the hens is possible only within the established Chaucerian rhetorical tradition, impossible without the prior existence of, for instance, a Troilus, a Pandarus or a Dorigen.

The confidence that self-styled fifteenth-century Chaucerians had in the epistemology of fiction can be seen in the manner in which they manipulate various processes employing autoreferential techniques. The remainder of this discussion is devoted to three of the most assailingly knowing poems of the period, widely divided by date and authorship, but all apparently responding to the same creative impulse. Dunbar's *The Goldyn Targe* and Skelton's *The Bowge of Court* deal specifically with the reflexive and parodic possibilities of the dream vision convention as mediated by Chaucer; the earlier poem, James I of Scotland's *Kingis Quair*, incorporates dream vision, but is more fundamentally autoreferential, collapsing in upon itself the whole question of the status of text.

Dunbar's *The Goldyn Targe* parades an ostentatiously literary language, making its concern not only the status of poetry, but its execution. The opening of the poem describes the effect of the sunrise upon the dreamer's landscape:

> Doune throu the ryce a ryvir ran wyth stremys
> So lustily agayn thai lykand lemys
> > That all the lake as lamp did leme of licht,
> Quhilk schadowit all about wyth twynkling glemis
> That bewis bathit war in secund bemys
> > Throu the reflex of Phebus visage brycht:
> > On every syde the hegies raise on hicht,
> The bank was grene, the bruke was full of bremys,
> > The stanneris clere as stern in frosty nycht. (28-36)

As the sun sheds reflected light upon the imagined landscape, the language which signifies that landscape for the reader is also adorned by the use of aureation, literally linguistic gilding. This self-reflexive conceit is signalled by the ostentatious paralleling of the rising of the sun and the first person narrator in the opening:

> Rycht as the stern of day begouth to schyne
> Quhen gone to bed war Vesper and Lucyne
> > I raise and by a rosere did me rest;
> Up sprang the goldyn candill matutyne. (1-4)

The relationship is re-emphasized at the opening of the dream by close verbal echoes of that first stanza (Ebin 1988, 76), complicating the interface between the poet and his matter through his intermediary fictional role as dreamer. These relationships are made explicit towards the close of the poem, as the metaphors of embellishment are less ambiguously applied to the poetic process. The dreamer awakens and addresses Chaucer directly as 'rose of rethoris all'

(253), who ' This mater coud illumynit have full bryght' (258), who was 'all the lycht' (259) of English. By adding Lydgate and Gower, who 'Oure rude langage has clere illumynate' (266), Dunbar acknowledges the tradition. The final stanza, the envoy, is addressed to the poem itself, ending with the instruction:

> . . . draw the out of sicht.
> Rude is thy wede, disteynit, bare and rent;
> Wele aucht thou be aferit of the licht. (277-79)

The core of the poem, the dream itself, has more complex reflexive properties. The persona of the dreamer parodies the usual naive figure in search of information about love. He is an eavesdropper, even a voyeur, of misogynistic tendencies, hiding in the bushes, watching beautiful ladies disembark from a ship. The fictional role of dreamer is never allowed entirely to usurp the actual role of poet, as the abrupt stanza of digression on the subject of the dreamer's inadequacies at relaying his dream (64-72) ensures. His activities as passive observer are interrupted by Venus, after which his Reason is assailed by a variety of ladies all having figural names closely allied to *Le Roman de la Rose* tradition. The dreamer-poet is thus drawn into his own aesthetic edifice, which takes on increasingly pageant-like qualities, suggesting yet another implicit metalanguage at work, for the course of the dream with its allegorical battle between ranks of emblematic adversaries is reminiscent of a court disguising. The disguising conventionally broke down the barriers between art and reality by formally embracing its audience, generally through a dance, at the end, in a manner comparable to the way in which this poem incorporates within the construction of its meaning the circumstances of its own creation (King 1984).

The poem not only explores the construction of dream vision, but simultaneously parodies it. The accepted decorum is reversed because here the dreamer is a reluctant lover who is assailed by predatory womanhood. This reversal is then exploited as a means by which the poem can not only celebrate poetic endeavour but also impart something ethical. The light image which links the creative process with the creative matter takes on a moral connotation within the dream, as the dreamer's Reason is blinded by the onslaught. This moment is marked by a withdrawal from poetic diction into Scots vernacular:

> Thai fyrit gunnis wyth powder violent
> Till that the reke raise to the firmament;
> > The rochis all resownyt wyth the rak,
> > For rede it semyt that the raynbow brak. (238-41)

Simultaneously as the collapse of the dreamer's moral edifice is signalled by the blinding of his Reason, the poetic edifice disintegrates. The former is not restored, but the dreamer awakes to resume and reassert his role of poet-creator at the end.

Skelton's *The Bowge of Court* uses the Chaucerian dream vision's characteristic placing of poetic matter at a remove from reality to more pointedly satirical ends. The poem exploits in particular the dream vision's defamiliarizing effects. The conventionally naive narrator, whose creation sets up a point of view which abstains from directing the reader, becomes here a failed or would-be courtier in order to expose the dog-eat-dog values of the Tudor court.

The dream in *The Bowge of Court* takes place in autumn, the season of unreliable dreams, so, for those well-versed in dream-lore (Spearing 1976, 197), the potential of this dream as a vehicle for meaning is undercut from the start. It is not inspired by an ancient authority, but occurs at a moment of failed creative inspiration: the narrator begins by lauding great authorities of the past but goes on:

> Wherby I rede theyr renome and theyr fame
> Maye never dye, bute evermore endure.
> I was sore moved to aforce the same,
> But Ignorance full soone dyde me dyscure
> And shewed that in this arte I was not sure;
> For to illumyne, she sayde, I was to dulle,
> Avysynge me my penne awaye to pulle . . .
>
> Thus up and down my mynde was drawen and cast
> That I ne wyste what to do was beste;
> Soo sore enwered that I was, at the laste,
> Enforsed to slepe and for to take some reste. (15-32)

The conventional relationship between dream and text is that the text recounts the remembered meaningful dream, whereas here the dream is an alternative to the generation of the text. The poem therefore ends at the point at which the narrator is able to write the poem. Like *The Goldyn Targe*, where lack of success in love is compensated by success in writing, here lack of success as a courtier and inability to find favour within the dream world leads to success in art. Of course the dream world here is the real world; the waking state and retreat into art is the escape:

> And as they came, the shypborde faste I hente,
> And thoughte to lepe; and even with that woke,
> Caughte pen and ynke, and wroth this lytell boke. (530-32)

The poem is akin to the so-called 'self-begetting novel', one which contains an 'account, usually first person, of the development of a character to a point at which he is able to take up and compose the novel we have just finished reading' (Waugh 1984, 14, quoting Kellman 1976, 1245). The poem is also self-undercutting, employing techniques not unlike those observed in *The House of Fame*: the time of year is unreliable, the narrator prey to Ignorance. Within the dream he is characterized as Dread, not only naive, but inadequate, not only unable to interpret what he dreams, but tantalizingly unable to mediate sufficient reliable information to make confident interpretation possible. The Tudor court is satirized through one excluded from it, one who fails to convey information because he is told obvious lies and excluded from conversations:

> But there was poyntynge and noddynge with the hede,
> And many wordes sayde in secrete wyse;
> They wandred ay and stode styll in no stede.
> Me thoughte alwaye Dyscymular dyde devyse;
> Me, passynge sore, myne herte than gan aryse;
> I dempte and drede theyr talkynge was not good. (421-26)

This leads to the construction of an artfully unreliable text, made up of fragments of incomprehensible information. Hence the poet ingeniously manages to construct informative satire whilst systematically de-authorizing his text. Although Skelton later abandoned the stylistic and formal solutions which the fifteenth century inherited from Chaucer (Ebin 1988, 193), he nonetheless developed the device of the naive narrator as the satirist's smoke-screen: the eponymous bird of *Speke Parott*, all-seeing but uncomprehending, is, in many respects, the apotheosis of the Chaucerian dreamer.

    The Kingis Quair, though much earlier than the other two poems discussed, has been reserved until last because its metatextual processes on Chaucerian models are most complex. It too borrows the ground of dream vision, as well as philosophical dialogue, complaint and autobiography, but it is fundamentally a celebration of poetic endeavour, entirely without parody. If the creation of *The Bowge of Court* begins at the end of the poem, it is difficult to determine where *The Kingis Quair* begins and ends, indeed, whether, according to its own logic, it begins at all. In autobiography, creator, narrator and protagonist are one, the narrative being constructed from memory in which the narrator's former self is the protagonist. When the former self, the protagonist, also engages in creative activity, the narrative becomes self-conscious artifice. Thematically the book is inspired by Boethius's *Consolation of Philosophy*, so its premise is that the events of the life described are to be paralleled with events in art and described in their terms (Ebin 1974, 322). In fact, the poem specifically suggests that poetic composition is a mirror of life's process (Quinn 1980, 337-38): youth is equated with compositional failure, as the poet laments that he has ' . . . in my tyme more ink and paper spent / To lyte effect' (87-88).

The equation of life with art, specifically the life described within the process of the poem, is sustained at all levels. The sea voyage, introduced at an early point in the narrative, is the actual sea voyage during which the protagonist was captured and imprisoned in his youth; it is also a stock literary metaphor for the voyage of life, and here, explicitly, a figure for the compositional process:

> The rokkis clepe I the prolixitee
> Of doubilnesse that doith my wittis pall:
> The lak of wynd is the deficultee
> In enditing of this lytill trety small:
> The bote I clepe the mater hole of all:
> My wit, vnto the saile that now I wynd
> To seke conning, though I bot lytill fynd. (120-26)

Literary authority and literary allusion become a mirror for life so that even the direct speech of the protagonist is borrowed from Chaucer's poems (Ebin 1974, 324; MacQueen 1961, 118). He is Palamon and Arcite in one, he is Troilus, he is the Man in Black of *The Book of the Duchess*. Experience and authority become one. The nightingales' song has revelatory force within the prison narrative: the setting for this is described but what is important is the 'text' (229). The text is virtually the same as the birds' roundel from *The Parliament of Fowls*.

The mirroring effect becomes more complex when the protagonist falls into his dream at the heart of the poem. He enters it from a 'real' world composed of literary allusion, so much of which has already resembled dream vision that the reader may be forgiven for forgetting that what has been presented so far was intended to represent recollected historical reality. Consonant with this, in the heavenly temple within the dream, the dreamer sees all of world history as a matter of art. Inevitably the dream at the centre of so textually conscious a poem draws upon *The House of Fame* in its continued foregrounding of the relationships between dream and reality, history and art:

> Here bene the princis faucht the grete batailis,
> In mynd of quhom ar mad the bukis newe;
> Here ben the poetis that the sciencis knewe,
> Throwout the world, of lufe in thair suete layes,
> Suich as Ouide and Omer in thair dayes. (591-95)

The past is peopled by poets, events are *topoi*.

Returning to the waking state, the protagonist, still the victim of unrequited love, is rewarded by grace, as a dove promises him delivery from his plight. That very promise takes the form of another piece of text, engraved on a branch, read, 'with hertfull glaidnesse' (1256), and pinned up in the prison. Paradoxically, of course, the protagonist is to be released from prison by being bound in love's chains, although the true prison is the prison of art from which life cannot escape. The poem presents the indissolubility of life and art which has caused problems in the interpretation of Jan Van Eyck's contemporary painting of the Arnolfini wedding, in which the mirror behind the couple shows not the artist as painter, but the artist as one of the pair of witnesses standing in the doorway (Panofsky 1966, 203). The picture both witnesses to the historical event and mirrors the 'real' witnessing of the same event.

In many ways, *The Kingis Quair* displays some of the techniques of The Wife of Bath's Prologue, where ostensible experience is in fact a paste-up of authoritative texts. In this poem, however, the situation is greatly complicated by the fact that the protagonist not only has no existence outside the literary allusions from which he is constructed, like the Wife of Bath, but that he is also presented as being the same person as the author. The poem is an autobiography as much about the maturation of the creative process as about the maturation of the narrator. The narrator is an older version of the protagonist who is both memory and fiction, the past is only the matter of art. At one further remove from that still is the poem, for it is presented in the beginning as a rewriting: it opens by describing the past circumstances in which the text we are about to read was composed; the narrator was reading a book in order to put himself to sleep, but its content made him too thoughtful for sleep so he wrote the poem instead.

If it may be argued that 'All the world's a stage, / And all the men and women merely players' (*As You Like It*, II, 7. 139-40), *The Kingis Quair* proposes that all the world's a book. Its thoroughgoing intertextuality is sophisticated and confident, for it celebrates an art form which regarded itself closely in many ways and for a long time, indeed one in which the process of writing poetry had become not only a legitimate subject for treatment by poets, but an element of convention in vernacular poetry of the Chaucerian tradition.

Queen Mary and Westfield College
University of London

REFERENCES

Aers, David, 1986	*Chaucer*, Brighton
Delaney, Sheila, 1972	*Chaucer's House of Fame: The Poetics of Sceptical Fideism*, Chicago
Ebin, Lois A., 1974	Boethius, Chaucer, and *The Kingis Quair*, *PQ*, 53, pp. 321-41
———— 1988	*Illuminator, Makar, Vates: Visions of Poetry in the Fifteenth Century*, Lincoln, Nebraska, and London
Kellman, Steven G., 1976	The Fiction of Self-Begetting, *MLN*, 91, pp. 1243-56
King, Pamela M., 1984	Dunbar's *Golden Targe*: a Chaucerian Masque, *SSL*, 19, pp. 115-31
Knight, Stephen, 1986	*Geoffrey Chaucer*, Oxford
MacQueen, John, 1961	Tradition and the Interpretation of the *Kingis Quair*, *RES*, 12, pp. 117-31
Panofsky, Erwin, 1966	*Early Netherlandish Painting*, I, Cambridge, Mass.
Payne, Robert O., 1963	*The Key of Remembrance: a study of Chaucer's Poetics*, New Haven and London
Quinn, William, 1981	Memory and the Matrix of Unity in *The Kingis Quair*, *ChauR*, 15, pp. 332-55
Spearing, A. C., 1976	*Medieval Dream Poetry*, Cambridge
Waugh, Patricia, 1984	*Metafiction: the Theory and Practice of Self-conscious Fiction*, London
Wellek, René, 1937	Literary Criticism and Philosophy, *Scrutiny*, 5, pp. 375-83
Wetherbee, Winthrop, 1984	*Chaucer and the Poets: an essay on Troilus and Criseyde*, Ithaca and London

MADNESS AND TEXTS: HOCCLEVE'S *SERIES*

James Simpson

The narrator of Hoccleve's *Complaint* is presented as having experienced a period of madness; in his recovery, he relates that he has received some consolation from a book:

> This othar day a lamentacion
> of a wofull man in a boke I sye,
> to whome word[e]s of consolation
> Reason gave spekynge effectually;
> and well easyd myn herte was ther-by;
> for when I had a while in the boke red,
> with the speche of Reason was I well fed. (309-15)[1]

What we seem to have here is reference to a situation in which a man, in his real life, was helped by a book. We might, not unreasonably, understand this as an autobiographical reference, since the narrator is called ' Thomas Hoccleve', and he is presented as a poet, with the same profession (a clerk in the Office of the Privy Seal) as the historical Hoccleve. Apparently uncontentious autobiographical readings of this kind were adopted by Hoccleve's first modern editor, F. J. Furnivall, who read ostensibly autobiographical passages in Hoccleve's work as in fact autobiographical (Burrow 1982b, 389-90).

In the light of the dominant currents in twentieth-century literary criticism, however, we might want to pause before reading this stanza as referential in the simple way an autobiographical reading would imply. New Criticism, Structuralism, and Deconstruction have each, for their different reasons, dislodged texts from their historical context. New Criticism privileges literary discourse by separating it from all other forms of discourse, including history: literature should be read on its own terms, 'as literature'; Structuralism begins from the premise that meaning is produced out of the play of conventions belonging to pre-established codes, rather than by reference to 'reality'; and Deconstruction focuses on the way in which texts call into question the very dynamics by which meaning is produced: the deconstructive act is to define how texts are ultimately expressive of nothing but their own textuality.

The net effect of this series of movements has been to render readers wary of any simple connection, or of any connection whatsoever, between 'literature' and 'life'. Looking back to the small passage cited above, we would not, in the light of these intellectual currents, read it as straight autobiography; in a structuralist reading, for example, we would instead look to the conventions which govern this scene. When we do so, we see that the very book which Thomas picks up (a consolation),[2] itself offers the model of a complaining man who is comforted by Reason. We see that the narrator's persona is itself shaped by a literary tradition. As soon as the *Complaint* has made its referential gesture, it falls into line as one further member of a specifically literary tradition, whose meaning is produced by reference to that tradition.[3]

Not only does the stanza seem to collapse back into a purely conventional world, but it also serves, ultimately, to draw the reader's attention to the *Complaint* as a text. It has recently been pointed out that while we read this particular stanza, we tend to ignore the textuality of Hoccleve's own poem: ' . . . as in Chaucer's *Parliament of Fowls*, the record of reading serves only to confirm the actual reader's tendency to forget that what *he* is reading is also, in fact, a book' (Burrow 1984, 262). This is certainly true of this stanza, and Hoccleve uses the same device in the *Dialogue*. But this tendency to forget that we are reading a text is only the prelude to our recognition that what we have before us is very much a text: in the *Dialogue with a Friend*, immediately following the *Complaint*, the *Complaint* is presented to us as a text, freshly written, and read out to the friend; the fiction of the poem suddenly becomes not so much that we have heard the record of Thomas's complaint, but rather that we have ourselves read Thomas's complaint as he wrote it. Just as the momentary gesture towards referentiality seems to collapse back into the conventional, so too does the momentary gesture towards the non-textual collapse back into textuality: Thomas's *Complaint* is as much a text as the 'lamentacion / of a wofull man' which he reads in the consolation.[4]

So our sense of the 'real life' gestured at in this stanza collapses under superficial scrutiny, as we recognize the stanza to be part of a literary tradition, and to be itself a text: as much as the book referred to, the apparent 'real life' in this stanza comes from the world of books, from, indeed, the very kind of book Thomas picks up. The fact that writing slips so readily and so constantly back into literary convention and textuality makes many readers, myself included, uneasy, since, for my part, what interests me is the ways in which literature springs out of, and answers to, conditions of lived reality.

In this essay I want to focus on Hoccleve's *Series*, since here Hoccleve points insistently to the textuality of his work. If ever there was a poem whose composition is part of its own subject, it is Hoccleve's *Series*. But when we look to this work, we see that Hoccleve is himself intimately aware of the kinds of problem I have raised, and that he so constructs his text in order to resist this 'collapse' into both textuality and the merely conventional.

In the first section, I will simply define the means by which Hoccleve insistently points to, or, in one case, effaces the textuality of the different parts of the *Series*; in Section II, I will attempt to define Hoccleve's strategy as a poet in either carefully drawing attention to, or effacing, the textuality of his writing. And in Section III, I will go on to show how the relationship of *Complaint* to *Dialogue* offers a critique of the literary conventions within which Hoccleve is working. Throughout the entire essay, I am far from wanting to deny the value of the categories 'textuality' or 'convention'; instead, I wish to deploy these categories to show how Hoccleve, at any rate, might resist their anti-historical implications.

I

The *Series* is a linked group of works in verse and prose, written probably between 1419 and 1422.[5] It proceeds in the following order:

(1) A Prologue, in which the narratorial 'I' (whom I shall call ' Thomas' throughout this essay) complains of his melancholy, and relates that he could no longer hold in his grief, such that the following morning he 'braste out'; there follows

(2) the *Complaint*, in which Thomas declares that God has restored his mental health after a period of madness; he complains that despite this he is alienated from his fellows: if he tries to talk with them, they look for signs of madness, and if he stays away, they assume he's mad again. He relates how he would examine himself in a mirror in private, searching for signs of instability in his face, which he could then work to change. He is powerless to change the public view of his instability; he feels like dying. After feeling like this, he says that he recently read a book, in which Reason comforted a grieving man by counselling patience. The *Complaint* ends with the narrator declaring his readiness to be patient in the face of what others say about his sickness, 'the peoples ymagination, / talkynge this and that of my sycknesse' (380-81). He thanks God for the gift of adversity.

(3) No sooner is the *Complaint* finished than a friend knocks at the door. This marks the beginning of the *Dialogue with a Friend*. Thomas reads out the *Complaint* he has just written, and the friend advises him not to publish it. Thomas argues for publication, in order to declare the fact that he has been cured of his madness — after all, he argues, the fact of having suffered madness is nothing to be ashamed of, like being a coin-clipper. The friend asks whether or not Thomas had intended to follow the *Complaint* with any other literary work. Thomas replies that he had intended to translate an *Ars Moriendi* from Latin. The friend tries to dissuade him from attempting this work, arguing that he will fall into madness again, since it was overmuch 'study' that had caused his madness in the first place. At this point Thomas reproaches the friend for not having believed the truth of the *Complaint* he has just heard read out to him. The friend, Thomas argues, is not acting like a true friend; this persuades the friend that Thomas is fit for further work. The clinching argument is Thomas's point that it is presumption to assume

complete knowledge of another person's state of mind. Agreeing that Thomas is sane, the friend now begins to co-operate in the planning of a new poem. They discuss the fact that Thomas owes a book to Humphrey Duke of Gloucester; Thomas says that he'd prefer to write something more cheerful than the *Ars Moriendi*, and also dismisses the idea of translating a work of chivalry, since Humphrey has no need of instruction in chivalry. The friend suggests something in praise of women, as a penance for Thomas's earlier work, *The Epistle of Cupid*. Then follows

(4) a story of a virtuous woman from the *Gesta Romanorum*, *The Tale of Jereslaus's Wife* (followed by a conversation with the friend, in which the friend points out that the work is unfinished, since it lacks its moralization, which the friend promptly gets and which is added to the tale);

(5) *The Art of Dying*; and

(6) a further conversation with the friend, in which the friend persuades Thomas to go on with his work, despite Thomas's sense that he has finished it. He persuades him to translate *The Tale of Jonathas*, again from the *Gesta Romanorum*. Finally, there follows

(7) an envoy to the *Series* as a whole.

It will be clear from this account of the *Series* that it is a work peculiarly concerned with the story of its own composition. This is as much the subject of the work as the subjects of the actual stories. The essential movement in this 'story of composition' is from an isolated and alienated poet, locked into solitary forms of address, and being dissuaded from publishing and even writing his work, to the poet standing confidently in relation to patron and audience, and being positively encouraged to write.

In this story, we are encouraged to pay particular attention to the textual status of different elements in the work. The Prologue presents itself as the memory of an unhappy time, and the introduction to something which is written: the *Complaint* which follows. But attention is drawn even to the Prologue's own status as a text: the rubric after the Prologue reads 'here endythe my prologe and folowythe my complaynt'; the 'here' can only refer to the place on a page before us, and the first person possessive adjective leaves us in no doubt that this 'textual deixis'[6] is not scribal (whether or not the authorial rubric is part of the fiction of the poem is another question). The textuality of the *Complaint* is insisted on in the *Dialogue*, where Thomas relates that he read it out to his friend. The *Complaint* is presented as an actual document here: as soon as the friend enters, Thomas says that he had no intention of hiding his work from him, 'and right anon I redd hym my "complaynt" ' (17).

Just as the elements of the *Series* are presented as texts, so too are they surrounded by, and fed by, other texts. The tales from the *Gesta Romanorum* are presented as coming from actual books. After the *Dialogue*, for example, Thomas says that he read a tale recently which he will now translate; the first line of the text insists on its textuality: 'In the Romain actes writen is thus . . . ' (1). During the tale, he constantly refers to his source's existence as a book: 'Nathelees of this tretith nat the book; / Wherfore to my tale wole I go . . . ' (264-65), and after he has finished this tale, his friend reads Thomas's work of translation (a couple of weeks later). The friend says that Thomas is missing the end, the moralization, which the friend fetches from his home and brings back to Thomas, who then translates it. Likewise, after *The Art of Dying*, Thomas thinks he has finished writing the whole *Series*, but the friend insists that he add a further story (*The Tale of Jonathas*), of which he (the friend) brings 'the copie verray' (34).

In respect of textuality being emphasized, the real exception in the *Series* is the *Dialogue*. Of course, if we think about it, the *Dialogue* is offered as a conversation remembered, and then written down. But by a sleight of hand, Hoccleve insistently effaces its textuality. This is done chiefly by the use of dramatic dialogue. The *Complaint* ends with a formal, rhetorically elaborate address to God:

> lawde and honore and thanke vnto the be,
> lorde god that salve art to all hevynes!
> thanke of my welthe and myne adversyte,
> thanke of myne elde and of my sek[e]nese;
> and thanke be to thyne Infinite goodnese
> for thy gyftes and benefices all[e],
> and vnto thy mercye and grace I call[e]. (407-13)

The highly wrought rhetorical patterning of this stanza marks it out as specifically literary language; and in the *Dialogue*, which immediately follows, we see that it is explicitly presented as written language. By contrast, the *Dialogue* begins in this way:

> And, endyd my 'complaynt' in this manere,
> one knocked at my chambre dore sore,
> and cryed a-lowde 'howe, hoccleve! arte thow here?
> open thy dore me thinkethe [it] full yore
> sythen I the se what, man, for god[de]s ore
> come out for this quartar I not the sy,
> by owght I wot' and out to hym cam I. (1-7)

This passage, characteristic of the *Dialogue* as a whole, draws on a range of devices to efface any sense either of 'literariness' or of textuality. Hoccleve cuts against the rhythmic expectations of the rhyme royal stanza to create the effect of the speaking voice, with the emphasis falling on this, rather than on the narrating voice. The enjambment in lines 4, 5 and 6, along with the colloquialisms 'for goddes ore', 'by owght I wot', sustain this sense of a speaking voice, while the deictic markers of the demonstratives ('this manere', 'this quartar'), the first and second person pronouns, and the adverbs of place ('arte thow here?') all serve to create the sense of a 'here and now'. They also serve to efface any sense of barrier between the reader and the scene he or she witnesses. Direct speech, unintroduced by any markers of speaker, characterizes the 798 lines of the *Dialogue*, with a single exception at line 659.

These formal devices serve to create the effect that the *Dialogue* is not itself a text. The very fact of conversation subliminally effaces textuality; in *The Regement of Princes* Hoccleve makes this point in his description of the privations of a scrivener, one of which is that while writing, the scrivener may not talk. Whereas workmen 'talk and syng', those who write 'labour in trauaillous stilnesse; / We stowpe and stare vp-on þe shepes skyn, / And keepe muste our song and wordes in' (1013-15). The impression of 'non-textuality' is created not only by these formal devices, but also through the many references in the *Dialogue* to actual texts outside it. This is most evidently true of the *Complaint*, which immediately precedes the *Dialogue*; but in fact there are many references to Hoccleve's other works, or intended works, in the *Dialogue*. Thomas refers to the *Ars Moriendi* he says he wants to translate; to the translation of *Vegetius On Chivalry* he wanted to translate for Humphrey (561); to *The Epistle of Cupid*, Hoccleve's earlier work in (he tells us) ironic praise of women; and, finally, to *The Tale of Jereslaus's Wife*, which is proposed as a way of expiating his sins to women, by writing about a good woman.

The cumulative effect of these references to texts outside the *Dialogue*, along with the formal presentation of the *Dialogue*, subliminally effaces the textuality of the *Dialogue* itself. Real texts are elsewhere, not here. The authenticating devices are so strong that we are persuaded to forget the textuality of the piece altogether.[7] The only time in the *Series* that the *Dialogue* is recognized as text is, I suppose, in the Envoy, where Hoccleve steps outside the whole work and addresses it as a text: 'Go, smal book to the noble excellence / Of my lady of Westmerland . . . (p. 242). By the 'small book', Hoccleve means the *Series* as a whole, including, of course, the *Dialogue*.

II

Hoccleve, then, writes a poem whose single unifying plot is the story of its own composition, and in this story pays particular attention to the textuality of individual elements in the *Series*, or, in the case of the *Dialogue*, goes to extraordinary lengths to efface any sense of textuality. What is his strategy in highlighting, or in effacing, the status of different parts of the *Series* as text?

One may suppose that Hoccleve learned the art of alternating the ostensibly 'non-textual' with the textual, or at least the literary artifact, from Chaucer: 'Mi dere maistir . . . And fadir, Chaucer' (*Regement of Princes*, 2077ff.; see also 4978-84). In *The Canterbury Tales*,

Chaucer's motive for creating this apparent distinction between 'real life' (in the link passages) and the literary artifact varies; but one common effect of the device is to destabilize the meaning of the literary artifact which follows, by making the teller as much the subject of the tale as is its ostensible subject. One need only mention the Wife of Bath, the Pardoner and the Merchant, I think, to gain general assent for this critical commonplace.

With Hoccleve, I want to argue that the reverse is true. Hoccleve's problem as an author is that his voice is publicly regarded as being unstable after his madness. What he tries to do in the *Dialogue* especially is to convince his public, in the person of the friend, that his voice is, in the most essential respects, stable. He does not want his madness to become the subject of his poetry; instead, he wants his position as teller to be regarded as stable, at least as regards his sanity.

If this is true, then it might be asked, why does Hoccleve not simply declare himself sane? But of course he does do precisely this: in the *Complaint*, he declares himself to be sane to his readers. But this, clearly, is insufficient warranty of sanity, as the friend's initial response demonstrates; the friend's immediate response on hearing the *Complaint* read out to him is to dissuade Thomas from his avowed intention of publishing the work:

> . . . 'Nay, Thomas, ware, do not soo!
> yf thou be wyse of that mattar hoo,
> reherse thow it not ne it awake;
> kepe all that cloos for thyn honours sake.' (*Dialogue* 25-28)

The friend, clearly, is 'reading' the *Complaint* both diagnostically (looking in it for signs of the narrator's ill health) and ironically (reading the professions of sanity as evidence of continuing mental instability). Implicit in this 'reading' is the idea embedded in any sophisticated literary culture that the narrator of a text is as much the subject of that text as is its ostensible subject. The problem for Thomas (and, presumably, for the historical Hoccleve) with this reading is that the public idea of his self is profoundly negative. Any text he writes in this context will simply be further grist for diagnostic readings, readings which give further evidence of Thomas's continued instability. Given the friend's implicit habit of such reading, then texts in themselves offer no solution to Thomas's painful situation. Just as in the *Complaint* Thomas defines the painful situation in which his attempts to socialize after madness were taken as evidence of his continuing madness, so too, we can see, will the publication of poetry serve as the occasion for diagnostic readings by his audience, as further proof of Thomas's insanity.

Given the automatically diagnostic reading of texts, then texts themselves can only serve to deepen, rather than relieve Thomas's predicament. What Hoccleve as a poet needs to do (and here it seems pointless to distinguish Thomas's interests from those of Hoccleve) is to create an extra-textual context for his poetry, in which readers will be persuaded that Hoccleve is sane.

21

This, of course, is where the *Dialogue* comes in; the consistently dramatic devices of the *Dialogue* are designed precisely in order to create this extra-textual effect, where the context for reading texts can be readjusted. The strategy is not to persuade readers that they should stop making the narrator part of the subject of the text; instead, Hoccleve simply wants questions of his own sanity to be excluded from such readings. But even in suppressing this line of reading, Hoccleve is at the same time acknowledging that texts are inevitably read in context. It is this sense of context, or 'extra text', which gives texts their dynamism, and, in the case of the elements following the *Dialogue*, which makes their publication possible.

If the extra-textual effect of the *Dialogue* gives the text of the *Complaint* its necessary context, it should also be noticed that the relationship also runs in the other direction. It is not simply the case that the extra-textual effect of the *Dialogue* achieves what the textual *Complaint* cannot. Earlier in the *Complaint* Thomas remarks that he had refused the chance of dialogue in the past, lest his talk give rise to 'diagnostic' reception:

> Sythen I recoveryd was have I full ofte
> Cawse had of angre and ympacience,
> where I borne have it esely and softe,
> sufferynge wronge be done to me, and offence,
> and nowght answeryd ageyn but kept sylence,
> lest that men of me deme would, and seyne,
> 'se how this man is fallen in agayne.' (176-82)

My argument in the previous paragraph was that texts affirming his sanity would be of no use to Thomas, since they would be read as further evidence of Thomas's instability; what he needs is the extra-textual effect of dialogue to give voice and direction to his poetry. But from this stanza it will be clear that neither is dialogue in itself immune from 'diagnostic' reception. It is only in the context of the *Complaint* that the 'extra-textual' *Dialogue* finds its 'voice and direction'. Texts and contexts require each other.[8]

So the story of the *Series's* own composition is really the story of a poet negotiating a new relationship with his audience. For this negotiation to proceed, Hoccleve needs to convince his audience that outside his texts there is a sane poet. The friend's advice not to publish is the obverse of the social relationship so often posited for medieval poetry, where writing is seen as essentially a social act (e.g. Burrow 1982a, 47-55). In the case of the *Dialogue*, where the audience (in the person of the friend) does not trust the poet, the audience equally does not trust the text (the *Complaint*), and so insists that Hoccleve remain silent, and publish no more. Clearly the text alone cannot convince the audience; what is needed is the extra-textual effect of the *Dialogue*. Of course the *Dialogue* is in reality a text, part of the 'small book' of the *Series*. But this is the merest truism, given the way in which Hoccleve has given dynamism to the texts surrounding the *Dialogue* by creating a sense of the extra-textual conditions in which texts were written and according to which they should be read.[9]

III

So far, my consideration of the 'story of composition' for the *Series* has remained within the question of textuality. Consideration of this question leads us to see how Hoccleve's status as author depends on his creating the extra-textual effect of the *Dialogue*, in which his fitness as an author outside and behind his texts is established. But the logic of movement from *Complaint* to *Dialogue* involves more than questions of authorship, and also raises questions of human identity more generally. The friend's acceptance of Hoccleve as author presupposes a larger acceptance of his coherence and stability as a person. I want to argue in this final section that Hoccleve convinces his friend, and his readership more widely, of his personal coherence by questioning the premises of the *Complaint* convention through the *Dialogue*.

In the *Complaint*, Hoccleve evokes both the style and the motifs of two discursive traditions: that of the Psalms, and that of consolation. He explicitly likens his situation to that of the narrative voice of the Psalms: 'As seide is in the sauter might I say, / they that me sye fledden a-wey fro me' (78-79), and he frequently evokes the exclamatory style of Psalmic complaint:

> O lorde, so my spirite was rest[e]les,
> I sowght[e] reste and I not it found,
> but aye was trouble redy at myn hond. (194-96)

And, as I have said, he also evokes the tradition of consolation by his reference to the book of 'lamentacion' he partly read, in which Reason comforts the 'hevy man, wofull and angwysshiows' (316). Both these authoritative traditions would seem to offer a complete answer to Hoccleve's state. And indeed the *Complaint* promises, and affirms, a sense of closure from within these traditions. It begins and ends with thanks to God for having restored his wits; the ending in particular suggests that Thomas has accepted the advice of Reason in the book he has borrowed; the borrowed text admonishes the grieving man to be patient:

> 'but thus thow shuldest thinke in thyn herte,
> and sey, "to the, lorde god I have a-gylte
> so sore: I moot for myn offensis smerte
> as I am worthy O lorde, I am spilt,
> but thow to me thy mercy graunt[e] wilt.
> I am full swre thow maist it not denye;
> lord, I me repent and I the mercy crye." ' (365-71)

This is the voice of traditional penitential authority, cited from an authoritative book. It implies a model of personal coherence based solely on one's relationship with God, in solitary acceptance of God's judgements. But such a model clearly does not answer completely to Thomas's condition. The book from which this advice is gleaned is, interestingly, an unfinished book: Thomas says that he did not read it right to the end, but that the person who owned it took it back again (372-75).[10] It seems to me that this sense of unfinishedness, or incompleteness, also applies to the *Complaint* itself, since the penitential wisdom of solitary patience on which it comes to rest is, so the following *Dialogue* would imply, an insufficient basis for human identity. The very fact that Thomas intends to publish the *Complaint*, as part of his poetic and social rehabilitation, itself implies the insufficiency of solitary resignation: any one who intends to publish his or her intention to suffer solitary patience is clearly not prepared to suffer solitary patience.

The insufficiency of the *Complaint*'s ostensible position of solitary resignation is clear from within the *Complaint* itself. What Thomas is really complaining about in the *Complaint* is not his madness, but the fact of his loneliness after having recovered from mental instability (cf. 118-19). If he tries to talk to his friends, they look for signs of madness, and if he stays away, they assume him mad again (120-210). Unsurprisingly, Thomas responds to this no-win situation by retreating into silence (176-82) and into his own room, where he looks in his mirror for signs of madness:

> And in my chamber at home when I was
> my selfe alone I in this wyse wrowght:
> I streite vnto my myrrowr and my glas,
> to loke how that me of my chere thowght[e],
> yf any [other] were it than it owght[e];
> for fayne wolde I yf it had not be right,
> amendyd it to my kunynge and myght. (155-61)

But this, clearly, is itself a no-win situation; by looking in his mirror, Thomas is treating himself purely as other: he tries to see himself only as others see him, and as a result evacuates any sense of personal coherence. Paradoxically, this place of greatest privacy is registered as being no defence against public scrutiny. He recognizes the inadequacy of this response further in the *Complaint*:

> Vpon a looke is harde, men them to grownde
> what a man is there-by the sothe is hid;
> whither his wittes seke bene or sounde,
> by cowntynaunce it is not wist ne kyd;

> thowghe a man harde have ones bene bityde,
> God shilde it shuld on hym contynue alway;
> by comunynge is the best assay. (211-17)

'By comunynge is the best assay': here Thomas not only enunciates the test of sanity, but he also points to the actual means to sanity, which lies in dialogue. If the thrust of Psalmic and consolatory literature is ultimately solitary resignation to the will of God, then we can see how the *Complaint* itself reveals the inadequacy of this acceptance. Whereas the *Complaint* ostensibly ends in humble, solitary resignation, the solution to Thomas's problems as both poet and person only comes in the *Dialogue*. It will be obvious now how the form of the *Dialogue* answers to, and questions, the *Complaint*: it offers the chance of dialogue, of not only convincing the friend of mental stability, but also of effecting that stability.

The unfinishedness of the consolation referred to in the *Complaint* spills over, then, into the *Complaint* itself. The authority for writing the *Series* as a whole comes not from within the authoritative conventions of consolation, as it does, for example, in Usk's *Testament of Love* (I. ii. 181-95), but rather from the every day world of the *Dialogue*, the world of human intercourse. It may be relevant here that the dialogue characteristic of Boethian consolation literature comes not from within the *Complaint*, which the tradition would lead us to expect as the prelude to dialogue with an abstract authority figure.[11] Instead, Hoccleve places the dialogue characteristic of the consolation tradition outside the *Complaint*, revealing that the dialogue he requires to re-establish his identity must be within the world of everyday life. Identity, Hoccleve seems to be saying, is intrinsically a social phenomenon.[12]

The real authority figure in the *Dialogue* is not the friend, but rather Thomas himself; and his authority derives not from his philosophic wisdom, but rather from the fact of his coherence as a person. The turning point of the *Dialogue*, when the friend is persuaded of Thomas's stability, comes when Thomas puts it to his friend that the friend should not presume to judge another completely:

> 'ffreend, as to þat, he lyueth nat þat can
> Knowe how it standith with an othir wight
> So wel as him self; al-thogh many a man
> Take on him more than lyth in his might
> To knowe, þat man is nat ruled right
> þat so presumeth in his iugement:
> Beforn the doom good were auisament.' (477-83)

Here Thomas is not seeing himself simply as 'other', through the eyes of other people. Instead, he is defending his intimacy and integrity. Paradoxically, at this very point when

Thomas asserts his identity as being unknown, and not completely knowable, does the friend agree that he should be allowed to publish his work. Whereas earlier in the *Complaint* Thomas had presented himself as subject to debilitating public scrutiny in the privacy of his own room (155-75), here instead he confidently asserts his privacy in public as a necessary element in the relationship between audience and author. Publication presupposes, that is, that an audience should respect the privacy of an author, and not presume to know him completely.

The fact that the pattern *Complaint* followed by *Dialogue* serves as a critique of the premises of consolation literature might suggest that any purely conventional reading of the Hoccleve persona will be wide of the mark: Hoccleve is deploying literary traditions to undercut the model of personality implicit in the consolatory tradition, and to create new models of personality, unauthorized by literary tradition.[13]

In conclusion, then, we can see that the categories of 'textuality' and of 'literary convention' are essential to understanding Hoccleve's enterprise as a poet in the *Series*; of all medieval poets, Hoccleve, perhaps, shows most awareness of the 'prison-house of language', in which literary representation constantly threatens to slide back into literary convention, and into decontextualized textuality. It seems to me, however, that in negotiating his way out of poetic and social alienation, he resists both these interpretative possibilities.

University of Cambridge
Girton College, Cambridge

NOTES

1. I have made some modifications to punctuation in quotations from the edition cited.

2. See Rigg (1970) for the actual source for this consolation, Isidore of Seville's *Synonyma*. It is interesting in the light of the issues raised by this essay that the *Synonyma* was itself very consciously a text. Rigg points out (566) that it was, as its title suggests, once classed as a rhetorical work.

3. Critics given to what Burrow (1982b, 394) has called the 'conventional fallacy' (treating all apparently autobiographical passages as conventional) have not made exactly the point I make here about Thomas as a Boethius figure. But the critic most insistently given to such readings, Penelope Doob, clearly sees the *Complaint* through a Boethian prism; according to her reading, the *Complaint* and *Dialogue* 'teach the need for patience and humility in a world where men must rely on true rather than false goods, on virtue and God rather than on money and friends' (1974, 220).

4. Attention has recently been drawn to the self-referential quality of the *Series*, by Burrow (1984, 260), who says that the work 'is to an unusual degree preoccupied with the business of its own composition'; and by Greetham (1989, 245), who points to the work's 'self-referentiality (not merely of the work to the artist but of the work to itself)'.

5. The date of the *Dialogue* has recently been established as between late 1419 and early 1421 (Burrow 1982b, 395), not 1422 as had previously been thought.

6. Wales (1989, 112) defines 'textual deixis' as markers within a text pointing to the text itself: 'since texts occupy time and space, it is also possible to have textual or secondary deixis'.

7. The term 'authenticating device' is drawn from Bloomfield (1970), who adduces many other examples of works which create a sense of real life outside the boundaries of what is presented as text.

8. This reciprocity between text and dialogue counters a potential deconstructionist account of the *Dialogue*. For if it were only the case that the *Dialogue* authenticates the text of the *Complaint*, then Hoccleve would seem an ideal locus for the deconstructionist point about the primacy of 'phonocentrism'. As Norris (1982, 28) says in his account of Derrida and the privilege granted to speech by Saussure (in this instance): '*Voice* becomes a metaphor of truth and authenticity, a source of self-present "living" speech as opposed to the lifeless emanations of writing. In speaking one is able to experience (supposedly) an intimate link between sound and sense, an inward and immediate realization of meaning which yields itself up without reserve to perfect, transparent understanding. . . . Writing, in short, is a threat to the deeply traditional view that

associates truth with self-presence and the 'natural' language wherein it finds expression'. At the same time, I hope it will be clear from this essay that the very concept 'text' necessarily implies the concept of the '*hors texte*'.

9. My argument here is similar to that of Burrow (1982b, 399), who says that 'even in medieval literature there are occasions when exclusive concentration on "le texte" or "the words on the page" leads to an impoverished and dehumanized reading of works whose true force and character can only be appreciated if their particular extra-textual reference is duly recognized and acknowledged'. What distinguishes my argument is that the model for this extra-textual reading is provided from within Hoccleve's own poem.

10. Interestingly, the *Series* contains other unfinished texts, and is itself, provisionally at least, an unfinished text: Thomas thinks that he has finished *The Tale of Jereslaus's Wife*, but the friend brings the moralization to him; the *Learn to Die* treatise offers only the first book of the Latin source, and leaves the others undone; and after the *Learn to Die*, Thomas thinks that he has finished the *Series* as a whole: ' This booke thus to han endid had y thoght' (*Tale of Jonathas*, Prol. 1), but the friend persuades him to add one further tale.

11. See Von Moos (1971) for the consolation genre, and I, 79-83 for the Biblical and Classical sources of dialogue in the genre. He remarks (I, 83) that ' . . . viele mittelalterliche Trostdialoge einen Gesprächspartner einführen, der die höhere Erkenntnisquelle personifiziert und der als geistige Macht dem verwirrten *affectus* des Trauernden aufklärend, sänftigend oder mahnend entgegentritt'. He particularly mentions Boethius's *Consolatio Philosophiae* and Isidore's *Synonyma* as influential in this regard.

12. The same critique of Boethian models seems to me apparent in Usk's *Testament of Love*, where Love's Boethian arguments about the insignificance of worldly fame (e.g. I. viii. 89ff.) are made as part of Usk's overall strategy to regain a name in the world.

13. My argument here is consonant with that of Kohl (1988), who argues that Hoccleve deploys two conventions of writing about oneself: 'medieval character portrayal' and 'autobiography'; he points out, interestingly, that it is only after Hoccleve has established his 'autiobiographical' credentials as a person who has overcome particular problems in the world of everyday reality, that he can again write 'poetry about Everyman' (124).

REFERENCES

Burrow, J. A., 1982a — *Medieval Writers and their Work: Middle English Literature and its Background 1100-1500*, Oxford

—— 1982b — Autobiographical Poetry in the Middle Ages: The Case of Thomas Hoccleve, *PBA*, 68, pp. 389-412

—— 1984 — Hoccleve's *Series*: Experience and Books, in *Fifteenth-Century Studies: Recent Essays*, ed. Robert F. Yeager, Hamden, Conn., pp. 259-73

Bloomfield, Morton W., 1970 — 'Authenticating Realism' and the Realism of Chaucer, in *Essays and Explorations*, Cambridge, Mass., pp. 174-98

Doob, Penelope B. R., 1974 — *Nebuchadnezzar's Children: Conventions of Madness in Middle English Literature*, New Haven

Greetham, D. C., 1989 — Self-Referential Artifacts: Hoccleve's Persona as a Literary Device, *MP*, 86, pp. 242-51

Kohl, Stephan, 1988 — More than Virtues and Vices; Self-Analysis in Hoccleve's "Autobiographies", *FCS*, 14, pp. 115-27

Norris, Christopher, 1982 — *Deconstruction: Theory and Practice*, London

Rigg, A. G., 1970 — Hoccleve's *Complaint* and Isidore of Seville, *Speculum*, 45, pp. 564-74

Von Moos, Peter, 1971 — *Consolatio: Studien zur mittellateinischen Trostliteratur über Tod und zum Problem der christlichen Trauer*, 4 vols, Munich

Wales, Katie, 1989 — *A Dictionary of Stylistics*, London

MORAL PATTERN IN *THE TESTAMENT OF CRESSEID*

Henrietta Twycross-Martin

To start with first things first: the date of this poem is uncertain, but, as Denton Fox suggests in his edition of Henryson's poems (p. xix), there is one piece of evidence that indicates it was probably written before 1492. There is a prose treatise, *The Spektakle of Luf*, dated by its author as from 10 July, 1492, that contains a list of notorious women who are briefly described in order to warn men to 'eschew þe delectatioun of luf'. Cresseid features in the list, with the comment that she abandoned Troilus for Diomede and then 'went common amang þe grekis / And syn deid in gret mysere & pane'. This sounds like an echo of two lines in the *The Testament of Cresseid*, where Henryson says of Cresseid ' Than desolait scho walkit vp and doun, / And sum men sayis, into the court, commoun' (76-77).

The Scottish printed editions of which we have certain knowledge are all much later: a lost edition is known to have been among the stock of the Edinburgh bookbinder Gourlay, who is recorded as having three copies at the time of his death in 1585, but the earliest surviving Scottish edition is the black letter quarto published in 1593 by Henry Charteris, correctly attributed to 'Robert Henrysone, Sculemaister in Dunfermling', and it is this edition that has provided the basic text for all modern editions. While the early Scottish editions correctly ascribed the poem to Henryson, English editions did not, for which Thynne's great 1532 edition of Chaucer is to blame: here Thynne added the *Testament* directly after the conclusion to *Troilus and Criseyde*, and before the following *Legend of Good Women*, without any note as to authorship, with the result that for a very long time Henryson's poem was accepted as part of the Chaucer canon, notwithstanding the complete difference in dialect and style. It was not until the nineteenth century that the *Testament* was generally recognized as not by Chaucer, and this early confusion as to the authorship of the poem is interesting in the light of Henryson's complex indebtedness to Chaucer, some aspects of which I shall trace in this discussion.[1]

While the 'last will and testament' motif occurs elsewhere in medieval poetry — one can compare, for example, Langland's fleeting use of it for Piers's will in *Piers Plowman*, passus vi, 85 ff. (Schmidt ed. 1978) — in *The Testament of Cresseid* Henryson expands the action to encompass the events leading up to this last earthly act of Cresseid, the culmination of her final self-assessment and self-condemnation. In reworking part of the action of Chaucer's *Troilus and Criseyde*, Henryson is of course following a very Chaucerian precedent, but the poem is more than yet another medieval reworking of a previous poet's work: by reworking only that section of time covered by Book V of *Troilus and Criseyde*, Henryson seems tacitly to accept Chaucer's version of events up to that point, but thereafter he supplies a supplementary narrative, with a complementary conclusion: he fills in the gaps, and hence his work seems to stand alongside Chaucer's Book V, as a kind of parallel text to be read in mental conjunction with Chaucer's version of events. Chaucer leaves Troilus dead and Criseyde alive and apparently happy with Diomede, however little we may feel such happiness is destined to last, while Henryson does the reverse: Criseyde dies and Troilus survives her to erect a tombstone over her grave. In Chaucer's version it is Troilus who receives enlightenment as, after his death, he looks down from the eighth sphere, whereas in Henryson's retelling it is Cresseid who reassesses her life, and who does so before death. In Troilus's case the change of perspective is shown by Chaucer to involve the reader as well in a general enlightenment concerning human affairs, but Henryson's Cresseid receives enlightenment only on the personal level of being brought to acknowledge her particular failings in contrast with the fidelity of her lover. In both cases the enlightenment received transforms the central character's attitude to past events, but Chaucer's conclusion presents a far more profound revaluation than does Henryson's: there is nothing in the *Testament* in the least like the shifting perspectives of *Troilus and Criseyde*, nothing that allows a final assessment of human life from a viewpoint comprehending but transcending earthly values. This should not be taken as a criticism: Henryson clearly set out to write a different sort of poem, with a different sort of theme, and the poem he wrote is brilliant; but its world view is closed and self-reflexive in a way that Chaucer's is not.

I have suggested that Henryson's narrative forms a kind of parallel text to Chaucer's, and so in many ways does Henryson's poetic technique: *The Testament of Cresseid* is full of echoes of Chaucer, not all of which are from Book V of *Troilus and Criseyde*, and the tracing of these echoes can often help to illuminate the way in which Henryson's poem works. What is clear to any reader of the *Testament* from the outset is the immensely detailed knowledge of Chaucer that Henryson possessed, a knowledge that shows itself not simply in verbal echoes of the more obvious kind, but also, and much more profoundly, in technique and structure. Henryson must have spent a great deal of thought on Chaucer, and yet the paradox is that the closer one comes to understanding how great Henryson's debt to Chaucer is, the more unlike Chaucer's work Henryson's becomes, and this like/unlikeness becomes more interesting the more closely the two poems are compared.

I want to start by considering how Henryson's treatment of sexual passion differs from Chaucer's treatment of the same topic, since both poems focus upon the sexual relationship between Troilus and Criseyde/Cresseid, and here one has to start, in fact, with the conclusion to both poems, since each poem ends with what appears to be a kind of 'author's message' in which a final moral conclusion is drawn from the foregoing action. I say appears, because of course Henryson is imitating Chaucer's use of a fictional narrating persona, and in neither case can one be sure how far the narrator's conclusion is or is not the poet's. Certainly, Henryson's narrator is reminiscent both of Chaucer's narrator in *Troilus and Criseyde* and of Chaucer's various dream-vision narrators with their less than perfect grasp of what is going on, and it can be very hard to tell when the narrator of the *Testament* is being used as a Chaucerian 'unreliable narrator', alerting the reader by his very obtuseness, or when he is being used, as it were, 'straight', and thus apparently speaking on behalf of the poet. Either is possible, and since Chaucer's own narrators notoriously oscillate between these two roles, one has to keep both possibilities in mind when responding to Henryson's narrator. Indeed, it is, I think, harder to make such judgements in Henryson's case than in Chaucer's, since Henryson's control over such oscillations seems to me less adept than Chaucer's, although not all would agree with me here.

Henryson uses his narrator first to set the narrative action of the poem in a particular context: in the first ten stanzas of the poem, the narrator relates the personal circumstances in which he came to read the story he will relate, giving the season, the weather and even the astrological conditions prevailing when he began to read first *Troilus and Criseyde*, and then 'ane vther quair' (61). As well as introducing the narrative proper, the first ten stanzas can also be taken as part of a framing device, the second element of which consists of the very last stanza of the poem, when the narrator, absent for a considerable period, reappears to exhort worthy women 'Ming not ȝour lufe with fals deceptioun: / Beir in ȝour mynd this sore conclusioun / Of fair Cresseid' (613-15). It does seem to me, however, that although the concluding stanza is from the formal point of view spoken by the narrator of the rest of the poem, Henryson is here imitating Chaucer's palinode in *Troilus and Criseyde*, and as it were coming out from behind his narrator to speak finally in what appears to be propria persona rather than what appears to be fictional persona (Tr 5.1772-1869). If I stress 'appears', it is, of course, simply to make the point that this change of role for the narrator is a poetic device, which may or may not have coincided with the author's personal opinion, about which we are in no position to know.

If one then looks at the palinode and compares it with this last stanza in the *Testament*, the ostensible 'author's messages' conveyed by each conclusion seem diametrically opposed to one another, for in the palinode the reader is advised to turn from the false love of passion to the true love of God, a change of perspective that calls into question the nature and value of passion itself. In contrast, Henryson's narrator, as he advises respectable women not to mingle deception with their love, seems to imply that love of the sort given and received by Cresseid in the *Testament* will bring only the inconstant lover to disaster and disrepute, while, if one wishes to be worthy, one must also be faithful. Fair enough, one may say, but I do not think this is the moral Chaucer is drawing in *Troilus and Criseyde*: there his point is the opposite one that love of this sort is likely to bring the lover to disaster whether he or she is faithful or not. Chaucer, it seems to me, is making a general point about the destructive nature of passion itself, and hence he emphasizes the suffering of his faithful lover, whereas Henryson by implication sees nothing wrong with passionate love per se provided the lover is faithful (he calls Troilus 'worthy', apparently without irony), and hence it is his unfaithful lover who must be brought to see the error of her ways. I am not, of course, suggesting that in *Troilus and Criseyde* Chaucer implies there is no moral difference between a faithful and an unfaithful lover, but I am suggesting a crucial difference in the way in which passion is presented by these two poets in these two poems: one presenting sexual passion as disaster-prone in itself, the other as disaster-prone if not loyally adhered to: Henryson is taking a moral line quite different from Chaucer's. The corollary, it seems to me, is that Henryson is looking at passion from the viewpoint of this world alone, and evaluating love without reference to any other value-system than that of the lovers themselves. Such a perspective, deliberately limited in its frame of reference, has no place for Chaucer's complex playing off of human and divine love against each other: being in and of this world alone, sexual love can have its own unambiguous value that must not be betrayed. Henryson thus looks at sexual passion from a much simpler and more limited viewpoint than Chaucer does, but can, as a result of this limitation, take a clear moral line according to which Troilus is worthy and Cresseid corrupt; Chaucer, on the other hand, is much less interested in apportioning blame.

Having suggested that, in this poem, Henryson's presentation of sexual passion is quite different from Chaucer's, I want now to return to the opening stanzas of the *Testament*, and look at some aspects of poetic technique, for however distinct their themes may be, Henryson's poetic technique is often deceptively similar to Chaucer's, showing an understanding of rhetorical effects and a desire to emulate them that comes close to plagiarism, were such a concept applicable to this period. If we look at the introductory ten stanzas from the point of view of rhetorical embellishment, we find that Henryson uses physical and astrological references much as Chaucer does, since such references not only have thematic relevance but also serve to heighten the style of what, in his first stanza, Henryson calls 'this tragedie', echoing the poetic envoy near the end of *Troilus and Criseyde* where Chaucer says 'Go, litel bok, go, litel myn tragedye' (Tr 5.1786). The first stanza of the *Testament* links the external weather of the world to the inner world of the tragedy about to be related, as the narrator comments that the cold winter weather around him is appropriate to his theme: 'Ane doolie sessoun to ane cairfull dyte / Suld correspond and be equiualent' (1-2). This seems, at first sight, merely an echo of the first and second stanzas in Book I of *Troilus and Criseyde*, where Chaucer's narrator invokes the aid of the Fury Thesiphone (instead of a Muse) in providing suitable poetic expression for his subject matter: 'help me for t'endite / Thise woful vers . . . / For wel sit it, the sothe for to seyne, / A woful wight to han a drery feere, / And to a sorwful tale, a sory chere' (Tr 1.6-14). However, there is a difference between Chaucer's metaphorical invocation of suitable poetic inspiration and Henryson's adjustment of his narrator's 'real world' to fit the world about which the narrator is reading. In Henryson's poem the sad fate of the woman about whom the narrator reads is mirrored in the cold world inhabited by the ostensibly 'real' narrator, to escape from which he starts to read the book that tells her story. Chaucer's imagery heightens the imaginative appeal of his prospective narrative, but also reminds us that there is a gap between his author-narrator and the story he is about to tell, for which telling he feels inadequate without help. Henryson does the reverse: his narrator inhabits a 'real world', the weather of which is somehow coloured by the coming narrative: both the narrator and his subject matter thus inhabit the same imaginative universe, the one reacting upon the other. The result of this adjustment of the narrator's external world to the inner world about which he is reading is that a distinctly claustrophobic touch is given to these opening stanzas, and we feel ourselves in an imaginatively closed world, the limitations of which suit the limitations of theme suggested above: this world is all we are concerned with.

The 'doolie sessoun' in which Henryson's narrator finds himself at the start of the *Testament* is the first month of spring (since the sun enters Aries on the vernal equinox), that spring setting so beloved of medieval writers on matters of love; but as befits a story of betrayal, the warmth of spring gives way to unseasonable hail and cold. If the spring setting is conventional for love-poems, there is also the less frequently used convention in medieval poetry whereby a cold and stormy season is used to open sombre or satirical poems, and behind both these complementary conventions there lies the standard equation of the seasons of the year with the periods of human life, according to which pattern a storm in spring becomes a well worn image for premature death, as, for example, in Aelfric's Homily on the Nativity of the Innocents (Whitelock ed. 1967, XIV. 108-18). We thus read the opening stanzas of the *Testament*, at least with hindsight if not with foresight, as presaging Cresseid's career: as the warmth of spring gives way to frost, so her warm youth and lust will give way to the physical blighting imposed at the later convocation of the gods by Saturn, whose arrows aré there described in terms reminiscent of this opening section, for they are 'fedderit with ice and heidit with hailstanis' (168). Nor should we be surprised that, at line 39, the narrator picks up a book ' To cut the winter nicht and mak it schort': the setting is wintery, and we will learn of the winter of Cresseid's life, as told by someone similarly in the winter of their days. That these opening stanzas can be read symbolically is made yet clearer by the astrological details of the second stanza, details which show how much Henryson had learned from Chaucer about such rhetorical embellishments: Titan, the sun, symbolizing in the central convocation of the planets the life force itself, 'Without comfort of quhome, of force to nocht / Must all ga die that in this warld is wrocht' (202-03), sets as Venus rises in opposition to him. This placing of the planetary Venus in opposition to the sun (which never occurs in reality) shows her in a position of malign influence: we are being given a picture of life in which the influence of Venus works against all that is truly life-enhancing, and can thus, paradoxically, be associated with the cold of winter and approaching death. Venus is nevertheless seen as 'fair', rising by night with her golden face in the west as the sun rises by day in the east, and, as the narrator tells us, she illumines his world for him: ' Throw out the glas hir bemis brast sa fair / That I micht se on euerie syde me by' (15-16), a non-naturalistic touch that may make us doubt the narrator's clear-sightedness as he first tries to pray to Venus, only to find that the cold overcomes him and he is forced to retreat to the fire. At this point we come back to the narrator, and to the question of how he is to be interpreted: my own view is that he conforms closely to his Chaucerian antecedents by functioning much more as a 'point of view' tool than as a character inviting psychological interpretation. Each time the narrator comments upon the action we, as readers, must decide how far we agree or disagree with the specific point of view suggested by his remarks; we should not assume such comments reflect 'his' character in any consistent way, much less suggest an authorial overview from which to interpret the entire poem.

In the course of the first ten stanzas we learn that this narrator is old, although he still owes some sort of allegiance to Venus, ' To quhome sum tyme I hecht obedience' (23), for he tells us he intended 'to pray hir hie magnificence' (26), and it sounds as though he wants to pray for sexual rejuvenation: 'For I traistit that Venus . . . / My faidit hart of lufe scho wald mak grene' (22-24), but instead the cold overcomes him and he retreats to the fire in his chamber: clearly, he can no longer warm himself at the fire of love. It seems as though here Henryson is giving us an image of the natural transience of sensual passion, a viewpoint sympathetic to, but essentially on the far side of love's excesses: a figure, that is, derived in the main from the narrators of Chaucer's dream-vision poems, who may present themselves as love-poets, in the sense that love is their subject, but who are always carefully shown to be not themselves lovers, or at least, in the case of *The Book of the Duchess*, only an unrequited lover. Chaucer's narrators are thus presumably distanced from their subject, a distancing that alerts the reader to a poetic viewpoint more objectively detached than one might expect at first sight. Do we see Henryson's narrator as implying a similarly sympathetically detached view, in which youthful passion, finally outgrown, yet leaves the topic with an abiding interest, so that given a night that cannot be spent in love, the narrator will spend it in reading about love? Such a position would be analogous to that which Africanus postulates for the narrator in *The Parliament of Fowls*, as the two of them stand looking at the two-faced inscription over the gate into the park of love: Africanus reassures the narrator-dreamer that the inscription both enticing towards and warning against love does not apply to him:

> For thow of love hast lost thy tast, I gesse,
> As sek man hath of swete and bytternesse.
>
> But natheles, although that thow be dul,
> Yit that thow canst not do, yit mayst thow se.

> For many a man that may nat stonde a pul
> Yet liketh hym at wrastlyng for to be. (160-65)

However, there is more to Henryson's narrator than this: though clearly he is partly derived from the detached yet sympathetic love-poet narrators of Chaucer's dream-visions, and also, obviously, from the sympathetic if not quite so detached narrator of *Troilus and Criseyde*, these antecedents alone would not account for those aspects of the narrator which, while equally Chaucerian in derivation, are unmistakably pejorative in effect. When, referring to Venus, the narrator says, in the line I have already quoted, that he trusted 'My faidit hart of lufe scho wald mak grene', his words recall the Reeve's ironic account of himself as one of those dirty old men who have 'an hoor heed and a grene tayl' (RvPro I.3878). Similarly, the Reeve's following comments on vicarious pleasure might strike a chord of recognition in Henryson's narrator: the latter says that to pass the night 'I tuik an quair — and left all vther sport' (40), a remark that has the reader wondering exactly what other sport the narrator had in mind, while the Reeve says of himself and other similar old men 'for thogh oure myght be goon, / Oure wyl desireth folie evere in oon. / For whan we may nat doon, than wol we speke' (RvPro I.3879-80). For 'speke', one might, perhaps, as well read 'Of fair Creisseid and worthie Troylus'? Admittedly the pejorative tinge to 'and left all vther sport' is very much in the eye of the beholder, but this is certainly how I would read the line.

Similarly dubious implications attend the narrator's remarks about bolstering his 'curage', presumably his sexual powers, with the outer heat of the fire and the inner comfort of 'phisike': ' To help be phisike quhair that nature faillit / I am expert' (34-35), might be innocuous in other contexts, but here it rings uncomfortably close to January's preparations for his wedding night, of whom we are told 'He drynketh ypocras, clarree, and vernage / Of spyces hoote t'encreessen his corage' (MerT IV.1807-08). On the other hand, unlike January, Henryson's narrator does set this experience in the past, even if he would still like to serve Venus if he could, and he does spend the night with a book. Hence although it is possible, as Denton Fox has done in his separate edition of the poem (Fox ed. 1968, 55), to see the narrator as an unambiguous image for fallen humanity, St. Paul's *Vetus Homo*, the Old (Unredeemed) Man as opposed to the New Man of the redeemed Christian life, an image, that is, of the sinner at home in this world, I find the moral status of the narrator more ambiguous than that. He seems to me more to hold in solution a number of potential viewpoints: that of the Venus-servant, the involved devotee; that of the detached sympathizer who has been, like Chaucer's Theseus in The Knight's Tale, a lover in his time; and that of the physically outworn who only leaves love because love has left him. All these viewpoints are part of the earthly spectrum of reactions to sexual passion, and one person could experience them all sequentially and through memory relive them simultaneously. Indeed, Cresseid does, I think, exemplify the same range of reactions to sexual passion in the course of the poem as the narrator foreshadows in the introductory ten stanzas; what is absent from this poem, as I have suggested above, is anything analogous to Troilus's moment of supra-earthly vision when, after his death, we are told of him that:

> ... in hymself he lough right at the wo
> Of hem that wepten for his deth so faste,
> And dampned al oure werk that foloweth so
> The blynde lust, the which that may nat laste,
> And sholden al oure herte on heven caste. (Tr 5.1821-25)

That shift lies outside Henryson's concerns in this poem, the focus of which is firmly on this world and on sexual passion as it is here experienced.

Reading 'to cut the winter nicht', Henryson's narrator also reminds us of the narrator of *The Book of the Duchess* passing his night's insomnia in reading the story of Ceyx and Alcione; Henryson is playing a neat variation on Chaucer's introductory book motif as his narrator takes a book 'writtin be worthie Chaucer glorious / Of fair Creisseid and worthie Troylus' (41-42), and the repeated adjective 'worthie' is illuminating. 'Worthie Chaucer glorious' is a conventional, and Chaucerian, acknowledgement of indebtedness and establishes a standard of artistic excellence against which to measure the new work; to call Troilus by the same epithet in the next line ensures, I think, that we take it at face value and without irony: in this poem, Troilus is to be seen as a standard of excellence in the moral sphere as Chaucer is in the artistic sphere. However, those familiar with *Troilus and Criseyde* might feel that Troilus's worthiness is far from convincingly demonstrated in that work: what does give him such worthiness as he has in Chaucer's poem is precisely his fidelity to Criseyde, albeit a fidelity that is clearly shown to be mistaken in its direction, and mistaken not because it was directed to an unfaithful woman, but to an earthly and transient good, the nature of which it is to be fleeting. For Henryson, Troilus becomes a type of fidelity, and such other aspects of his character as we do see, his nobility and generosity towards the poor, for example, are firmly linked to his status as a faithful lover.

When Henryson's narrator takes up his copy of *Troilus and Criseyde*, he gives us a resumé of Troilus's grief at Criseyde's defection, before turning to read his second volume, 'In quhilk I fand the fatall destenie / Of fair Cresseid, that endit wretchitlie' (63). This initial account of Troilus, given in the narrator's précis of Chaucer's poem, shows him not only as a faithful lover, but also as a wheel-of-fortune victim: we are told that despair renewed his tears while hope made him happy again, ' Thus quhyle in ioy he leuit, quhyle in pane' (49), and all the time he longed for Cresseid's return, 'For quhy scho was his only paramour' (53). Both these views of Troilus derive directly from the poem the narrator purports to be reading, with this important difference: Chaucer makes plain the causal connection between Troilus's enslavement to an earthly good, and his consequent vulnerability to changes wrought by Fortune, whereas Henryson's narrator makes no such connection; the implication behind the narrator's compressed account of Troilus's fate seems to be that 'worthie Troilus' simply chose the wrong kind of woman, not that he made essentially the wrong kind of choice. We are back with the limitation of vision I described above: this poem looks at the earthly experience of love, of passion and fidelity or infidelity, and does so without any exterior yardstick against which to measure the entire experience in a wider context.

In other words, the Boethian line of thought, so marked in *Troilus and Criseyde*, is entirely absent from the *Testament*, with the result that as we read Henryson's poem we enter a world in some ways much more 'pagan' than the mental world of *Troilus and Criseyde*. When reading Chaucer's poem we are always aware of philosophical and religious perspectives brought deliberately to our attention by Chaucer's Boethian additions, and by his manipulation of narratorial 'point of view'. What makes *Troilus and Criseyde* so richly complex is precisely this insistence by Chaucer that we read as both inside and outside the action simultaneously; Chaucer's audience (as medieval Christians) had an orientation towards experience that was not open to Troilus, and it is this inevitable limitation to his vision, but not to the reader's, that gives Chaucer's Troilus his paradoxical nobility and pathos: no higher view was available to him, he did the best he could with what he had; but he was blind. Henryson's Troilus, on the other hand, is seen from a fixed point of view, from within a world in which love can and should have the value that the first Troilus, mistakenly, thought it had. From this fixed point of view, Henryson's Troilus can be seen as 'worthie' from first to last, as Cresseid is unworthy by virtue of her infidelity. However, to return to a point made earlier, Henryson is not just writing a simpler poem than Chaucer's: he is using his simpler perspective to make a point complementary to Chaucer's conclusion. In Chaucer's version, after his death, Troilus finally learns a spiritual lesson concerning the absolute nature of heavenly love and the relative nature of earthly love; whereas Henryson's Cresseid learns, during her life, a physical lesson commensurate with her physical faithlessness. Presumably this is a connection we are intended to make, since I assume Henryson was writing for an audience very familiar with *Troilus and Criseyde*, and it may serve to explain the strict limitation of Henryson's world-view in the *Testament*. Henryson's Cresseid has to learn the elementary lesson that fidelity, commitment, to relationships is the starting point for any moral progression in this world, whereas Chaucer's Troilus learns a more advanced lesson about the limitations of what he has been faithful to, and in this way the *Testament* reads as a very careful moral comment upon *Troilus and Criseyde*: Henryson seems to be reminding us not to undervalue fidelity to the lesser good; if it is all we have, then let us be faithful to it, and receive honour therefore.

There is a strong suggestion from Henryson himself that he is going to give us a viewpoint very different from Chaucer's, when his narrator cautiously remarks, as he comments upon the second book he takes up, 'Quha wait gif all that Chauceir wrait was trew?' (64) adding 'Nor I wait nocht gif this narratioun / Be authoreist, or fenȝeit of the new / Be sum poeit, throw his inuentioun' (65-67). Both works are works 'be sum poeit', relative, personal views, that is; and this view of poetry is one that Chaucer himself seems to have promoted, to judge from the strong sense of poetic relativity in his writing: the version of the *Aeneid* found in *The House of Fame* gives a view of Aeneas's relationship with Dido quite unlike that found in Virgil, a comic comment on poetic 'truth' that would be lost on any reader of Chaucer's version not already familiar with his source, while in *The Book of the Duchess*, Chaucer reworks Ovid's story of Ceyx and Alcione to promote an exactly opposite view of bereavement from that found in the *Metamorphoses*.

I want now to look in more detail at how Henryson uses his narrator as a point-of-view tool, a function in which he can be very close to Chaucer's narrator in *Troilus and Criseyde*: as I have said before, one of the interesting things about the *Testament* is how precisely Henryson can imitate some of Chaucer's techniques, while at the same time being so divergent in theme. Henryson's narrator commences the account of Cresseid he says he found in his second book by giving new information about Cresseid's career post-Troilus, in the famously nasty lines beginning 'Quhen Diomeid had all his appetyte, / And mair, fulfillit of this fair ladie' (71-72). We are told that she is 'divorced' from her lover, 'excludit fra his companie' (75), and then in thoroughly Chaucerian self-exculpatory tones the narrator implies that she became a prostitute: ' Than desolait scho walkit vp and doun, / And sum men sayis, into the court, commoun' (76-77). This is very reminiscent of the moment in *Troilus and Criseyde* when the narrator comes as close as he can apparently bring himself to admitting that Criseyde has betrayed Troilus with Diomede: when Diomede has been wounded by Troilus, Criseyde 'took, to kepen hym, good hede; / And for to helen hym of his sorwes smerte, / Men seyn — I not — that she yaf hym hire herte' (Tr 5.1048-50). Chaucer's narrator follows this with the excusing lines 'But trewely, the storie telleth vs, / Ther made nevere womman moore wo / Than she, whan that she falsed Troilus' (Tr 5.1051-53), and Henryson's narrator follows his powerfully unpleasant suggestion concerning 'the court, commoun', with two stanzas of emotional sympathy for Cresseid, a reaction which has been condemned by Denton Fox (ed. 1968, 56) as 'morally imbecilic', and which he paraphrases as follows: 'Poor girl, she's so pretty she shouldn't have been faithless, but anyway it's all the fault of Fortune'. Fox sees the narrator as one of the distinctly unreliable kind, and certainly a narrator who can say in one line 'Sa giglotlike takand thy foull plesance!' (83), only to follow in the next line with 'I haue pietie thow suld fall sic mischance!' (84), is bound to puzzle, if not infuriate, any reader looking for a clear moral lead to follow, especially when he concludes his comments by saying:

> I sall excuse als far furth as I may
> Thy womanheid, thy wisdome and fairnes,
> The quhilk fortoun hes put to sic distres

As hir pleisit, and nathing throw the gilt
Of the — throw wickit langage to be spilt! (87-91)

The simplest interpretation of these lines is indeed to see them as of the 'unreliable narrator' kind: as intended, that is, to provoke a reaction from the reader, to alert the reader to just how impossible it is to defend Cresseid, and thus to lead the reader into prejudging the issue and into condemning from the beginning both narrator and heroine as sharing a blindness to moral responsibility that the rest of the poem will illuminate. Certainly, later on in the poem we do see Cresseid sharing the viewpoint here put forward by the narrator, when she blames an apparently external agency, rather than herself, for what has happened to her; but although these comments by the narrator serve to point up a certain moral blindness he shares with his heroine, and thus isolate for us as readers where we start from, morally speaking, I think they also have another function. The narrator here is not entirely 'unreliable', for we are reminded by his remarks that we are dealing with a wretchedly unhappy story, in reaction to which it is not sufficient to dismiss the narrator's viewpoint as 'morally imbecilic', and to see him simply as missing the essential point that Cresseid brought it all on herself and thus deserved her fate. While the suggestion that Cresseid's fate was 'nathing throw the gilt / Of the' is clearly wrong, the comment 'I haue pietie thow suld fall sic mischance' is not necessarily inadequate: the narrator's moral muddle invites us to think things out for ourselves, certainly, but we are also being invited to be compassionate.

It is time now to turn to Henryson's central character, and look at what he makes of Cresseid, for she is, after all, the focus of his narrative. As the story proper gets under way, stress is laid on Cresseid's isolation, and on her fear of public exposure: excluded from Diomede's company, she goes to her father without companions and in disguise. When the 'solempne day' comes on which the people honour Venus and Cupid at her father's temple, she 'into the kirk wald not hir self present, / For giuing of the pepill ony deming / Of hir expuls fra Diomeid the king' (117-19), and, secluded in a private chapel, the burden of her complaint against the deities of love is that far from being, as they had promised her she would be, 'the flour of luif in Troy' (128), she is now 'ane vnworthie outwaill' (129). Chaucer's Criseyde feels herself dependent on the men in her life for help and support: her reliance upon Pandarus is one factor leading to her acceptance of Troilus as a lover, and Henryson takes up this reading of her character. When his Cresseid asks 'Quha sall me gyde? Quha sall me now convuoy, / Sen I fra Diomeid and nobill Troylus / Am clene excludit' (131-33), she is seeing herself as passive, as 'done to', rather than acting on her own behalf, and thus she takes no responsibility for herself either physically or morally. When she asks 'Quha sall me gyde?', it seems a comprehensive rejection of physical autonomy, just as she denies any moral self-determination when she says 'O fals Cupide, is nane to wyte bot thow / And thy mother, of lufe the blind goddes' (134-35). Her following reference to the 'seid of lufe' which they had led her to believe was sown in her face, and which she now says is slain with frost, suggests the traditional rose of earthly love, and echoes the opening stanzas where the warm spring gives way to sudden unseasonable frost, just as Cresseid's beauty will soon be frozen by Saturn, but at this stage in the poem it is her isolation that makes her feel betrayed: 'Bot now, allace, that seid with froist is slane, / And I fra luifferis left, and all forlane' (139-40). Beauty has seemed to her a passport to protection, a possession that has meant security, an attitude that also explains why she can lump Diomede and Troilus together: 'And I fra luifferis left' — the point of a lover is that he should be there with her, and not left behind in Troy while she is in the Greek camp.

After this outburst, Cresseid falls 'doun in ane extasie, / Rauischit in spreit' (141-42), and has in effect a traditional dream-vision, complete with cosmic range (Cupid rings a bell audible from Heaven to Hell), divine authority figures debating the point at issue, and finally a judgement being given which effects a change in the person of the dreamer. But the change brought about in Cresseid by the judgement upon her is of course entirely physical; what is lacking is any development in her own view of herself at this point in the poem.

I must diverge here for a moment to look at the literary background to Henryson's convocation of the planets. Although there are several poems surviving from the medieval period in which an offence against love is punished by a quasi-legal court made up of the pagan gods, in such poems, with the exception of The Knight's Tale (see below), the gods are not usually given an astrological frame of reference: they tend to function simply as literary devices for clarifying the issues involved. Nevertheless, the tradition of seeing the planetary bodies as astrological forces endowed with the names and characteristics of the pagan pantheon is thoroughly medieval, and since the planets were believed to have profound influence upon human affairs, and to be in effect part of the physical cause-and-effect machinery of God's universe, such a fusion allowed a poet to set a story in a pagan past and yet to suggest that his motivating forces might have more than simply historical relevance. In such a view, the planets become physical causation writ large, and what they do not necessarily have, used in this way, is any suggestion of autonomy as spiritual forces analogous to their original role as pre-Christian deities. They operate on the material rather than the spiritual plane. Thus, in a story set in the pagan past, the characters within the story may well view the planets as truly 'gods', and offer prayers to them, but such a direction for prayer would serve to remind the Christian reader that the pagan world was a world limited to an essentially physical viewpoint, beyond which it could not move. Hence, when Cresseid, within the pagan world of the *Testament*, invokes her particular deities, who are 'gods' to her, the deities she sees in her dream are the planetary forces whose influences rule this world in complex chains of causality.

Here, I think, we leave *Troilus and Criseyde* as a direct source for the *Testament*, and turn instead to Chaucer's Knight's Tale, in which the treatment of the gods is very different from that found in *Troilus and Criseyde*. In *Troilus and Criseyde*, the deities invoked by the characters themselves within the story seem to be invoked simply as deities, without astrological undertones or overtones, unlike, for example, the narrator's complex invocation of Venus as both goddess and planet in the Proem to Book III of this poem; but prologues, by definition, stand apart from the action proper, and different techniques can be employed there. On the rare occasions when the gods do take a hand in the action of *Troilus and Criseyde*, as when Troilus is struck by Cupid's arrow and falls in love with Criseyde, their function is metaphorical rather than causative: much of the poem is concerned with free will and its abuse, and there is a down-playing of any suggestion, except as the characters' own wish-fulfilment, that they are not at least partly responsible themselves for what happens to them. The reverse is true of The Knight's Tale, which, as Spearing has pointed out (1972, 157-92), presents a fusion of pagan and planetary deities very similar in poetic effect to that of the *Testament*. Although in both poems the protagonists intially lay themselves open to disaster by a misdirection of moral choice (Palamon and Arcite allow their passion for Emelye to break their fraternal devotion; Cresseid abandons Troilus), once free will has been so misdirected they apparently become the victims of implacable forces who take over their destinies and against whom there is no appeal. In both poems Saturn acts as the malevolent solver-of-problems, devoid of any humane compassion, and the reader is faced with a bleak vision of 'things as they are in this world', and none the more comforting for that.

If we now look at Henryson's presentation of the planetary deities in his convocation, it is clear that we are dealing with a manifestation of the physical universe, for the planets appear in order of spheres, the outermost first, which order also allows for a balancing of astrologically malevolent forces against (usually) benevolent ones: Saturn, who comes first, is astrologically speaking the major infortune, being cold and dry, symbolizing age and death; after him comes his opposite, Jupiter, a benevolent force, traditionally warm and moist, promoting growth and vitality; then Mars, second only to Saturn in malevolent influence, as is shown by Chaucer's use of him in The Knight's Tale, where his protégé Arcite does indeed win Emelye, only to die immediately after his fruitless victory. After Mars comes 'fair Phebus . . . causing . . . lyfe in all eirdlie thing' (197-201); we remember how he is setting in opposition to Venus as the poem opens, and appropriately enough she comes next; but I will consider her role later, as her complex antecedents, both Chaucerian and otherwise, take some unravelling. Mercury follows her, and although he has in fact a confused astrological tradition behind him, his significance in this poem seems clear enough, since he acts as parliamentary Speaker for the convocation. Last comes the moon, Lady Cynthia, whom Henryson seems to distinguish from the 'Diane', goddess of hunting and chastity, whom Cresseid later invokes as she dies penitent. Astrologically the moon is neither malevolent nor benevolent, but takes her quality from any planet with which she is in conjunction, and her sphere of influence (note the image) is particularly over the body: her blotched raiment images not only the moon's spots, but also the leprosy with which she will afflict Cresseid.

To return now to Venus: according to traditional astrological lore, Venus was one of the most benevolent of the planetary forces, but Henryson departs from this tradition to present her much as Chaucer does, as a highly ambiguous figure. This potential ambiguity in the significance of Venus developed simply because the astrological, benevolent, Venus was traditionally different from the figure of the pagan deity, who came to symbolize lust and sensuality, at least as far as most medieval commentators on the pagan gods were concerned. Chaucer can certainly present Venus according to this latter tradition: Venus as she appears within the park of love in *The Parliament of Fowls* symbolizes a life dedicated to sensual pleasure; but he can also present her, far more profoundly, as partaking of both the characteristics of the benevolent planet and of the goddess of sensuality, so that she becomes the embodiment simultaneously of the life-enhancing and the destructive aspects of sexuality. In the pre-dream opening to the *Parliament of Fowls*, just before Africanus shows the dreamer-narrator the gate with its dual inscriptions promising love as either life-enhancing or destructive, the narrator invokes Venus in a similar double-edged vein:

> Cytherea, thow blysful lady swete,
> That with thy fyrbrond dauntest whom the lest . . .
> Be thow myn helpe in this, for thow mayst best!
> As wisly as I sey the north-north-west,
> Whan I began my sweven for to write. (113-18)

Here she has the firebrand of the goddess, together with a planet's position in the heavens, and her significance is thus wider than when we meet her within the park. Similarly, the Proem to Book III of *Troilus and Criseyde* is a tour de force of simultaneous reference, serving either to link earthly and heavenly love, or alternatively, to suggest how fatally easy it is to make this presumably erroneous identification: one is not sure which attitude one should adopt, which viewpoint is the more valid. Henryson's Venus is certainly related to Chaucer's Venus, but one might say she is straightforwardly ambiguous rather than ambiguously ambiguous in the Chaucerian manner. This simpler ambiguity seems to derive from the way in which Henryson's Venus is very close indeed to an image of Fortune: in the convocation portrait of her, we are told:

> Vnder smyling scho was dissimulait,
> Prouocatiue with blenkis amorous,
> And suddenely changit and alterait,
> Angrie as ony serpent vennemous, (225-28)

while the sexual force she rules over is 'Richt vnstabill and full of variance' (235); in her instability she is an obviously appropriate mentor for Cresseid, who has, after all, shown the same characteristics.

As the convocation opens, Cupid (who, as Venus's son, is literally a deity and not a planet) accuses 'ȝone wretchit Cresseid' of blasphemy against her 'awin god' in blaming 'hir greit infelicitie' upon him, and of calling his mother 'ane blind goddes'; he concludes ' Thus hir leuing vnclene and lecherous / Scho wald retorte in me and my mother, / To quhome I schew my grace abone all vther' (285-87). In other words, he is accusing her of a two-fold fault, defamation of Venus, and moral buckpassing. The detail about calling Venus blind depends upon traditional imagery: the god of love (whether Amor, Cupid or Eros) was traditionally called blind when he represented 'blind passion' (we use the image to this day), and Henryson may have intended a conscious irony when Cupid accuses Cresseid of applying such an epithet not to him but to his mother. Difficult though it might be, however, to defame the Venus Henryson has just described, the irony is that Cresseid has exactly lived out the characteristics of her planetary patron, and is herself blind to what she has done: whatever potential there might have been initially in Cresseid's experience of sexual love has by now shrunk to nothing more than 'blind lust'; she has herself been inconstant and deceptive, and cannot complain if others are inconstant to her, or if her expectations deceive her. I want now to suggest that the assembled planetary deities in this poem in fact represent Cresseid's 'universe', the inner world of how she sees life, and that far from being external determining forces in the manner of The Knight's Tale, they function as an externalization of what she has made of herself and her opportunities: the forces of love act uncharitably by her because she has acted so by them; they are an image of what she is herself. (I should add that this 'inner' element is also present in The Knight's Tale, since Palamon is obviously more of a lover and Arcite more of a fighter: Palamon, for example, could not be under the patronage of Mars without wrecking the symbolic structure of the tale; but the impression of mankind as victim of external forces is perhaps stronger in The Knight's Tale than it is in the *Testament*.) Cupid's point about moral buckpassing similarly draws our attention to Cresseid's own nature: when he says she blames her 'leuing vnclene and lecherous' on him and his mother, he is pointing out that she rejects her own responsibility for what has happened to her, and thus it is symbolically appropriate when she loses autonomy and has punishment involuntarily inflicted upon her from without by Saturn and Cynthia, the former pronouncing sentence and the latter inflicting the penalty. The actions of the gods show how she interprets her life: she sees herself as an injured, and innocent, victim of circumstances, and so her leprosy is presented as a further infliction upon her 'from outside' as it were, instead of being recognized for what Henryson's age might well have thought it, a venereal disease literally caused by, as well as symbolically appropriate to, her corrupt way of life (Fox ed. 1968, 27-30).

When Saturn passes judgement on Cresseid, he does so in a series of contraries directly reminiscent of the moment in *The Book of the Duchess* when the Man in Black describes the change wrought in him by the death of his lady White (BD 599ff.), and even more reminiscent of a single stanza in the formal *Litera Troili* (Tr 5.1317ff.), the letter that Troilus sends Criseyde, lamenting the change her departure has made to his life, in which Chaucer uses, much more briefly, the same technique of contraries as he had used before for the Man in Black's lament. The single stanza from the *Litera Troili* is remarkably close to Henryson's stanza that begins at line 316 of the *Testament*, as we can see if we put the two versions together: Henryson's stanza has Saturn saying:

> 'I change thy mirth into melancholy,
> Quhilk is the mother of all pensiuenes;
> Thy moisture and thy heit in cald and dry;
> Thyne insolence, thy play and wantones,
> To greit diseis; thy pomp and thy riches
> In mortall neid; and greit penuritie
> Thow suffer sall, and as ane beggar die.' (316-22)

Troilus writes:

> 'Myn eyen two, in veyn with which I se,
> Of sorwful teris salte arn waxen welles;
> My song, in pleynte of myn adversitee;
> My good, in harm; myn ese ek woxen helle is;
> My joie, in wo; I kan sey yow naught ellis,
> But torned is — for which my life I warie —
> Everich joie or ese in his contrarie.' (Tr 5.1373-79).

Even Chaucer's more discursive two-line opening that provides a rhythmic contrast to the oppositions to come has been imitated by Henryson, as has, very obviously, the dramatic mid-line caesura driving home the before and after contrasts. What Chaucer's Criseyde did to Troilus, Saturn is now doing to Cresseid, and if we know Book V of *Troilus and Criseyde* well enough we recognize the stylistic allusion, as Henryson may have hoped his original audience would do.

At this point we get another interjection from the narrator, of the unreliable or 'morally imbecilic' variety, when he denounces Saturn's judgement:

> O cruell Saturne, fraward and angrie,
> Hard is thy dome and to malitious!
> On fair Cresseid quhy hes thow na mercie,
> Quhilk was sa sweit, gentill and amorous?
> Withdraw thy sentence and be gracious —
> As thow was neuer . . . (323-28)

This evokes a picture of the innocent victim, the passive sufferer, plainly at variance with Cresseid's career as the narrator has himself given it, but we should not, I think, make any reflection on the narrator's mental powers: he is not a 'character'. This interjection invites us to see Cresseid once more as she sees herself, and by so doing it points up the sheer implausibility and partiality of such a view, while suggesting also the genuine tragedy of what her life has become. Furthermore, the plea to Saturn to 'be gracious — as thow was neuer', perhaps suggests more than just the moral escapism of astrological determinism: if the planetary deities do on one level symbolize what Cresseid is, then they cannot be other than they are, because she is not other than she is, and grace does not enter into it.

The dark and spotted moon then appropriately enough inflicts Cresseid with the 'spottis blak' of leprosy, remarking ironically 'Quhair thow cummis, ilk man sall fle the place' (341), and she awakes to take a mirror in which she sees 'hir face sa deformait' (349), but the image is literally taken at face value only, and Cresseid does not yet 'see' herself in a moral sense: the deities have shown her that she is what she is because she was what she was, but she does not accept the harsh truth of what she has been shown. Instead, she reacts once more as to an external infliction, accepting responsibility only in the facile sense of admitting to an error of judgement: 'Lo, quhat it is,' quod sche, / 'With fraward langage for to mufe and steir / Our craibit goddis' (351-53), and this view of Cresseid as the victim of superior, exterior and malevolent forces is maintained by the unconscious irony of Chalcas's remark, reported by the boy sent to summon her to dinner, that she is taking too long with her prayers, since ' The goddis wait all ȝour intent full weill' (364), and also by the narrator's paraphrase of what she told her father about her dream: 'scho can all expone, / As I haue tauld, the vengeance and the wraik / For hir trespas Cupide on hir culd tak' (369-71).

Once conveyed by her father to the lazar house (and we should note that the only selfless examples of love in the poem come from the two men in it, Chalcas's affection preparing us for Troilus's later devotion), Cresseid is given a formal seven-stanza complaint (407-69), marked out by Henryson with a change of stanza form: instead of seven lines rhyming *ababbcc*, the complaint stanzas have nine lines rhyming *aabaabbab*. The first stanza of Cresseid's complaint is a bitter lament for the loss of happiness: 'Fell is thy fortoun, wickit is thy weird, / Thy blys is baneist, and thy baill on breird' (412-13), in which it is significant that Cresseid can still feel concern for her reputation rather than her actions: 'Vnder the eirth, God gif I grauin wer, /

Quhair nane of Grece nor 3it of Troy micht heird' (414-15). In the second stanza, which
opens 'Quhair is thy chalmer wantounlie besene' (416), Cresseid lists her lost luxurious
comforts, her chamber, her embroidered bedding, gold cups for wine, rich clothing and
'plesand lawn pinnit with goldin prene' (423), in a lament cast in the same traditional *ubi sunt*
form that Chaucer uses twice for laments uttered by Troilus in Book V of *Troilus and Criseyde*.
In the first of these, just after Criseyde's departure to the Greek camp, Troilus laments her lost
physical presence, saying ' Wher is myn owene lady, lief and deere? / Wher is hire white brest?
Wher is it, where? / Wher ben hire armes and hire eyen cleere' (Tr 5.218-20). On the second
occasion, he laments not only her physical but her spiritual loss, when he is finally forced to
recognize her untruth after he finds on Diomede's abandoned coat the brooch he had once given
Criseyde. At this point Troilus says 'O lady myn, Criseyde, / Where is youre feith, and where
is youre biheste? / Where is youre love? Where is youre trouthe?' (Tr 5.1674-76). There is a
large gap between Cresseid's grounds for complaint in the *Testament* and Troilus's grief in
Troilus and Criseyde: she laments lost comforts, he laments her loss, body and soul, and I
should like to think that Henryson intended his audience to pick up this contrasting use of the
ubi sunt formula; it may, of course, be an unconscious echo, but I doubt it: the positioning
seems too precise for that. The possibility becomes stronger that Henryson is not merely
imitating rhetorical patterns, but is using specific stylistic devices to recall precise moments in
Book V of *Troilus and Criseyde*, when we remember the passage in the convocation of the
gods to which I referred earlier. There, Henryson closely imitates Chaucer's language by
giving Saturn's judgement upon Cresseid the same pattern of contraries Chaucer had used for
Troilus's expression of bereavement in the *Litera Troili*. It is interesting that both these stylistic
echoes, if we are able to place them against their counterparts in Book V, work to the discredit
of Cresseid: Saturn's words remind us that she is merely suffering as she once caused Troilus
to suffer, while her use of the *ubi sunt* formula shows her superficiality in lamenting the loss of
possessions, whereas Troilus used the same rhetorical pattern to lament the loss of a personal
relationship. On these two occasions, close comparison with Book V seems to enhance our
understanding of the *Testament*, and it is tempting to suppose that Henryson hoped his
audience would recognize his stylistic allusions.

By the end of her complaint, Cresseid sees herself as embodying an important truth when
she exhorts the fair women of Troy and Greece to make a mirror of her in their minds, in which
mirror they may see the grim reflection that as she is, so may they become. However, this
mental image merely reflects the generalizing truism that 'Fortoun is fikkill quhen scho beginnis
and steiris' (469); Cresseid may see herself as a living *memento mori*, but at this stage in the
poem she perceives no deeper significance to her story than that it exemplifies the transience of
all human happiness. She expects the ladies to see in the mirror of their minds no more than
she saw in her mirror on awakening from her swoon: physical beauty fades, and with it, the
happiness it bought. In Cresseid's view of herself as typifying no more than the common

human predicament of subjection to time and chance, there is nothing of individual self-knowledge: by seeing herself as a 'type' in this way, Cresseid once more refuses to accept personal responsibility for what has happened to her, and this view of herself precludes moral development. If her fate represents no more than the general fate of womankind, then lament is pointless, as the leper woman who has overheard her complaining suggests 'Quhy spurnis thow aganis the wall / To sla thy self and mend nathing at all?' (475-76). Given such a view of life, unquestioning and stoical resignation is the most practical reaction one can have, as the leper woman goes on to advise Cresseid, when she concludes:

> 'Sen thy weiping dowbillis bot thy wo,
> I counsall the mak vertew of ane neid;
> Go leir to clap thy clapper to and fro,
> And leif efter the law of lipper leid.' (477-80)

If as one of the leper band Cresseid is, for the first time in this poem, no longer effectively alone in her misery, she is also no longer an individual: she has become one of the mass of humankind who suffer for no reason beyond the incomprehensible one that life is like that; but it is this view that Troilus's sudden appearance destroys once and for all, in a recognition scene in which ostensible lack of recognition symbolizes far deeper revelation.

When Troilus does not recognize Cresseid, it is presumably because of her outer deformity, a deformity which accurately reflects the inner reality of her character, to which Troilus was blind while he loved her; but this failure of recognition also emphasizes the symbolic anonymity of what Cresseid has become, being now in her own mind no more than one among many. Yet what Troilus sees in his mind as he looks at Cresseid is a specific image of the woman he loved, always and uniquely an individual to him: '3it than hir luik into his mynd it brocht / The sweit visage and amorous blenking / Of fair Cresseid, sumtyme his awin darling' (502-04), and whom he still recalls as physically beautiful. Troilus's reactions to this memory show the symptoms of passionate sexual desire: 'Ane spark of lufe than till his hart culd spring / And kendlit all his bodie in ane fyre' (512-13), but this intense love then moves him to an act of pure charity towards an unknown stranger:

> For knichtlie pietie and memoriall
> Of fair Cresseid, ane gyrdill can he tak,
> Ane purs of gold, and mony gay iowall,
> And in the skirt of Cresseid doun can swak. (519-22)

These lines seem to most readers to create a particularly powerful effect: the initially sexual basis for Troilus's 'knowledge' of Cresseid is suggested by the physicality of 'And in the skirt of Cresseid doun can swak', but here even the memory of Cresseid's beauty issues in a gesture of, one might say, blind generosity, as blind as Troilus's love had once been, and in giving Cresseid the worldly wealth she has always associated with love, he finally and unconsciously demonstrates to her that love has a spiritual as well as a physical dimension.

The reaction of the other lepers to what has happened emphasizes through its balanced rhythm and repetition of words that there must be a bond between the apparent strangers: 'ʒone lord hes mair affectioun, / How euer it be, vnto ʒone lazarous / Than to vs all' (530-32), and Cresseid's enquiry as to the identity of her unknown benefactor shows that she has at least recognized his salient characteristic: 'Quhat lord is ʒone . . . / Hes done to vs so greit humanitie?' (533-34), before she has any idea of who he is. Her failure to recognize Troilus is as evidently symbolic as was his failure to recognize her: she has never 'known' him, in the sense of recognizing what he was, and what she was, relative to him; and there is a neat touch of irony as a leper replies to her question by saying 'I knaw him weill; / Schir Troylus it is, gentill and fre' (535-36). Cresseid is the last to recognize in Troilus the 'gentill and fre' qualities which also, once seen, show her to herself, and lead to her reiterated refrain 'O fals Cresseid and trew knicht Troylus'. In her lament she contrasts two types of earthly love, with Troilus and herself as the respective archetypes of fidelity and infidelity: if she still sees herself as a 'type', this time the perception is as valid as the earlier suggestion was limited; instead of typifying the lesson of earthly and inevitable transience, generalized without reference to her own moral responsibility, now she has become a 'type' for the specific instability of infidelity and can at last admit 'Nane but my self as now I will accuse' (574).

As the title implies, the whole poem is summed up in Cresseid's concluding 'testament', in which her body is left 'With wormis and with taidis to be rent' (578), her goods merely serve to provide for her burying, and she returns to Troilus the ring he gave her, the one love token she has not given to Diomede. When Cresseid finally bequeathes her spirit to Diana, goddess of chastity and solitariness, the gesture symbolizes Cresseid's acceptance of what she is now, and ought to have been in the past; she has accepted her lesson and the justice of her destiny: she leaves her corrupt body and all it stands for to be buried 'withouttin tarying', and the moral needs no further pointing than Troilus's brief comment when he hears of her death 'I can no moir; / Scho was vntrew and wo is me thairfoir' (601-02).

If Chaucer's poem ultimately sets earthly love in the context of heavenly love and finds the former wanting, Henryson's poem sets fickle earthly love against stable earthly love, and acts, not surprisingly, as a defence of the latter. What his poem does not touch on, as I have suggested earlier, is Chaucer's implication that it is specifically the most passionate earthly love that may be the most misguided, and that leads the soul most astray from God. It is characteristic of Henryson's vision that illumination does not come from any divine intervention or any apprehension of divine reality, for in his poem the planetary deities function as reflections of Cresseid herself, thrown as it were on the walls of her universe, just as in the opening stanzas the planets seen setting and rising presage the course of her life. In such a closed world as this, devoid of any yardstick other than this present life, human beings are all we have to go by, and illumination will come through them or not at all. It therefore seems to me that, in spite of the often very close reworking of many aspects of *Troilus and Criseyde* (among other of Chaucer's poems) which underlies the *Testament*, Henryson is here putting a much greater premium on the experience of earthly love than Chaucer does: in this poem, there is no alternative value-system.

Goldsmiths' College
University of London

NOTE

1. For further bibliography and a range of previous criticism see: Jack ed. 1988; Scheps and Looney eds 1986; Yeager ed. 1984.

REFERENCES

Fox, D., ed., 1968 — *Testament of Cresseid*, London and Edinburgh

Jack, R. D. S., ed., 1988 — *The History of Scottish Literature*, Volume I, *Origins to 1600*, Aberdeen

Scheps Walter, and J. Anna Looney, eds, 1986 — *Middle Scots Poets: A Reference Guide to James I of Scotland, Robert Henryson, William Dunbar, and Gavin Douglas*, Boston, Mass.

Schmidt, A. V. C., ed., 1978 — *The Vision of Piers Plowman*, London

Spearing, A. C., 1972 — *Criticism and Medieval Poetry*, 2nd edn, London

Whitelock, Dorothy, ed., 1967 — *Sweet's Anglo-Saxon Reader*, Oxford

Yeager, Robert F., ed., 1984 — *Fifteenth-Century Studies: Recent Essays*, Hamden, Conn.

WOMEN AS EXEMPLA IN FIFTEENTH-CENTURY VERSE OF THE CHAUCERIAN TRADITION

Janet Cowen

Chaucer in his *Legend of Good Women* places a series of tales ostensibly in praise of women within a fictional framework which radically complicates the work's declared purpose. He draws, furthermore, on divergent traditions in which women, sometimes the same women, figure on the one hand as praiseworthy, on the other hand as blameworthy. It is the purpose of this essay to outline these traditions which converge in *The Legend of Good Women*, and to trace their appearance in some of Chaucer's fifteenth-century English imitators. The story of Medea will be used as a specific example.

One such tradition is addressed by the Wife of Bath when she voices a critical protest at the book which was the favourite fireside reading of her fifth husband: Jankin's 'book of wikked wyves' (WBT III.685), a collection of exemplary stories about bad women. She says:

> By God, if wommen hadde writen stories,
> As clerkes han withinne hire oratories,
> They wolde han writen of men moore wikkednesse
> Than al the mark of Adam may redresse. (WBPro III.693-96)

Her specific point is not that neither sex can find anything good to say about the other, but that scholars writing in the privacy of their studies can find nothing good to say about women, and that if women had written in similar circumstances they would find just as many bad things to say about men. She is referring primarily to the tradition of antimatrimonial satire which was developed within Christian traditions of monastic asceticism and clerical celibacy (see Rogers 1966; Utley 1944). Staple notions in this tradition were those of women's insatiable lasciviousness and instability. The examples in Jankin's book, some biblical: Eve, Delilah; some classical: Pasiphae, Clytemnestra, were often retold and cited in this tradition.

But it was a tradition which generated good examples as well as bad: the good ones were dedicated virgins and chaste wives. One of the sources of Jankin's book, a treatise by St Jerome which was an early and formative text in the tradition (see Bryan and Dempster 1941,

208-12; 395-97 for translated extracts), includes a set of such 'good' examples. The point of introducing these is to show that chastity was esteemed even before the days of Christianity. The argument is of the 'how much more so' type: 'if pagan women could be so virtuous, how much more so should good Christians'. But if these examples were in Jankin's book they were not among those he chose to read aloud to Alison of an evening.

In one of the versions of the Prologue to *The Legend of Good Women* the God of Love refers to this latter aspect of Jerome's work:

> What seith Jerome agayns Jovynyan?
> How clene maydenes and how trewe wyves,
> How stedefaste widewes durynge alle here lyves,
> Telleth Jerome, and that nat of a fewe,
> But, I dar seyn, an hundred on a rewe,
> That it is pite for to rede, and routhe,
> The wo that they endure for here trouthe. (G 281-87)

The God of Love is, for his own purposes, being as selective as Jankin: where Jankin cites only bad examples, he cites only good. *The Legend of Good Women* itself is a collection of good examples, specifically examples of women faithful in love.

There are several collections of exemplary stories which provided or could have helped to provide Chaucer with a model for this work, although he is not following one model or source exclusively or exactly. One such important medieval collection comprising mainly classical subjects is Boccaccio's work on famous women, *De Claris Mulieribus*. It cannot be definitely proved that Chaucer used this as a source for the *Legend*, but it is of considerable interest as an analogue, and it was known in England in the fifteenth century. Like Jerome's treatise, Boccaccio's collection is double-edged: of his 104 examples, some are good and some are bad, and sometimes he uses the same story to make a double point, as with Hypermnestra, the last of the heroines of Chaucer's *Legend*, whose story Boccaccio uses as an example of the infamy of the forty-nine sisters who did murder their husbands, as well as of the good fame of the one who did not. Ovid's *Heroides*, a collection of love epistles incorporating retrospective narrative, provides part of the source material for six of Chaucer's legends: Dido, Hypsipyle, Medea, Ariadne, Phyllis and Hypermnestra. It is relevant to note that the *Heroides* was given an explicit exemplary status in the Middle Ages by the addition of commentary and annotations. In manuscripts such as Chaucer most probably used as a source the text was accompanied by prefaces and marginal glosses explaining and supplementing it. By these means the work as a whole is presented as a set of positive and negative examples designed to commend chaste love and discommend impure love. Thus, of the subjects used by Chaucer in his *Legend*,

Hypermnestra is often cited as an example of licit (chaste) love, and Dido, Hypsipyle, Medea, Ariadne and Phyllis as examples of foolish (illicit) love (Edwards 1970).

Another form of exemplary tale collection which Chaucer employs in *The Legend of Good Women*, although in a parodic way, is the saints' legendary. This parodic framework for the poem derives, of course, from the familiar metaphor of the religion of love, and it is an extension of the dream encounter between the poet and the God of Love which takes place in the Prologue and which provides the fictional pretext for the tales which follow: the poet Chaucer is accused of 'heresy' against the 'law' of the God of Love for having translated *Le Roman de la Rose* and for having given an example of inconstant love in his *Troilus and Criseyde*. The tales which follow are the fictional penance for this fictional charge: Chaucer undertakes to write a set of stories, 'a glorious legende' (Pro F 483), of women who were faithful in love and of the false men who betrayed them. One of Chaucer's chosen subjects for the legends, the story of Medea, provides a particularly apt example of a story shaped to divergent ends within the classical and medieval texts which recount it, some of them falling within traditions outlined above. I refer here mainly to those texts which provided source material for the *Legend* and to examples from fifteenth-century texts in the Chaucerian tradition. A comprehensive survey of classical and medieval forms of the story is given in Feimer 1983.

The elements of the story as available in the Middle Ages are these. Medea, daughter of the king of Colchis, a country east of the Black Sea, a woman skilled in magic arts, used her skills to assist Jason to win the Golden Fleece from her father. She then fled with Jason back to Greece, impeding her father's pursuit by scattering the dismembered limbs of her brother in the way. She rejuvenated Aeson, Jason's father, who had been excluded from the throne by his half brother Pelias, and in an attempt to obtain the kingdom for Jason she tricked the daughters of Pelias into killing their father, but she and Jason were then banished by Pelias's son. They went to Corinth where Jason deserted her to marry the daughter of King Creon. Medea, in revenge, sent Jason's new wife a poisoned garment which burnt her to death, and then she killed her own children by Jason. She escaped to Athens, married Aegeus, and attempted to poison his son Theseus. Finally, according to some versions, she fled and was reconciled with Jason, returned to Corinth and restored her father to his throne. But of course this compendious summary is misleading as an account of the story as told. These episodes are not present all together in any of the Greek or Latin sources, and they are variously selected and emphasized in the medieval accounts.

There is, however, a central theme in all the versions: Medea's consuming passion for Jason, which is always represented in some way as beyond reason, though the terms and tone in which this is done vary considerably from text to text. Complementing this is the theme of Jason's ingratitude, the provocation for Medea's acts of vengeance, which match in violence and destructiveness those prodigious acts she had performed on his behalf.

Two of the classical examples better known to us are the plays of Euripides and Seneca. The *Medea* of Euripides had no direct influence on the medieval versions. Seneca's *Medea* was known in the Middle Ages and is the probable source of some details in the medieval versions of the story.[1] The action of both plays is set in Corinth and extends from Jason's marriage to Creusa to Medea's killing of the children and escape. In Euripides the Chorus is the mouthpiece through which moral scrutiny of Medea's vengeance is conducted and her moral rights weighed against Jason's. At first the Chorus is sympathetic to her, agreeing that revenge on Jason would be just. In a comment which interestingly anticipates the line from the Wife of Bath's Prologue quoted above, they say that if women had the gift of song they would tell as long a tale of treachery as men do about women: in the store of tales which time has there are men and women of equal fame and infamy (p. 29). It is when Medea's plan for revenge takes the form of killing her children that the Chorus tries to dissuade her. Thus the notion of justifiable revenge is complicated by the use of innocent instruments and by the horror of infanticide. Her vengeance also becomes, as the Chorus points out, an act of self-destruction, for in choosing the means which will most injure Jason she chooses those which will most injure herself. In Seneca the Chorus does not play the role of moral counsellor, but reacts to Medea as an object of fear and horror throughout. This play develops the theme of madness stemming from the twin root of love and hate, the antithesis which dominates the speeches of Medea herself: in executing her hatred she will copy her love: both will be limitless (lines 397-98). Both plays allude, as an essential part of their argument, to Medea's earlier murder of her brother and her instigation of the killing of Pelias.

This last incident is prominent in Ovid's story of Medea in the *Metamorphoses* (a major source for medieval versons). This account begins with the arrival of Jason and the Argonauts in the kingdom of Medea's father, who imposes prodigious tasks on Jason as a condition of obtaining the Golden Fleece. Medea, represented as inexperienced in love, is stirred by Jason's handsome person, his noble birth and youthful bravery. She debates the risk of helping him, the betrayal of her family and country, analysing the contradictions of her own feelings: why be so concerned for someone she has only just met? why choose a stranger when her homeland could provide her with a suitable match? This internalization of considerations which in some later accounts are voiced as authorial criticism lends a certain dignity to the character at this point, although of course the story shows her in the last analysis as subdued to and activated by passion. Ovid goes on to relate their meeting in a sacred grove and Jason's oath to marry her in return for her magical aid. There is a graphic account of Jason's subjugation of the fire-breathing bulls, the host of warriors sprung from the earth, and the unsleeping dragon, all of which stand between him and his prize, but the episode which receives the greatest amplification is the rejuvenation of Aeson. After their flight to Greece Jason asks Medea to prolong his aged father's life; she does more: she restores his youth. Ovid's account of this weird process is the core of his story. He relates in terms at once fascinating and alienating how Medea goes out at full moon bare-headed and bare-footed, prays to the spirits of the night and the elements, and rides in a dragon-drawn chariot to many regions to gather herbs. Returned home, she avoids all male contact, sets up two altars in the open air, sacrifices and pours libations. She has the old man brought out and charms him asleep while a liquid containing herbs and parts of animals, birds and reptiles is brewing. With this she replaces the old man's blood, pouring it in through the mouth and through the slit in the throat from which she had drained the blood. As she does so his white hair darkens, his wrinkled skin fills out and his limbs become strong. But this life-giving act is hinged to its death-dealing counterpart: Medea ingratiates herself with the daughters of Pelias and persuades them to try the same trick, but of course when they do it it doesn't work. There is a grisly account of how Pelias, mutilated by his daughters' blows but not quite dead, tries to rise to his feet to appeal to them; Medea slits his throat and throws him into the boiling cauldron. Ovid goes on to a more summary account of her flight to Corinth, her killing of Jason's new wife and the children and her escape to Athens, but the themes of vengeance and disappointed expectation of gratitiude, though implicit in the story, are not amplified by him here.

In Ovid's *Heroides*, however, Jason's ingratitude is the whole subject of Medea's complaint. Regret and reproach inform the entire epistle: why did she take delight in his golden hair and smooth speech? (a plaintive cry which Chaucer echoes in the *Legend* in his much abbreviated rendering of the Ovidian letter); the only pleasure she can now gain from him is that of reproaching him with favours done. Her complaint alludes darkly to her killings of her brother and Pelias: her pen fails as she recalls her brother; what her hand could do it cannot write of; she should have been torn limb from limb with him; why rehearse how the daughters of Pelias laid a knife to their father's limbs? The writing of the letter is placed after Jason's second marriage: Medea speaks of having seen the wedding procession. The closing statement of the letter is an anticipation of her revenge: she will follow where her anger leads, though she may repent it (*Heroides* XII. 209-12).

One of the earliest medieval versions of the Medea story is in the *Historia Destructionis Troiae* written in 1287 by a Sicilian, Guido delle Colonne. This was a source both for Chaucer's legend of Medea and for the *Troy Book* of John Lydgate, the most prolific of Chaucer's fifteenth-century admirers and imitators. The story forms part of the history of Troy in that before his arrival in Colchis Jason's voyage had taken him to the shores of the first city of Troy, where he was badly received, an encounter which led subsequently to a war in which the first city of Troy was destroyed and rebuilt by Priam. Medea's part in this story extends from Jason's arrival in Colchis to her flight with him after winning the Fleece. There is a brief narratorial reference forward to Jason's later betrayal of her.

Guido used as his main source *Le Roman de Troie* of Benoit, dated about 1165, in which the Troy story is set in the social and ethical world of medieval chivalric romance, projected back, as if timeless, on to ancient story. Thus the first meeting between Medea and Jason in

Benoit and Guido is set in a splendid courtly feast in which Medea (here represented as her father's only child: no brother to murder) is summoned to entertain the guests. On the second such occasion she and Jason contrive a private talk amidst the company. Failing to dissuade him from his dangerous mission she offers her help in return for marriage, and makes an assignation for him to come to her room the following night to solemnize his promise.

But though both adopt a courtly setting, Benoit and Guido handle these hall and bed-chamber scenes quite differently. Benoit delineates the love of Medea for Jason as a pleasure arising from his appearance and bearing, a pleasure which becomes a painful preoccupation, an enchainment of feeling (lines 1261-95). Desire strives with decorum in her, and decorum only just wins, as when the woman she sends to fetch Jason to her room says it would be more seemly if she were to get into bed first, rather than appearing to have been waiting up half the night, as she has been. But this suggestion of lack of restraint appears itself restrained beside Guido's treatment of these scenes. For Guido, Medea is primarily an example of women's insatiable sexual appetite. Among his several comments to this effect is a reproach to Medea's father for his carelessness in allowing his daughter to sit beside a stranger in the hall, given the weakness and dissemblance of the female sex: female desire seeks a man as matter seeks form, and as matter takes different forms, so the dissolute desire of women proceeds from one man to another (p. 15). (Chaucer, in his *Legend*, neatly turns this simile round and applies it to Jason.)

Guido is also disparagingly sceptical about Medea's powers of enchantment, emphasizing that though she was skilled in magic arts, Ovid is quite mistaken in asserting that she had actual power to alter nature: all her work was by illusion (pp. 14-15).

Such rationalization of the mythic elements in ancient stories is particularly evident in Boccaccio's *De Claris Mulieribus*. Here Medea is introduced uncompromisingly as 'the most cruel example of ancient wickedness . . . best trained in evil doing' (p. 35). Boccaccio offers a naturalistic explanation of all her strange feats: she helped Jason win the Fleece by causing a war to break out among her father's people as a distraction; Aeson was so happy at his son's return that he 'seemed' to regain his youth; she 'armed' the daughters of Pelias against their father. He concludes with a moralization: we should not give too much freedom to the eyes, through which lust sends messages to the mind; if Medea had closed her eyes instead of turning them longingly on Jason, her father's power, her brother's life and her own virginity would have remained intact.

Standing in apparent contrast to such harsh moralizations, which delineate Medea's story in terms of the destructive effects of lust, are the numerous instances where her name figures in lists of examples of women renowned for fidelity in love. Such allusive lists, consisting of names without accompanying narrative, are found in texts both before and after *The Legend of Good Women*, and constitute the paradigm which the *Legend* ostensibly fits. It has been argued (e.g. Lowes 1909) that such 'stock exempla' constitute a distinct medieval tradition in which a high valuation of human love enabled certain literary examples to be employed according to a convention which threw the loyalty of the subjects into high relief without reference to other implications of their stories. But attention to the context of such lists can bring such singleness of interpretation into question. The paradigms of fidelity can at the same time be examples of the short-lived benefits of love, as in Gower's *Confessio Amantis*, Book VIII; of the sorrow of love, as in Lydgate's *Temple of Glass*; or of the harm that befalls lovers, as in Lydgate's *Reson and Sensuallyte*.

The versions of the Medea story in fifteenth-century narrative texts continued to exploit its ambivalent potential. Before referring to three of these I want to mention a work which, since it is neither English, nor verse, nor Chaucerian, nor a source for any fifteenth-century English works, is not an immediate part of my subject, but I refer to it not only for its intrinsic interest as a work of the period dealing with exemplary women, but also for its interest as a self-conscious corrective to Boccaccio's *De Claris Mulieribus*. This is *The Book of the City of Ladies* by Christine de Pizan, a French writer of the late fourteenth and early fifteenth centuries, notable not least as a woman who, after being early widowed, earned a living as a professional writer. Her *Book of the City of Ladies* takes the form of an allegorical vision arising from its author's solitary reflections on its subject. In the opening chapter she recalls a time when, reading in her study, she became weighed down by her recollections of the low view of women voiced by so many philosophers, poets and orators. Though it did not accord with her own experience and observation, she lacked the confidence to ignore the view of so many famous men, and found herself filled with depression to think that God had formed so vile a creature as woman. Into this scene of reflection and self-doubt enter three female figures, Reason, Rectitude and Justice. They tell her that with their help she must construct a city to be both a home and a lasting enhancement for women of fame and virtue. The city is the book. The book stands in an allusive relationship to Boccaccio's *De Claris Mulieribus*, of which it is essentially a critical rewriting. Christine rearranged Boccaccio's more or less random sequence of examples into thematic groups. This grouping is itself a part of the argumentative project, the examples fitting into the question and answer process which is conducted between the author and her spiritual visitants. For instance: why is it that women appear to know less than men? Because they are often required to do no more than sit at home performing undemanding tasks; yet there is no doubt that nature endowed them with the same potential as men: witness Sappho, Minerva, etc.. It is in this group that Medea appears, as one surpassing all women in learning, whose skills won Jason his quest (p. 69). She also appears in the group of examples designed to rebut the charge of women's natural sexual inconstancy. The defence is qualified by the implication of excessive feeling: she loved Jason with 'too great and too constant love' (p. 189), the results of which are tactfully generalized: when Jason deserted her, Medea 'who would rather have destroyed herself than do anything of the kind to him, turned despondent, nor did her heart ever again feel goodness or joy' (p. 190). Though this may seem rather a mealy-mouthed evasion in the light of fuller versions of the story, it is, as a rhetorical strategy, no more than the equivalent in understatement to the overstatement of Guido and Boccaccio noted above.

Christine's *Book of the City of Ladies* was not translated into English until 1521, and there is no equivalent in English literature of the fifteenth century to a rewriting of Boccaccio on this scale. But it is worth taking note here of an anonymous verse translation of parts of *De Claris Mulieribus* dating from about 1440 (Schleich ed. 1924). The poem is in rhyme royal stanzas, and is clearly the work of a writer familiar with the poetry of Lydgate and Chaucer. It is a deliberate selection from Boccaccio, dispensing with the more lurid examples and diverting some of Boccaccio's back-handed compliments to slightly different effect: where Boccaccio concludes that his more outstanding experts in learning and warfare were really acting like honorary men, this author has a slightly jokey aside warning men to take care lest women beat them on their own ground (Schleich ed. 1924, lines 1776-78). Medea here is among the great enchantresses, and although the author does not remove her crimes of murder, the killing of the children is presented less as a calculated act than as a descent into madness (line 1359). This Middle English rendering softens its original, and is an interesting testimony to the argumentative potential of Boccaccio's subject, and to the potential of his text for adaptation and modification, though it is by no means the kind of radical revision which Christine made.

John Lydgate uses the story of Medea both in his *Troy Book* (dated 1412-20) and in his *Fall of Princes* (dated *c*. 1431-39). The two versions vary from one another in a way which displays the antithetical potential found in the story in its successive retellings. In *The Troy Book* Lydgate takes over Guido's interpretative emphasis and amplifies it. Like Guido, Lydgate uses authorial commentary to promote Medea to exemplary status, to make her conduct emblematic of that of women in general. He does so in such a way as to open up a palpable gap between story-matter and interpretation. He extends the equation of female sexual appetite with promiscuity to a point where the strain against the tenor of a story in which a woman will be deserted by a man becomes patent. In elaborating Guido's comment that women know how to cloak immodest desires under a veil of modesty he inverts Medea's express wish for marriage into a concealed act of treachery, a painted floral screen hiding the serpent of 'new-fangelness' (I. 2072-92). Anticipating objection, he professes to be reporting what Guido says (when in fact he exceeds it), and he proffers mitigating arguments of his own which serve only to compound the misogynistic rhetoric: women are often led astray by the bad example of men (wantonness is commuted to weakness); since it is not fitting for women to live alone, it is not such a serious matter if they have more than one man (moral status is reduced by mitigation).

In *The Fall of Princes*, all the characters, both male and female, have exemplary status insofar as they are instances of the arbitrary motions of Fortune. Lydgate's poem is a version of Boccaccio's *De Casibus Virorum Illustrium*, of which he used a French translation made between 1405 and 1409 by Laurent de Premierfait, who expanded some of the examples, including that of Medea, with material drawn from other sources.

It is not Medea herself who is the principal subject of the exemplum, but her father Oetes, who appears to Boccaccio in a crowd of weeping people (the underlying structure is that of a vision poem in which the subjects appear in the author's presence); he steps forward to lament the arrival of Jason on his shores, which led to the loss of the Fleece, of his son and his daughter. Boccaccio's account (I. cap. VII) is very summary, commenting only that Medea was led into 'a mad love and flight'. The French translator expands Boccaccio's epitome with details of the betrothal of Medea and Jason and her scattering of her brother's limbs in the way of her father's pursuit. He goes on to relate from other sources Jason's desertion, Medea's revenge, and Medea's eventual reconciliation with Jason (he implies that he finds this improbable), her return to her homeland and restoration of her father's kingdom.[2] A particular feature of this account is the attempt to rationalize the mythological background by taking the Golden Fleece as a figure of speech: the king's treasure was so great that people used to call it 'the Golden Fleece'. To this French source Lydgate adds, from the *Metamorphoses*, the rejuvenation of Aeson and the killing of Pelias. While this could be seen simply in terms of his tendency, evident in other parts of the poem, to add material from other sources (Schirmer 1961, 211), I think there is more to be said about it. The piece is shapely: the three stanzas describing the rejuvenation of Aeson (I. 2241-61) are mirrored by three stanzas describing the killing of Pelias (I. 2290-2310), and these paired episodes form the centrepiece of the exemplum, flanked on either side by Medea's murder of her brother and her murder of Jason's second wife. The whole exemplum is marked out by the figure of Oetes at the beginning and end. It traces his arbitrary fall and equally arbitrary rise, in which Medea is instrumental. Set in the middle is a pair of episodes demonstrating her power of life and death over two other old men, rulers and fathers. I think Lydgate's shaping of the piece is a sign both of the potential fascination of the Medea story and also of the reason why it could be turned so easily into a negative exemplum. The story had become, with its accumulated episodes, that of a woman who by her skills could give men success and power, children, even prolongation of life, and by her self-assertion could take these things away. Here in his description of the rejuvenation of Aeson, Lydgate seems to have yielded to the fantasy of the renewal of youth. Although he locates his report in ancient authority, there appears none of the scepticism one might expect in a medieval writer transmitting an account of such a magical event, especially in a writer who, as we have seen, had earlier striven to out-do Guido. There is a striking difference between the tone and attitude of this passage and the passage in *The Troy Book* (I. 1707-98) where Lydgate had followed Guido in emphasizing that though Medea was skilled in magic arts, Ovid was quite mistaken in asserting that she had power to alter nature. The passage in *The Fall of Princes*, in surprising contrast, works not to alienate but to involve the reader:

A yerde she took, that was drie and old,
And in hir herbis and commixciouns
She made it boile, in Ouide it is told,
And bi carectis and incantaciouns
And with the crafft off hir coniurisouns
The yerde began [to] budde & blosme newe
And to bere frut and leuys fresh off hewe.

And semblabli with hir confecciouns
His olde humours she hath depurid cleene,
And with hir lusti fresh[e] pociouns
His empti skyn, tremblyng & riht leene,
Pale and wan, that no blood was seene,
But as it were a dedli creature—
Al this hath she transfformyd bi nature.

Made hym lusti and fressh off his corage,
Glad off herte, liffli off cheer and siht,
Riht weel hewed and cleer off his visage,
Wonder delyuer bothe off force & myht,
In all his membris as weeldi & as lyht
As euer he was, and in the same estat,
Bi crafft off Mede he was so alterat. (I. 2241-61)

Lydgate defers to Ovid (line 2243), but where Ovid's account of Medea whirling before her altars like a Bacchante incorporates its own distancing devices, Lydgate's rendering does not defamiliarize, but transmutes the unacceptable into the acceptable, the alienating into the desirable. The reader is drawn into sympathetic witness of a tenderly described process of cleansing and renewal.

If a single point can be drawn from this survey of examples it is that we see how the story, or rather, aspects of the story, came to be used primarily for its argumentative potential. (This is, of, course, a point which applies to a good deal of medieval narrative, not just to examples about women.) We see the tendency for the argumentative potential to be polarized: by a selection of different aspects, the story can be deployed in rhetoric of praise or blame, and yet it remains a configuration of paradoxes, pulled apart in all its tellings by the tensions within it. What links the differing interpretations of a subject such as Medea, and what, at the same time, makes the polarization of different aspects of it possible, is the idea that the subject is dominated by love. She is made pre-eminently an instance of a notion with roots in western literature which can be traced particularly clearly in Ovid: the notion that women are the natural victims of passion, which, although it may lead to the commendable virtue of fidelity, is a weakness.

It is against this background that I would like to return to the relation between the legends and the Prologue in Chaucer's *Legend of Good Women*. Behind the God of Love's fictional charge of heresy against the poet lies the real question of how *Le Roman de la Rose* and *Troilus and Criseyde* should be read. *Le Roman de la Rose* was to become a subject of controversy in the early years of the fifteenth century (Luria 1982)—indeed, to judge from Chaucer's Prologue to the *Legend*, it may have already become one. And anyone who has ever taken part in a class on *Troilus and Criseyde* knows that that is still a subject of controversy. But however we read *Troilus and Criseyde*, most would surely agree that the reader whom Chaucer's God of Love is so anxious to protect, the reader who will trust women less after reading the poem, would be not only a naive reader but a poor one. The God of Love posits a readership which read Criseyde in the light of a misogynistic tradition, and then he demands that the poet counter that tradition by writing a poem in which all women are good—'good' that is, in terms of their devotion to love. Chaucer responds by drawing on traditions which themselves contained and generated contradictions (Delaney 1986).

There is an interesting comparison to be made between Chaucer's procedures here and those in the series of poems by Thomas Hoccleve which begins with his *Letter of Cupid*. The *Letter of Cupid* is a freely handled translation of Christine de Pizan's *L'Epistre au Dieu D'Amours* (*Oeuvres Poétiques*, vol. II—the spelling 'Pisan' is not now preferred). Christine's poem, written in 1399, is a literary defence of women cast in the form of a letter from Cupid to his earthly subjects in which he addresses complaints made to him by honourable women about slanderous allegations against them, particularly in the writings of Ovid and Jean de Meun, the author of the second part of *Le Roman de la Rose*. There is an intriguing similarity between the fictional construction of this poem and that of the Prologue to *The Legend of Good Women*, though a direct dependence on the *Legend* cannot be proved (Ames 1986).

Hoccleve perceived the similarity quite clearly, and he grafts one on to the other, not only by introducing into his translation of the French poem some verbal echoes of *The Legend of Good Women*,[3] but by having Cupid refer to 'my legende of Martres' (316), clearly Chaucer's poem: as nice a medieval example of intertextuality as one could hope to find.

As James Simpson points out in his essay in this volume, *The Letter of Cupid* is referred to in Hoccleve's later *Dialogue with a Friend*, and the reference there serves to generate a further poem, *The Tale of Jereslaus's Wife*. The friend says that Hoccleve's *Letter of Cupid* contains some things against women. It does, of course, in the citation of arguments and examples against which counterarguments and examples are proposed. This is Hoccleve's defence: he was only reporting other views in the course of an argument which concluded in favour of women: ' The book concludith for hem / is no nay' (779). He asks helplessly: 'What world is this / how vndirstande am I?' (774). The friend admits he hasn't read the poem (781), but says that some people who have read it are offended, so Hoccleve had better be on the safe side and make amends.

The problem, presented with the self-deprecating air which Hoccleve learned in part from Chaucer, but to which he adds his own voice and inflection, is that of making oneself understood to an audience determined to misunderstand; it is that of the ease with which an example cited can be converted to its opposite use, of the way in which a framework of interpretation can mark out a work in a manner quite contrary to its author's intention: the problem which, as I would argue, Chaucer is dramatizing in *The Legend of Good Women*.

But whereas Chaucer, in addressing this problem, compounds it by producing a work which is itself problematical, Hoccleve appears to do the opposite: he writes *The Tale of Jereslaus's Wife* as an unexceptionable example of wifely virtue. His tale is a version of the Constance legend, of which Chaucer had used a version in his Man of Law's Tale. Hoccleve draws on a different strand of the tradition, taking his source from the *Gesta Romanorum*, a collection of exemplary tales in wide circulation at the time (Mitchell 1968, 86). His tale satisfies more than doubly the desire for restoration, justice and symmetry which is answered by the narrative forms of romance. Where Chaucer's Constance suffers two wicked stepmothers, two solitary voyages of exile, and enjoys two rescues, Jereslaus's wife not only resists seduction by two treacherous stewards, at the cost of two successive periods of homelessness, but escapes another seduction collaboratively planned by two further wicked men, and finally, when she has retired to a convent and acquired a reputation for healing, confronts all four of her betrayers, now sick, who have come to her, not recognizing who she is, in search of a cure. This she says she cannot provide unless they confess the evil in their lives. They do so, and she is fully vindicated before her husband, who is present as escort to his brother, who was the first wicked steward.

But this shapely tale, quite untinged by irony, is not the end of the matter. A prose moralization follows the tale. This concludes by equating the lady's retreat to the abbey with the turning to holy life of the soul, after which it may be led to the joy of paradise. This is the cue for Hoccleve to add to the *Series* his verse translation of a Latin work on the art of dying (he had earlier spoken in the *Dialogue* of his ambition to compose such a work). After this he writes that he intended to bring the book to a close, but his friend prevailed upon him to translate another tale from the *Gesta Romanorum*, to serve as a warning to his wild fifteen-year-old son. This is the tale of a young university student who becomes involved with a prostitute, who tricks him out of the magic gifts inherited from his father, including a flying carpet, which she makes off with, leaving him stranded at the ends of the world. He makes a painful return home, assumes the guise of a physician, and poisons her. Before acceding to his friend's request Hoccleve had demurred, saying that the friend seemed to be giving him contradictory advice, and he would undo all the good he had done for his reputation in writing

The Tale of Jereslaus's Wife; but the friend retorts that criticism of evil women is no shame to good ones.

And so Hoccleve too, in the end, produces his set of good and bad examples, but I think that the framework of discussion in which he places it shows that he realized there was more at issue than recruiting examples for a rhetoric of praise or blame, and in this it seems likely he was influenced by the rhetorical strategies of *The Legend of Good Women*, even though he did not use its subjects or its formal model.

As mentioned above, one of the formal models of *The Legend of Good Women* itself, though used in a parodic way, is the saints' legend collection. It is appropriate in the context of the present discussion to refer to the tradition of English vernacular saints' lives in the fifteenth century. Space does not permit an extended discussion of this further area of exemplary narrative, a very important area of medieval writing, but it is to be noted that Chaucer's influence is clearly discernible in the development of this genre in the fifteenth century, albeit in ways quite different from that considered above. Despite his parodic use of the form in the *Legend*, Chaucer did, of course, write a straightforward example of the genre in his life of St Cecilia (The Second Nun's Tale). His Prioress's Tale belongs to a related genre, the miracle of the Virgin, and he introduces religious motifs and hagiographical conventions into his two tales of exemplary women in the romance tradition, The Man of Law's Tale and The Clerk's Tale. Notable stylistic features of these tales are the rhyme royal stanza, and, in The Second Nun's Tale and The Prioress's Tale, the use of a formal prologue and of embellished rhetorical language. Fifteenth-century poets, who looked to Chaucer's work for what was serious and elevated in style as well as in subject matter, developed these elements of style in verse saints' lives to produce a particular form and style of hagiographical writing distinctive within what had, of course, been a popular vernacular genre from the early Middle English period onwards. It was distinctive by its use of formal prologues, sometimes marking a division into books, by its use of rhetorical figures and ornate language, and occasionally by echoes of Chaucer's phraseology. Examples noteworthy in the context of the present topic are Lydgate's *Life of Our Lady* and his *Legend of Seynt Margarete*, which contains a number of clear echoes of The Clerk's Tale; Capgrave's *Life of St. Katharine of Alexandria*; and Bokenham's *Legendys of Hooly Wummen* (see further Pearsall 1970; Stouck 1982).

King's College London
University of London

NOTES

1. See Feimer 1983, 272. In the early fourteenth century Seneca's text was provided with an influential commentary which included a summary of the argument of the play (see Franceschini 1938).

2. See Lydgate's *Fall of Princes*, Part IV, pp. 146-48 for the text of Boccaccio and Laurent. The story of Medea's eventual return to her father's kingdom and his restoration is related or alluded to by several writers of antiquity: Apollodorus, *The Library*, chs 16-28; Hyginus, *Fabulae*, edited by H. I. Rose (Leyden, 1933; rpt. 1960), ch. XXVI; Justin, *History of the World*, in *Justin, Cornelius Nepos, and Eutropius*, translated by John Selby Watson (London, 1853), p. 279; Valerius Flaccus, *Argonautica*, V. 683-87. I am grateful to Olga Illston for enabling me to trace some of these references.

3. The reference to hell in line 3 of *The Letter of Cupid*, not present in the French source, may be derived from the mention of heaven and hell which opens *The Legend of Good Women*, though the context of the two references differs; Hoccleve's line 41 sounds like an allusion to line 1254 of the *Legend*.

REFERENCES

Ames, Ruth M., 1986 — The Feminist Connections of Chaucer's *Legend of Good Women*, in *Chaucer in the Eighties*, ed. Julian N. Wasserman and Robert J. Blanch, Syracuse, New York, pp. 57-74

Bryan, W. F., and Germaine Dempster, 1941 — *Sources and Analogues of Chaucer's Canterbury Tales*, New York

Delaney, Sheila, 1986 — Rewriting Woman Good, in *Chaucer in the Eighties*, ed. Julian N. Wasserman and Robert J. Blanch, Syracuse, New York, pp. 75-92

Edwards, Mary Carol, 1970 — A Study of Six Characters in Chaucer's *Legend of Good Women* with reference to Medieval Scholia in Ovid's *Heroides*, unpublished B. Litt. thesis, University of Oxford

Feimer, Joel Nicholas, 1983 — The Figure of Medea in Medieval Literature: A Thematic Metamorphosis, unpublished Ph. D. thesis, City University of New York

Franceschini, Ezio, 1938 — Glosse e commenti medievali a Seneca tragico, in *Studi e Note di Filologia Latina Medievali*, Milan, pp. 1-105

Lowes, John Livingston, 1909 — Is Chaucer's *Legend of Good Women* a Travesty?, *JEGP*, 8, pp. 513-69

Luria, Maxwell, 1982 — *A Reader's Guide to the Roman de la Rose*, Hamden, Conn.

Mitchell, Jerome, 1968 — *Thomas Hoccleve*, Urbana, Chicago and London

Pearsall, Derek, 1970 — *John Lydgate*, London

Rogers, Katharine M., 1966 — *The Troublesome Helpmate*, Seattle and London

Schirmer, Walter F., 1961 — *John Lydgate*, trans. Ann E. Keep, London

Schleich, Gustav, ed., 1924 — *Die mittelenglische Umdichtung von Boccaccios De Claris Mulieribus*, Leipzig

Stouck, Mary-Ann, 1982 — Chaucer and Capgrave's *Life of St. Katharine*, *The American Benedictine Review*, 33, pp. 276-91

Utley, Francis Lee, 1944 — *The Crooked Rib*, Columbus

BIRD POEMS FROM *THE PARLIAMENT OF FOWLS* TO *PHILIP SPARROW*

W. A. Davenport

I

Bird poems provide a measure of the variety and enterprise of fifteenth-century poetry. In his edition of *The Harmony of Birds* and *The Parliament of Birds* Malcolm Andrew (ed. 1984, 27) says: 'their mode is predictable, their structure unoriginal, their outlook conventional' and sums up (justly as far as these two sixteenth-century bird poems are concerned) by saying 'they manifestly do not exemplify the bold innovation and growing individualism which characterizes much of the best shorter poetry written during the English Renaissance'. While some of the poems considered below are predictable and conventional, others are not and the general impression of bird poetry in the fifteenth century is that there was bolder innovation than the period is usually credited with, and that, in some works, individualism is already growing. *The Parliament of Fowls* is a suitable starting point not only because its liveliness stimulated later poets to imitation and emulation but also because it displays the interesting mixture of traditions of literary birds already available to Chaucer in the 1380s. One main tradition may be identified in Chaucer's use of lists and categories of birds. The mixture of natural and legendary bird characteristics visible in lines 330-64 of the poem is taken over from encyclopaedias such as Vincent of Beauvais's *Speculum Naturale* and its derivative Bartholomaeus Anglicus's *De Proprietatibus Rerum*. The scientific classifications of Aristotle and Pliny merge with bits of folk-lore, literary traditions, fables and historical allusions to form a body of 'bird-lore', which moves comfortably between natural observation of such things as the different habitats of birds and the bestiary symbolism of the pelican in her piety and the unique phoenix burnt to ashes and newly born. Chaucer begins his bird description with a scientific classification into birds of prey, worm-eating birds, water birds and seed-eating birds, placing them high, low, on the water and on the grass, and so combining a grouping based on food with one based on habitat. Aristotle, Vincent of Beauvais and Bartholomew can all be detected. Once Chaucer begins to describe the members of his parliament he makes the traditional hierarchical start with the royal eagle ' That with his sharpe lok perseth the sonne',

and gives generous space to the birds of prey, before moving on to briefer characterizations of
a more random collection of mainly familiar birds, with only the 'popynjay, ful of delicasye'
providing a touch of the exotic. This is a more natural assembly than many others one meets in
medieval poetry, more natural too than the literary list of trees earlier in the poem, where olive
and vine, palm and sibyl's laurel give an obviously Mediterranean ring. The choice of birds
reflects the social theme of the poem and the influence of *De Planctu Naturae*; it also prepares
for Chaucer's later effects of playing off the language of formality and status against the
language of down-to-earth common sense, even to the extent of using the bathos of bird noises:

> 'Wel bourded,' quod the doke, 'by myn hat!
> That men shulde loven alwey causeles!
> Who can a resoun fynde or wit in that?
> Daunseth he murye that is myrtheles?
> Who shulde recche of that is recheles?'
> 'Ye queke,' seyde the goos, 'ful wel and fayre!
> There been mo sterres, God wot, than a payre!' (589-95)

Other writers, more interested in the homiletic moralization of animal examples and the use of
birds as religious symbols, were apt to extend Nature by the inventions of fantasy and legend.

A second tradition drawn on by Chaucer in *The Parliament of Fowls* is that of companies
of birds, especially in joint song, found in the medieval *locus amoenus*. The harmony of the
world under Nature's control is illustrated by an idyllic, amorous chorus singing, as, for
example, in the Garden of Deduit in *Le Roman de la Rose*; the singing sometimes consists of a
repertoire of courtly lyrics illustrating the realization of joy in love. The bird company and their
song are frequent decorative motifs associated with spring, well-being, impulses towards love,
young heroes seeking adventure in the early morning, the beginning of new enterprises, and
the start of spiritual enlightenment (as in the dream landscape in *Pearl*). The choristers of
Nature or of Venus may be seen celebrating divine service and joining in a Mass of Birds, as in
Jean de Condé's *Messe des Oiseaus*. In the final roundel of Chaucer's poem, 'Now welcome,
somer, with thy sonne softe', differences are forgotten, the separate bird voices become a
chorus to do 'honour and plesaunce' to Nature.

Thirdly in *The Parliament of Fowls* there is the obvious literary idea of the debate or
parliament of birds, in which birds, doubtless because they are vocal creatures of intriguingly
distinct and varied sound, are used as substitutes for human beings and either thronged to
suggest the mixture of human society or paired to represent the rivalries and polarities of human
attitudes. Andrew (ed. 1984, 28) distinguishes three versions: bird versus human, bird versus
bird, and the parliament. Apart from the question of speech and song, the particular appeal of
birds to the imagination of medieval writers was a basic similarity of form and life which made

them a definable population sharing characteristics and so forming a coherent basis for the mirroring of human activity, together with great richness and variation of detail in colour, size, temperament and so on, which meant that they demonstrated God's skill as endlessly inventive creator. Chaucer's comedy and miming of human poses gives a particular sharpness and vigour to his version of the debate. The association with St Valentine's Day (found also in *The Complaint of Mars*, *Complaynt d'Amours*, and the poems of Grandson) turns the birds into representatives of human beings as lovers and sets up a double game whereby the aristocratic aquiline rivalry of a contest in a court of love is played off against the medley of commentating voices on the ways of love; Chaucer nicely exploits the court game of choosing partners, echoing the French *demandes d'amour* and the rivalries of *Florence and Blancheflor* and *Melior and Ydoine*,[1] but enriches the debate by letting it spill over into a wider discussion which explores the range of bird species and their variety of voice. It is through weaving together literary traditions that Chaucer makes *The Parliament of Fowls* work simultaneously as argumentative, courtly game, philosophical discussion of Nature, love, seasonal order and law, and a graceful lyrical celebration of springtime and the mating instinct. The variety within the comparatively brief poem explains why it is one of Chaucer's most imitated works.

Direct influence is most obvious in John Clanvowe's *The Book of Cupid* (*The Cuckoo and the Nightingale*). Clanvowe returns to the simple pattern of two spokesbirds for different ideas of love, placing his debate within a framework composed of initial praise of love, springtime and the perfect joy of the birds singing their hours and the final plan to arraign the Cuckoo at a bird parliament before the window of the Queen at Woodstock on the next St Valentine's Day, followed by the poet's waking. Outwardly Clanvowe discards Chaucer's imaginative mingling of ideas and accepts the most courtly and conventional aspects of his form and theme: the praise of love taken from The Knight's Tale, the poet-lover's sentimental attitudes, the court-poet's ending. But the challenge to love by the 'lewed' Cuckoo, who scorns love not just by association with cuckoldry and faithlessness, but by refusal to accept the value of love, by pouring ridicule on its folly, wildness, instability, jealousy, quarrelling and despair, amounts to a sturdy, rational scepticism and he is unabashed by opposition. The Nightingale puts up the expected defence of ideal love and its joys, virtue, courtesy and trust, its rewards, its honour and beauty. The Cuckoo is unconvinced and there is no weak yielding to the privileged attitude. The Cuckoo sees merely wilful randomness in love and can be quelled only by the author-dreamer's interference; the throwing of a stone drives off the Cuckoo, who cries scornfully 'farewel, farewel papyngay' and leaves the poet to reaffirm pastoral beauty, truth and ceremony, without sounding very convincing to the reader.[2] The poem is typical of a Lollard arguer at least to the extent of expressing the objections of common-sense and experience. Clanvowe has learned from the pragmatism of the lower-class birds in Chaucer's poem, not merely from the courtly tone of the eagles.

While not exactly a bird poem, *The Kingis Quair* also shares material with Chaucer (and with Gower and Lydgate and other courtly dreams and allegories) and shows an intelligent absorption of Chaucerian complexity of attitude and intention. It is one of the few medieval courtly allegories based on autobiographical fact, and a striking quality of the poem is the fusion of symbolism and actual circumstance; the black rocks, borrowed from The Franklin's Tale as an image of the dangers of life's treacherous sea and the Boethian theme of danger, reversal and mutability, also refer literally to the voyage on which James was taken prisoner. The whole poem interprets the experience of the youthful voyage, imprisonment in the tower, falling in love and eventual liberation as the fulfilment of a Boethian process, and the poet's use of birds is in tune with this fusion of the circumstances of life with an intellectual design, drawing, in Chaucerian manner, on several different aspects of bird imagery. The narrator in prison, 'Bewailing in my chamber thus allone' (line 204) and inviting comparison with Palamon, Arcite and Troilus, sees through the window a fair May garden in which the birds hop and play and the nightingales are singing hymns of love. He is led to muse on love and the contrast between the freedom of the birds and his own state: ' That I am thrall, and birdis gone at large' (263). The use of birds as part of the spring landscape, images of natural liberty, and of nightingales as choristers whose voices can be used for an inset lyric hymning the power of love again effectively combines the natural and the artificial; the words of human song are conventionally put into the beaks of birds but the natural idiom used elsewhere encourages one to hear them as the human narrator's interpretation of natural birdsong. A little later in the poem, when he has seen the fair maiden with whom he falls in love, the nightingale becomes the addressee for the narrator's own enhancing rhetoric as he exhorts her (in lines 372-413) to express his feelings for him, to find the pathos of Procne's suffering, to chide the false with Philomena's poignancy and then, as the lady approaches, to leave sorrow and 'Opyn thy throte'. The nightingale does sing and is joined by other birds in joyful music. The poet then uses the music, rather than the supposed words, of 'the philomene' as accompaniment to his own words ('the ditee there I maid'), a lyrical stanza craving mercy (435-41), and then the birds take up another song and again are given words (442-55) proclaiming their joy in their mates, the service of love, and welcoming May: ' This was thair song (as semyt me)'. In this passage birds are used as a reflection of the poet's mood; the ostensible object of his chiding and his pleading, they are in effect a peg on which he hangs his aroused feelings of joy, anxiety and sorrow. The passage cleverly mixes lyricism, images of spring and love, and myths from Ovid which transform human beings into birds; so the poet's voice becomes the bird's voice, the bird his other self giving public expression to the state of his inner soul. A third appearance of bird material in the poem comes towards the end when, after a vision of Fortune and her wheel, the poet laments (with another echo of Troilus) his doubts and fears, and asks for a token of the grace of the gods, whereupon at the window a turtle-dove lands on his hand, holding in her bill a spray of flowers which bears a message of comfort. This last use of the bird as divine messenger adds to the overall quality in the poem of birds as part of an expressive language of emblems and figures, illustrating human feelings; birds do not take over the poem here and become substitutes for human characters but show Chaucer's poetic vocabulary being intelligently adopted and extended.[3]

II

Not all fifteenth-century bird poems belong to the Chaucerian tradition of courtly narrative and lyric, obviously. If nightingales are messengers of love in *The Kingis Quair*, as in *Troilus and Criseyde*, they appear in a different guise in several poems where they reprove lamenting lovers and attack women and the folly of love.

> 'A woman is a wonder thyng,
>> þow sho be fayre & stille,
> She nys trwe to kny3t nor kyng;
>> clerke, to 3e she nylle.'
>> (' The Clerk and the Nightingale' I, Robbins ed. 1955, No. 179)[4]

The story of Philomena and her suffering makes available the image of nightingale as sacrificial victim and hence as a figure of the bleeding Christ. The medieval tradition of complaint includes the use of bird voices to stir pity and devotion, and the figure of bird and tree appears in several poems as a representation of Christ on the cross. Two fifteenth-century expressions of this literary theme are *The Nightingale* and *A Saying of the Nightingale* , both formerly attributed to Lydgate. *The Nightingale* (see *Lydgate's Minor Poems*, ed. Glauning, 1900) is a direct paraphrase of *Philomena*, a thirteenth-century Latin poem by John Pecham (a Franciscan friar who became Archbishop of Canterbury, and died 1292) in which the nightingale sings before her death, first at the top of a tree and then on gradually lower branches at the canonical hours, Prime, Tierce, Sext and Nones, singing her heart out and dying. The poem is a commemoration of the Passion, expressed in intense affective verse characteristic of Franciscan piety. The English version is a compact, neatly constructed poem, written for the Duchess of Buckingham after 1446, presenting the allegory of the life of Christ, the life of man and the ages of the world, clearly and systematically; it doesn't sound like Lydgate. *A Saying of the Nightingale* (see Glauning ed. 1900 and *The Minor Poems of John Lydgate*, Part I, ed. MacCracken, 1911) is an independent work, a more likely product of Lydgate's pen not just because it is, according to MacCracken, 'digressive, indirect and incompact' (ed. 1911, xxxiv; see also Pearsall 1970, 266-67), but because of its resemblances to other poems by him. This poem opens with a bold picture of sunset as birdsong fades away, leaving only the voice of the nightingale singing the enigmatic 'occy, occy', as in *The Book of Cupid*. The Poet thinks she is crying 'O sle theym' to alert Venus to punish false lovers. In the dream that follows a strange messenger comes:

> Nought from Cupide, but fro the lord above –
> And, as me thought, ful fayre and fressh of chiere,
> Whiche to me sayde, 'Foole, what dostow here
> Slepyng allone, gapyng vpon the mone?
> Rise, folowe me.' (45-49)

The nightingale's song is then 'unclosed' to the dreamer as pure love and glossed as a mnemonic of Christ's love and suffering. After a process of teaching, which uses the wounds of Christ, Isaiah's image of the winepress, a Complaint of Christ, and the theme of the cross as a specific against the sins, the sinful soul is exhorted to forsake the world for the garden of 'perfite paramours' (340), where Christ the nightingale calls to man's soul 'Com to my gardyn and to myn herber grene' (359). The poem uses from *Philomena* only the initial idea of the nightingale's song; after that it becomes a mixture of well-rehearsed religious themes and moments of sensitivity. *A Saying of the Nightingale* has successfully borrowed from the Chaucerian idiom its secular frame, as well as the rhyme-royal stanza and the machinery of the courtly dream. Instead of the close pattern of figure and interpretation in *Philomena*, the poet creates the antithesis between worldly and spiritual values; the religious meaning achieves power by its contradiction of vain folly based on the bodily senses. In the scene of listening to the song before sleep the poet alludes perhaps to Criseyde and certainly to a whole tradition of courtly association which is tartly rejected in the dream messenger's words:

> 'For trust me wele, I cast the nat to leede
> Nothyng towardes the gardyn of the Rose.' (52-53)

Later this particular rejection is given point by the use of the rose image as an affective emblem: the dreamer is exhorted to make of the five wounds of Christ a rose:

> Make of these fyve in thyn hert a Rose
> And lete it there contynuauly abyde;
> Forgete hym nought, where thow go or ride,
> Gadre on an hepe these rosen-floures fyve,
> In thy memorye prynt hem al thy lyve. (115-19)

The poem shows us a different face of post-Chaucerian verse, the adoption of Chaucerian diction and situations for the purpose of contrast, to provide a touchstone for explicit emphasis on spiritual themes, which for Chaucer were more often matter for epilogues and retractions or part of a debate than the main burden of the song.

Some of Chaucer's birds were teachers, of course: the eagle in *The House of Fame*, the crow (in its way) in The Manciple's Tale. Fifteenth-century poets make use of the tutorial role in various ways. Straightforwardly didactic poems include ' The Bird with Four Feathers' (Brown ed. 1924, No. 121) in which a lamenting bird teaches the wandering poet the vanity of worldly things: the four feathers that have been plucked were youth, beauty, strength and riches, and each is the occasion for a confession, first of folly, then of pride in appearance, thoughts of lechery, worldly power and possession, the pursuit of wealth; all benefits have gone and the bird's complaints accumulate into a miniature, one-role morality play describing the rise and fall of the worldly life. 'Revertere' expresses a similar theme rather more urgently, at least in the short version in Richard Hill's commonplace book (Oxford, Balliol College MS 354), which contains several homiletic bird poems:

> In a tyme of a somers day,
> > The sune shon full meryly þat tyde,
> I toke my hawke, me for to play,
> > My spanyellis renyng by my syde.
> A fesavnt henne than gan I see;
> > My howndis put her to flight;
> I lett my hawke vnto her fle,
> > To me yt was a deynte syght.
>
> My fawkon flewe fast vnto her pray;
> > My hownd gan renne with glad chere;
> & sone I spurnyd in my way;
> > My lege was hent in a breer;
> This breer, forsothe, yt dyde me gref;
> > Ywys yt made me to turn a-ye,
> For he bare wrytyng in euery leff,
> > This latyn word: 'Revertere.'
>
> I hayld & pullid this breer me fro,
> > & rede this word full meryly;
> My hart fell down vnto my to,
> > That was before full lykyngly.
> I lett my havke & fesavnt fare;
> > My spanyell fell down vnto my kne;

It toke me with a sighyng sare,
    This new lessun: 'Revertere.'

Lykyng ys moder of synnes all,
    & norse to euery wykyd dede;
To myche myschef she makyth men fall,
    & of sorow þe dawnce she doth lede.
This hawke of yowth ys high of porte,
    And wildnes makyth hym wyde to fle,
& ofte to fall in wykyd thowght,
    And than ys best: 'Revertere.' (Dyboski ed. 1907, 80-81)

Here moral warning develops neatly from pleasant natural description as the flight of the hawk acquires the sense of the reckless, youthful pursuit of pleasure, and being caught in headlong chase by a briar vividly expresses the tug of the awakening conscience. All is gathered into the bird imagery of ' This hawke of yowth', which draws on the accumulated associations of depictions of youth's characteristic occupations in literature and art (Cummins 1988, ch. 20). The longer version (120 lines) of the poem in Lambeth Palace MS 853 (Furnivall ed. 1867, 91-94) labours the point, but makes the moral meaning quite clear:

This hauke is mannis herte, y vndirstonde,
    For it is ȝong & of hiȝ romage. (59-60)

This hauk of herte in ȝouþe y-wys,
    Pursueþ euere þis feisaunt hen;
þis feisaunt hen is likingnes,
    And euere folewiþ hir þese ȝonge men. (73-76)

The Balliol version manages it with a lighter hand, using birds as hunter and prey, suggesting worldly pursuit and youthful liberty, and briar as an image of moral restraint, and leaving the rest to our own response.

    The meeting between the foolish human being and the didactic bird provides the material for one of Lydgate's best short poems, *The Churl and the Bird* (MacCracken ed. 1934).[5] The prologue identifies this as a moral fable but the rhyme-royal stanza indicates Lydgate's choice of the Chaucerian courtly narrative as his point of reference and the dialogue between the ignorant peasant and the shrewd bird is enlivened by a sense of scene and some terseness of speech. As with many other bird poems, the narrative begins in an elaborate garden where the golden bird is singing on a laurel before being caught and caged. Though the making of the garden is a sign of the peasant's 'lust and gret corage' to create a thing of beauty, as well as of his 'diligent travaile' (45-46), these ambitious stirrings do not go far enough; they do not stretch to generosity of mind and his response to the bird's pleas for freedom and refusal to sing in captivity is merely to threaten to eat the bird, until the bird offers him three nuggets of wisdom in exchange for liberty. The lessons are apparently simple and within the range of a schoolroom fable: don't believe everything you are told, don't wish for impossible things, and don't cry over spilt milk. The second half of the poem is, though, more subtle than one expects. With freedom the bird gains in confidence and ruthlessly plays with the churl's credulity, telling him that he was a fool to release her, since she had a precious, magic stone ('iagounce', 232) in her body, which would have brought prosperity and happiness, and then, when the peasant immediately accepts this implausible story and complains of Fortune in hopeless passion, unsparingly bringing him to realize how he has failed to acquire any of the wisdom offered him:

> 'O dulle cherl! wisdames for to leere
> That I the tauht, al is left bi-hynde,
> Racid awey, and cleene out of thi mynde.' (299-301)

Credulity, vain regret and impossible desire all expose the inadequacy of the man to whom all birds are alike. The simple moral lesson thus proves to have an interesting twist in the bird's offering a test to the churl and the dialogue of teacher and pupil is not the expected ritual but a failed lesson, a comic debacle in which a reasonable morality of contentment and self-discipline is demonstrated not by the learner's acquisition of it, but by his simplicity and failure. The dialogue becomes at times a dramatic confrontation using the language of taunt rather than of reason and instruction:

> ' To heeryn a wisdam thyn eris ben half deeff,
> Lik an asse that listeth on a harpe.
> Thou maist go pypen in a ivy leeff.' (274-76)

The tones of the eagle in *The House of Fame* and of the scornful upper-class birds in *The Parliament of Fowls* have schooled this bird and Lydgate makes intelligent use of the animal/human relationship, with the bird standing for imagination and understanding, associated with beauty and colour, while the ignorance of the churl is reflected in his actions, crude, aggressive, physical, self-pitying. The moral convincingly arises out of the narrative, rather than being tacked on, except, of course, for the question of why the churl wished ' Tarray his gardeyn with notable apparaile' (47) in the first place.

A more powerful use of bird-fable is Henryson's excellent poem The Preaching of the Swallow (*Fables* VIII). This is a brilliant combination of the usual fable pattern of anecdote and concluding moralization with a picture of man's life and the life of the world through the sequence of the seasons. Drawing on the encyclopaedists' surveys of God, man and the calendar, Henryson describes seasonal activities (especially of the winter months, bird-catching, preparing flax) and uses traditional images, such as that of Satan as a bird-catcher, to extend the sense of the fabulous tale of the swallow's attempts to forewarn the other birds of the danger of the fowler's net. Here birds appear both in the role of preacher and as representatives of general vulnerability and short-sightedness. The swallow is a melancholy Cassandra-figure, observant and imaginative, while the folly of the rest is exposed as limitation of vision, the inability to conceive of any time but the present, the imprudence of lack of foresight. With Henryson's usual sleight of hand, human beings, who in the fable are the enemies of birds, are transformed in the *Moralitas* into the real subject, while the fowler is translated into the Devil. As with *The Kingis Quair*, one would not describe this exactly as a bird poem, but Henryson imaginatively uses naturalism with fable conventions to create through bird figures an ironic and elegiac picture of human failure, labour and idleness. Burrow (1984, 150) points to Henryson's vivid picturing of the sudden, darting movements of the flock, which both define the space within which the action occurs, and 'suggest exhilaration, hysteria and finally panic'. The dwindling of the birds, seen through the eyes of Henryson's observer, to the lonely swallow, who takes her flight and disappears, makes its moral point but works on the reader, in conjunction with the winter scene, largely through pathos. Behind Henryson's perceptive development one can see the raw material of the conventional springtime description of nature and birdsong, of the bird dispute, of *chanson d'aventure* and courtly dream, but the transforming intelligence has turned the parable into a satisfying exploration of landscape, the pattern of the year and of wisdom and folly.

More central to the tradition of bird poetry is a less often read Scots poem, Richard Holland's *The Buke of the Howlat*, written about 1450 in the alliterative thirteen-line stanza with nine long lines and wheel. The poem is an exemplary fable, telling the story of the owl who first complains of its ugly appearance and then, when clad by Nature in borrowed plumage, becomes too proud and is stripped by the other birds. Holland has transferred this story to the owl from the crow, perhaps with the image of the mobbing of the owl in mind, and fused it with the lively tradition of the bird parliament to produce a particularly rich comic fantasy. True, the poem is a hotch-potch as a result of Holland's introduction of lengthy praise of the Douglas family in a heraldic digression in the style of the dynastic epic, but even here there is heroic bravado recalling earlier alliterative paeans and laments. The main current of the poem moves on the two levels of the fable and the assembly of the birds. The fable begins in the springtime wandering mode, reminiscent of *The Parliament of the Three Ages*, and the owl's lament is heard against the pleasant background of birds preening in a May landscape; the lament is expressed as an accusation of Nature for which the owl is reproved by the papal peacock who calls together his cardinals, council, patriarchs and prophets. Holland now lets the poetry flow into the second channel and vastly enjoys himself in describing first a religious and then a secular assembling of birds, in which he finds bird equivalents for human offices and roles. This is comparable to Chaucer's listing of birds in *The Parliament of Fowls* but Holland makes comic, satirical use of bird appearances. The view is not critical, more fantastic, with cranes as cardinals, swans as bishops, magpies, partridges and plovers as abbots of different orders, seagulls as monks, crows and jackdaws as friars begging corn, 'schir Gawane the drak' (210) as treasurer wearing the green amice, and so on. However, there is some variation of treatment: with some birds it is the appearance that makes the effect, as with the heron:

> Heronnis contemplatif, clene charterouris,
> With toppit hudis on hed and clething of hair,
> Ay sorowfull and sad at evinsang and houris
> — Was nevir leid saw thaim lauch, bot drowp and dar. (185-88)

With others the opportunity for social satire is taken, as with the raven:

> The ravyne, rolpand rudly in a roche ran,
> Was dene rurale to reid, rank as a raike;
> Quhill the lardner was laid, held he na hous
>> Bot in uplandis townis
>> At vicaris and personnis
>> For the procuracounis
>>> Cryand full crows. (215-21)

This ecclesiastical assembly decides that since Nature is involved the opinion of the secular estate is required and Holland moves on to the birds of prey who represent the rulers and nobles, with goshawks as army commanders ('marchonis in the mapamond', 328), sparrowhawks as keen knights, the woodpecker as pursuivant riding before the emperor in coat-armour; eventually (after the Douglas diversion) we come down to mere soldiers and packhorse drivers (kites), robin redbreast as page and the 'little wee wren' as the poor dwarf. The fantasy culminates in a colourful and humorous banquet with bird attendants and bird minstrels (thrushes, starlings and nightingales), who sing an aureate celebratory lyric to Mary ('Hale, temple of the Trinite . . . ' 718ff.), a virtuoso performance by the juggling jay (who has learned his party tricks from the magician in The Franklin's Tale and creates illusions of hunting, ships and battle), the rook as an Irish bard spouting gobbledegook and getting involved in flyting with the raven, and a rough and tumble, full of joking alliterative exaggeration, with two fools, the lapwing and the cuckoo ('the tuchet and the gukkit', 821). Here Holland appears simply to be having fun, exploiting the animal disguises to caricature aspects of social life; the poem allies itself not only to the 'Who killed Cock Robin?' tradition, but also to Dunbar's flytings and cartoons of court life and to Skelton's gabbling grotesqueries. Holland returns to the fable of the owl and completes the story with vigour and humour, pointedly picturing the owl's besotted vanity and arrogance towards the other birds as a Lucifer-like excess and Nature's response as an ironic percipience. At the end only poet and owl are left, the bird offering himself as an example and uttering the moral, not merely a warning against pride but showing the pattern of all human life:

> ' Think how bair thow was borne, and bair ay will be
> For oucht that sedis of thi self in ony sessoun.
> Thy cude, thi claithis, nor thi cost cummis nocht of the . . .
> We cum pure, we gang pure, baith king and commoun.' (976-78, 983)

Holland's imaginative use of bird qualities turns this fable into a richer experience than the message might suggest: we begin and end with the owl's wretched ugliness and the bleak lesson but the central part of the poem has taken on coloured plumage, like the owl, and luxuriates in comic ingenuity and zestful invention of correspondences, jokes, ceremonies and rituals. The moral fable has a satisfying irony in that the owl, obsessed with his own ugliness, imagines that he will be mobbed by the other birds, out of loathing and scorn, but it is only when proud of his own beauty that the owl is punished. The sequence of thought and the presentation of Jonah in *Patience* provide an interesting parallel in alliterative poetry; the pattern of accusation, assembly of judges and eventual repentance has an intriguing similarity to *The Testament of Cresseid*.

The mere massing together of many individual birds becomes a pleasure in *The Buke of the Howlat* because the different species are ingeniously used as equivalents to human uniforms or functions. The catalogue of birds is used in a more explicitly didactic manner in *The Court of Sapience* (*c.* 1450), a poem characteristic of fifteenth-century interest in lengthy educational allegory; the youthful hero's vision of the wonders of creation is a process of learning and the list of birds (1387 ff., based on *De Proprietatibus Rerum*, but with a few Chaucerian touches) is part of a demonstration of the harmony and ordering of Nature, simply part of the syllabus of wisdom and virtue for the ignorant dreamer. Its literary interest is the sign of the continuity of a tradition, encyclopaedic in origin but part of the material of moral epic which links Langland, Spenser and Milton.

Similarly *The Plowman's Tale*, added at the end of *The Canterbury Tales* in Thynne's second edition of 1542 but probably written early in the previous century, is less interesting in itself than as an example of birds used for religious and political allegory in the mode employed more famously by Dryden in *The Hind and the Panther*. *The Plowman's Tale* is a hybrid in which a 'preaching' of didactic satirical intent is cobbled together with a journalistic cataloguing of abuses by the church and a *contentio* for two opposed animal speakers. The debate is more reminiscent of *Winner and Waster* than of *The Owl and the Nightingale*; the Lollard pelican, who lengthily, diffusely and repetitively harangues priests for worldliness for over six hundred lines, could have any identity, and the Catholic gryphon, when at last allowed to present some counter-arguments, has no animal identity. It is only at the end of the poem, when the pelican is left alone with the Plowman, that the poet justifies his choice of speakers by drawing on bestiary lore to associate the pelican with Christ's sacrifice and to give moral significance to the hybrid eagle/lion nature of the gryphon, who combines Lucifer's evil pride with misused temporal strength. Finally the gryphon's company of ravens, rooks, crows, magpies, *et al.* is defeated by the Christ-figure of the phoenix. This is an arbitrary and patchy poem in which invective is allowed to distort the literary purpose, but it is an indicator of awareness in the period of ways of extending the usefulness of the bird debate and drawing on inherited symbolism.

III

At the end of the century two major poets, Dunbar and Skelton, demonstrate the rich resource which bird-lore and the forms of bird poems had become. In his court poetry Dunbar presents animals and plants in their heraldic and allegorical guises. In *The Thrissil and the Rois* the eagle is proclaimed king of birds, and enjoined to be just to the birds who are his subjects. At the beginning and end of the poem birds are used decoratively in the courtly vision company of Aurora and May; birdsong is scattered through the poem as part of a picturesque rendering of Nature into highly coloured illumination of ceremony and aristocratic display. It is the lark on Aurora's hand that bids the narrator and all lovers awake, the birds that register the joy of spring and, at the end of the poem, lead the celebration, first singing one by one and then together, hailing the Rose and waking the dreamer with their joyful noise. A poem about King and Queen requires courtiers as well as royalty: lion, eagle, thistle and rose represent the honoured and celebrated by heraldic emblems, and Dunbar turns the birds into the courtiers, through whom the honouring is expressed. In *The Goldyn Targe* he employs the same vocabulary with splendidly rich effect and his depiction of 'Venus chapell clerkis' skipping and hopping on the boughs among the jewelled dewdrops is one of his most living, alert pieces of writing; tapestried artifice and the delicate natural animation of the poet's imagination work together. It is in this company that his exercise in bird debate, *The Merle and the Nychtingall*, belongs. It is a polished example of the contention between secular and religious values, displaying Dunbar's unfailing sense of adopting the right poetic language for a particular formal purpose. Constructed as a double ballade in Monk's stanza, the poem has alternate refrains for blackbird and nightingale to act as the poles between which the argument moves. The blackbird speaks up for the spirit of springtime, youth, woman's beauty, love's virtue and its inspiration of honour and courage, while the nightingale responds with scorn for time wasted in vain pursuits, pleading for love of God, truth and a recognition of the relative inferiority of love of woman. The arguments are sensibly expressed but Dunbar treats the theme as the occasion for a formal dance of alternate steps which, when a certain point is reached, must join, as the last four stanzas do in the nightingale's refrain: 'All lufe is lost bot upone God allone'.

Dunbar's acceptance of the formal decorum of the lyric pattern may be placed in contrast to his use of bird-lore in his satirical jibe against John Damian in *Ane Ballat of the Fenȝeit Freir of Tungland.* Damian's attempt at flight gives Dunbar the excuse for a fantasy picture of this usurper-bird mobbed by the genuine creatures of the air:

> The myttane and Sanct Martynis fowle
> Wend he had bene the hornit howle;
> They set aupone him wyth a ȝowle
>   And gaif him dynt for dynt.
> The golk, the gormaw and the gled
> Beft him with buffettis quhill he bled;
> The sparhalk to the spring him sped
> Als fers as fyre of flynt. (73-80)

The list of birds here is used to good satirical effect to accumulate a mass of natural richness against the unnatural pretender who is seen as blasphemously assaulting the region which belongs to the birds. The birds' representation of Nature repelling an attack on order takes us back to the concepts which in *The Parliament of Fowls* Chaucer showed he had absorbed from Alain de Lille. Dunbar has turned this philosophical and literary material, together with the bird-lore of the mobbing of the owl, to the purposes of attack on corruption at court, again demonstrating the colourful flexibility of bird material.

Skelton provides two major instances of bird poetry, *Speke Parott* and *Phyllyp Sparowe.* In these two poems he shows himself to be, like Chaucer, a transforming genius. Here the bird material, which can be seen to be growing more complex and interesting in fifteenth-century poetry, looks suddenly quite different, even though one can identify in the two poems many familiar ideas. Skelton's Parrot has some of the qualities already present separately in Chaucer's eagle, in Chauntecleer, in the lamenting falcon in The Squire's Tale, and echoes other fifteenth-century feathered moral commentators, but by making Parrot the poet's voice in the poem, Skelton significantly enlarges the bird role. No longer is the bird voice overheard and then dismissed in a return to the poet's or the dreamer's terms of reference; here the human beings are merely the admiring feeders of the bird's cleverness, or, in Galathea's case, questioner, attendant priestess and stimulator of Parrot's prophetic powers. Skelton has enriched the bird role by drawing on Ovid and Boccaccio to give complexity of reference to his Psittacus, but the actual qualities and poses of Parrot could equally be seen as a compound of characteristics found in Chaucer's crow, Holland's juggling jay, Lydgate's golden bird, and so on; indeed Skelton encourages the reader to recognize this compositeness by alluding to other bird poems and making passing references to Hoccleve, Lydgate, Hawes and others, as when the following commendation of Parrot invites us to recall *The Churl and the Bird*:

> For trowthe in parabyll ye wantonlye pronounce
> Langagys divers; yet undyr that doth reste
> Maters more precious than the ryche jacounce. (364-66)

As the comments in the poem make clear, Skelton found reactions to his writing as stupid as Lydgate's bird thought the churl, and the reference to the fictional jacinth is a suitable tongue-in-cheek way of indicating it. Parrot's role as satirical truth-teller achieves, by such complexity, greater authority and comic interest than is possible for such a limited satirical voice as that of the pelican in *The Plowman's Tale*.

Skelton has also liberated the bird voice from the confines of the formal structure of fable or dream poem or debate. The satire against the abuses of the age was often loosely constructed and Skelton's combination of monologue, dialogue and poet's envoys has similarities to *The Plowman's Tale*. We can find echoes too of other satirical works on the times, such as Lydgate's ' The Cok Hath Lowe Shoone' (MacCracken ed. 1934; see also Heiserman 1961, 177-86). But Parrot's voice becomes that of the scourge of his age, speaking out against abuse, only in the final monologue. Readers have found in the movement from the vain, flamboyant display of tricks and wit in the first monologue to the catalogue of contemporary troubles in the last the most interesting exploration of the court poet's role since Chaucer's dream poems; Parrot is court jester and Old Testament prophet rolled into one, a caged wit prodded from a round of dates and kisses to rail against the world. *Speke Parott* shows the range within which a poet moves when he takes on a bird voice. He can 'Sette asyde all sophysms, and speke now trew and playne' (448), and show the usefulness of the disguise in narrowing and concentrating the observer's view. Or he can fantasize, be whimsical, and use the disguise to create pretty pictures, as Skelton does in his opening view of his pampered self as court pet:

> A cage curyowsly carven, with sylver pynne,
> Properly payntyd to be my coverture;
> A myrrour of glasse, that I may tote therin;

These maydens full meryly with many a dyvers flowur
Fresshely they dresse and make swete my bowur,
With 'Speke, Parott, I pray yow,' full curteslye they sey,
'Parott ys a goodlye byrde and a pratye popagay.' (8-14)

It is fantasy that dominates *Phyllyp Sparowe*, which displays even more strikingly a
variation of voice, between Jane Scrope's deliberately naive innocence and the commentating
poet's knowing experience. Considered as a bird poem, it draws on one main tradition, the
Mass of Birds, and shows a fusion of classical literary allusion to Catullus and Ovid with
medieval bestiary traditions and popular bird-lore (Scattergood ed. 1983, 406). Its most
striking effect is based on reversal: here a human voice laments a bird, rather than, as in *The
Kingis Quair*, bird voices being used to express human feeling; this turning inside out of
courtly poetic relationship is the basis for the poem's effect of mock heroic, even at moments of
parody. Here the bird is the love object on which a child practises expression of human love
and loss with all the resources that medieval rhetorical patterns of lament, imprecation,
remembrance, commemoration, digression and amplitude can supply. In the Mass section
Skelton goes back to the endlessly rich literary device of the list, used not for scientific or
microcosmic purpose, but for sheer display; birds are used exuberantly to embellish the theme
and characterize the innocent garrulity of the speaker. Seventy-five birds are named.
Recognizable in this comic version are the encyclopaedic and hierarchical catalogue, the
mirroring of liturgical ceremony in the phenomena of Nature, the satirical resemblances to
human activities used in *The Buke of the Howlat* and in 'Who killed Cock Robin?', and
bestiary traditions turned into whimsical fantasy rather than into exemplary symbolism: so the
phoenix is reduced to a mere thurifer waving incense at the funeral. Adding to the richness of
effect is a layer of naturalism observant of the variety of bird sound: ' The starlyng with her
brablyng', ' The fleckyd pye to chatter', ' The owle . . . to houle', ' The bitter with his bumpe /
The crane with his trumpe', and so on. The bird world is not made merely to mirror human
activity but is presented in its own nature in relationship to human feeling.

Phyllyp Sparowe is very different from *The Parliament of Fowls*, not least in the contrast
between Chaucer's poised rhyme-royal stanzas and Skelton's short-breathed couplets, but they
have in common bird lists, the association between birds and the theme of love, and a quality of
medley. Birds did not have to be taken seriously and part of their usefulness to poets was as a
means of distancing human experience; human characteristics could be simplified into
extremes, antitheses, caricatures, pastoral idealisms, and placed in patterned and schematic
views of the world. Many bird poems make use of ceremony and ritual, and many fifteenth-
century examples present strongly moral creatures offering lessons. But medieval poets do not
long forget that birds are beautiful and varied creatures, active and quick, and that their song is
full of possibilities to the human hearer. This aesthetic appeal is reflected even in the

encyclopaedias: 'foules ben more pure and liȝt and noble of substaunce and swift of meuynge and scharp of siȝt', says Bartholomew (in Trevisa's translation, Seymour ed. 1975, I, 602). The general qualities of birds distinguished in *De Proprietatibus Rerum* include their lightness and flight, their 'honestee of kynde', the variety of their habitat, and of their food and eating habits, though not their song. Chaucer and Skelton in different ways respond to the multiplicity of bird qualities. These are reflected in a prose work of the period, *The Boke of St Albans*, which includes among its hawking and hunting lore the following terms for 'Compaynyes of Beestys and Fowlys':

> A mustre of pecockys. An exaltyng of larkis. A wache of nyghtingalis. A cherme of goldefynches. An unkyndenes of ravenes. A clateryng of choughes. A pride of lionys. A besynes of ferettis. A noonpaciens of wyves. A doctryne of doctoris. A sentence of juges. A glosyng of taverneris. A melody of harpers. A tabernacle of bakers. A rage of maydenys. An uncredibilite of cocoldis. A skulke of foxis. A gagle of women. A pepe of chykennys. An eloquens of laweyeris. A blast of hunteris. (Gray ed. 1988, 144)

In this weaving together of human and animal society it is indicative of the interest of poets in birds and other animals that it is qualities of sound and movement which mainly take the attention, in contrast to the satirical edge apparent in the human groups. Birds are useful to writers as mirrors of human activity but it is their natural qualities of colour, grace and sweet sound which explain why they so often appealed to the poet's imagination, and are described waking dreamers up or lulling the lovelorn to sleep. Some poems of the fifteenth century support the view that 'Literary forms based on or around bird and animal lore tend to be didactic or sententious in nature' (Andrew ed. 1984, 30). But some of the poems discussed above, even one or two of the sententious ones, show that bird poems could be sensitive and truthful about feelings and ideas, and that poets, encouraged by Chaucer perhaps, could use bird poems to be sophisticated and funny.

Royal Holloway and Bedford New College
University of London

NOTES

1. See translations of these and other French love debates, including Jean de Condé's *La Messe des Oisiaus* and Oton de Grandson's *Le Songe Saint Valentin*, in Windeatt ed. 1982, 85ff.

2. See Lampe 1967 and Spearing 1976, 176-81 for two different 'ironic' readings of the poem.

3. Bain 1964 attributes also a cohesive structural importance to the use of nightingale and dove in the poem.
4. See also Robbins ed. 1955, No. 180.
5. The bare bones of the story occur in several collections of exempla: e.g. as no. 28 in *The Exempla of Jacques de Vitry*, edited by T. F. Crane (New York, 1890, reprinted 1967).

REFERENCES

Andrew, Malcolm, ed., 1984   *Two Early Renaissance Bird Poems*, Washington, Toronto and London

Bain, Carl E., 1964   The Nightingale and the Dove in *The Kingis Quair*, *TSL*, 9, pp. 19-29

Brown, Carleton, ed., 1924   *Religious Lyrics of the XIVth Century*, Oxford

Burrow, J. A., 1984   Henryson's *The Preaching of the Swallow*, in *Essays on Medieval Literature*, Oxford, pp. 148-60 (first published in *EC*, 25, 1975, pp. 25-37)

Cummins, John, 1988   *The Hound and the Hawk*, London

Dyboski, Roman, ed., 1907   *Songs, Carols, and other Miscellaneous Poems from Balliol MS 354, Richard Hill's Commonplace Book*, EETS, ES 101, London

Furnivall, F. J., ed., 1867   *Hymns to the Virgin and Christ*, EETS, ES 24, London

Gray, Douglas, ed., 1988   *The Oxford Book of Late Medieval Verse and Prose*, Oxford

Heiserman, A. R., 1961   *Skelton and Satire*, Chicago

Lampe, David, 1967   Tradition and Meaning in *The Cuckoo and the Nightingale*, *PLL*, 3, Supplement, pp. 49-62

Pearsall, Derek, 1970   *John Lydgate*, London

Robbins, Rossell Hope, ed., 1955   *Secular Lyrics of the XIVth and XVth Centuries*, 2nd edn, Oxford

Seymour, M. C., *et al.*, eds, 1975   *On the Properties of Things: John Trevisa's Translation of Bartholomaeus Anglicus De Proprietatibus Rerum*, I, Oxford

Spearing, A. C., 1976   *Medieval Dream-Poetry*, Cambridge

Windeatt, B. A., ed., 1982   *Chaucer's Dream Poetry: Sources and Analogues*, Woodbridge

CHAUCERIAN PRISONERS: THE CONTEXT OF *THE KINGIS QUAIR*

Julia Boffey

It is generally recognized that for English writers of the late fourteenth and fifteenth centuries, Chaucer's writings provided models of form, content, and style (Hammond 1927; Pearsall 1966; Fox 1968; Strohm 1982; Ebin 1988, ch. 1). I propose in this essay to explore the creative use made by later authors of something rather harder to define: a situation, derived in part from Chaucerian sources, namely that of imprisonment. I shall examine this situation as it is represented in a range of late fourteenth- and fifteenth-century works. There is of course a tantalizing ambiguity in the idea of 'imprisonment in Chaucerian verse', for the works I shall be dealing with not only borrow from Chaucer narrative incidents of imprisonment and images developed from these, but also, in their debt to his inescapably copious oeuvre, they are in a sense 'imprisoned' in his models; their authors struggle to come to terms with 'the anxiety of influence' which A. C. Spearing has recently explored (1985, ch. 3). Starting with a very brief sketch of the range of prison-scenes and prison-images which appear in Chaucer's writing, I hope to isolate some particular patterns of emulation in later works, and to consider the extent and manner in which they build on Chaucer's examples, whether adopting them uncritically or using them as creative inspiration. The combination of motifs and metaphors which informs *The Kingis Quair* will provide a particular focus.

Chaucer's works unsurprisingly make reference to prisons of different kinds. Some prisons feature as simple circumstantial locations, necessary to the functioning of plot, but of no deeper symbolic resonance. We might cite the occasional hospitality which Newgate prison offers to Perkyn Revelour, the hero of the unfinished Cook's Tale (I.4402); the tower which forms the grisly setting of the Monk's acccount of the 'tragedie' of Hugolino (VII.2409); the prisons of Theseus and Philomela in *The Legend of Good Women* (1960-62; 2335-36). Other prisons are purely figurative, concerning ontological states in which human capacity is somehow restricted. In The Knight's Tale, for instance, Theseus speaks of 'this foule prisoun of this lyf' (I.3061). Frequently, these states of metaphorical imprisonment are connected with the experience of love. One of the inscriptions over the gate to the dream-garden in *The Parliament of Fowls* threatens entry to 'the sorweful were / There as the fish in prysoun is al drye' (138-39),

suggesting the barren or life-devouring outcome of misdirected love, while the speaker of the
humorous lyric *Merciles Beaute* asserts 'Sin I fro Love escaped am so fat, / I never thenk to
ben in his prison lene' (27-28 etc.). The appurtenances of love's prison are sometimes
envisaged in alarmingly concrete detail, as in the cynical advice against marriage in the *Envoy
to Bukton*:

> But thilke doted fool that eft hath levere
> Ycheyned be than out of prison crepe,
> God lete him never fro his wo dissevere,
> Ne no man him bewayle, though he wepe, (13-16)

or in the case of Troilus, who, ensnared by his first crucial sight of Criseyde, gnaws the chain
which binds him (Tr 1.509).

Circumstantial function and figurative potential are combined in such prisons as that which
holds Arcite and Palamon in The Knight's Tale. In terms of the literal events recounted in the
narrative, the young men are imprisoned by Theseus until (in one case legitimately and in the
other by stealth) they eventually escape. In terms of the focal or governing images of the tale,
which V. A. Kolve has recently explored at length (1984, ch. III), their prison becomes an
image firstly for the confinement to which love subjects them, and secondly for the constriction
which results from their subjection to the whims of hostile pagan gods. The force of
combining such literal and metaphorical significances must have been apparent to Chaucer as he
read and worked on his translation of Boethius's *De Consolatione Philosophiae*, one of the
most widely-known medieval explorations of the correspondence between earthly life and
confinement. Here, the Boethian prisoner's efforts to transcend the oppression of the 'solitarie
place of myn exil' (Bo 1.pr3.10) take on an extra level of meaning in the light of the author's
own biography: he was imprisoned and put to death in Pavia in 524, after a life of active public
service.

In *Boece*, of course, Chaucer was translating directly from a Latin source, and the prison
setting of the dialogue in which Philosophy's consolation is offered can hardly be attributed to
his own invention. So too, to a greater or lesser extent, some of his other prison locations are
derived from specific sources: the incarceration of Palamon and Arcite from Boccaccio's
Teseida; the humorous love-prisons of *Merciles Beaute* and the *Envoy to Bukton* from an
ancient nexus of conventional images of love which were influentially incorporated in *Le
Roman de la Rose* (Chaucer's *Romaunt of the Rose*, 1967-72; Barney 1972; Leyerle 1974). In
many cases neither the prison situations, nor their exploitation in figurative terms, are in
themselves new. Chaucer's primary audience, and those of his successors literate in Latin and
French, could have encountered amatory and philosophizing prisoners not only in Chaucer's
own writings but also in his source-texts and in other works accessible to cultivated English

readers: Froissart's *Prison Amoureuse*, for example, or Baudouin de Condé's *Prison d'amour*.[1] For the purposes of my argument, I merely want to emphasize that Chaucer's own various works established and formalized, in the vernacular, and in a body of influential and widely circulating texts, a cluster of related structural, rhetorical and metaphorical possibilities.

The tradition of the prisoner of love surfaces in different kinds of post-Chaucerian writing, particularly in love lyrics, such as 'O Lady, I schall me dress with besy cure' (Robbins ed. 1955, No. 196), whose refrain begs pity for the 'cative bound & thrall', and in love allegories like Dunbar's *Bewty and the Presoneir*. The tradition of philosophical Boethian prisoners is activated in an anonymous 'Lament of a Prisoner against Fortune' (edited by Hammond 1909; see also Green 1976), in a debate between 'the playntif' and 'fortune' which opens with the question 'Fortune alas . alas . what haue I gylt / In prison thus to lye here desolate . . . '. It proceeds to detail the prisoner's bitterness at what he feels to have been his wrongful accusation and his loss of good name, and his disillusionment with his former friends, who no longer visit him. The philosophy which his situation generates is unsubtle. Fortune tells the plaintiff that although he may be innocent of the specific felony for which he was imprisoned he nonetheless deserves punishment for other sins which he has forgotten:

> Wenest thou . þat god chastith þe for nought
> Though þou be giltles I graunt wele of this vyce
> Hit is for synnes þat thou hast foredrought
> That now peraunter full litell are in thi thought. (37-40)

And his own conclusions are commonplace: abandoning Fortune ('ffare wele fortune þan & do right as þe liste', 50), he castigates the Fates, and declares:

> ffy on this world it is but fantesye
> Seurete is non . in no degre ne state
> Aswele a kyng as a knafe shal dye
> Not wetyng wher ne whan erly or late . . .
> ffortune & eke the Sustresse I defie
> ffor I will go to him . þat me hath bought, (106-09, 122-23)

and concludes by praying for Mary's intercession on his behalf.

There is little sense here of the forward intellectual movement of Boethius's *Consolation*, and the plaintiff cannot rise much beyond his victimized perception of Fortune's essential malevolence. But the author must surely have derived the form and setting of his dialogue either from Boethius directly or from some vernacular rendering: perhaps *Boece*, or more probably Chaucer's distillation of Boethian philosophy in his short poem *Fortune*, whose form the 'Lament' closely mimics.[2] There is, furthermore, specific verbal evidence for the author's acquaintance with *Troilus and Criseyde*. A line from the parenthetical castigation of Fortune in the proem to Book IV of *Troilus* is quoted ('Lament' 18; Tr 4.7), and a reference to Lachesis 'twining the thread of life' echoes a description of Troilus's approaching 'fatal destyne' at the start of Book V ('Lament' 62; Tr 5.7). The Boethian inspiration is in effect jumbled with recollections of Troilus's prison of love: a fruitful conjunction in Chaucer's poem, where the Boethian material extends the significance of Troilus's predicament, but here left somewhat inert. We might feel that this prisoner, and his poem, are best left confined.

One essential difference between the portrayal of Troilus and the Boethius-figure of the *Consolation* as prisoners is of course the latter's status as first-person narrator of a vision exploring his predicament, and the consequent apparent authentication of his tribulations and discussion of them as 'real' experience — something which persuades us to think of the work as part-autobiography. Troilus's extended soliloquies considered alone do something similar, but they belong to a larger narrative context, delivered to us through the agency of another narrator whose presence (although not without some complication) confirms their status as fiction. The speaker of the 'Lament', like Boethius's prisoner, defines his prisoner-status in his own words, but makes no allusion to a precise 'real' identity, and since the poem is anonymous we cannot be tempted to adopt the author's name to do duty for this. Some of the complications introduced into prison-poems by devices which suggest the imprisoned narrator's identity are apparent in the lyrics attributed to Charles of Orleans, which provide a gloss on my Chaucerian examples, and illustrate the pervasiveness in both French and English lyric writing of images of the lover as prisoner.[3] In a sequence of ballades and rondeaux, the author explicitly names himself as Charles of Orleans and speaks of his service in love to a distant lady who apparently dies, then of love's eventual renewal and the cultivation of a new object of affection. The order of the lyrics, as they survive in the unique manuscript of the English poems, indicates clearly enough that they were intended to be read as a sequence, with an ongoing narrative thread (Burrow 1988).

Especially in the first sequence of ballades, Charles cultivates the metaphor of the prisoner of love:

> . . . yowre plesaunt body and fawkoun
> Hath me thus tane / maugre alle my might
> For prisoner abidyng day and nyght. (249-51)

His separation from the lady condemns him to 'the prison of grevous displesaunce' (1012ff.), and the only virtue he can find in his incarceration is that it allows leisure for letter-writing (491-518; 824-57). What he barely mentions at all is the historical fact that at the time of writing he was indeed a prisoner: taken by the English after Agincourt and held in England during twenty-five years of complicated negotiation. From what we know of the conditions of his captivity it was not physically barbaric, but it was long, and undoubtedly unsettling; the prisoner seems to have been continually moved around the country, lest he should cultivate friendships which might facilitate attempts to escape.

None of this would be guessed from the poems, which exploit the image of the prisoner almost solely for its metaphorical value. The single allusion is brief and unspecific:

> Alle be that of my fare or sely case
> I gesse ye take fulle litille remembraunce
> Yet if to wite hit lust yowre good grace
> My poore estat and nakid gouernaunce
> As wite ye welle that ferre from alle plesaunce
> Am y and garnysshid with aduersite
> As moche . nay more than eny wrecche of fraunce
> God wot in what afore cursid parte . . . (858-65)

and the poignancy of the coincidence of factual and figurative situations is left implicit. Would the author have expected an audience to import the biographical information for themselves? An illustration to a late fifteenth-century copy of the French versions of the poems made for Henry VII and his sons, which depicts the prisoner-narrator in the Tower of London (reproduced as the frontispiece of Fox 1969) suggests that some readers at least did so. Although we cannot be sure exactly how the reception of the poems was affected by their status as covert autobiography, it seems likely that the metaphor of the prisoner of love may here have awakened responses beyond those associated with literary tradition, and have brought into the process of evaluation questions of social or political loyalty.

The *Prisoner's Reflections* of George Ashby, which deploy the philosophical rather than amatory tradition of the prison-complaint, amalgamate biographical fact and literary tradition in a much more clearly personal way. Ashby names himself in the poem, gives details of the place and date of his imprisonment: the Fleet, in 1463, and hints darkly at the injustice of his committal, carried out 'by a gret commaundment of a lord' (9) who remains unnamed. As Ashby was clerk of the signet to Henry VI and Margaret of Anjou, and responsible for the education of their son Prince Edward, it is hardly surprising that his life became complicated in the Yorkist dispensation of the early 1460s. His poem is essentially a combination of autobiographical self-justification and moral exemplum, partially shaped by the conventions of genres such as the consolation. He writes from prison, after a year's incarceration, and having signalled his innocence and lamented the extent of his accumulating debts, proceeds to instigate a kind of internal dialogue, in which his rhetorical questions: 'What may I do? to whom shall I compleyn?' (50) are answered by his own counsel of patience in the face of adverse fortune:

'Set the neuyr thy full wyll here / In worldly ioy and in felycyte' (162-63). The philosophy
inspired by his reflections is, like that of the 'Lament', unremarkably commonplace, but it
contains some Boethian echoes: the strength which Boethius takes from his virtuous youth, for
example, is echoed by Ashby's remembrance of 'my bryngyng vp from chyldhod hedyrto'
(58) (here put to the admittedly different purpose of comparing past happiness with present
sorrow, and reminding former friends of their fickleness); the potential troubles of family life,
cited in the *Consolation* in a demonstration that even the apparent blessing of children can bring
anxiety (in Chaucer's version, Bo 2.pr4), are not evaded:

> Yef thow haue chyldren ryght plenteuously
> Haply suche may be theyr gouernaunce
> That they woll dysplese ryght greuously. (176-79)

Given that Ashby writes appreciatively in his *Active Policy of a Prince* of his debt to Chaucer,
Lydgate, and Gower, praying for their salvation 'In recompense of many a scripture / That ye
haue englisshede' (20-21), it seems likely enough that he knew Boethius in Chaucer's
translation. His *Reflections* nicely illustrate the ready way in which those compelled to write
by circumstance in the fifteenth century turned almost automatically to Chaucer, or to Chaucer's
sources, for help.

The speed with which Chaucer's works established themselves as models is illustrated in
Thomas Usk's *Testament of Love*, a prose justification-cum-consolation whose exploration of
the speaker's confinement by the force of circumstance is shaped both by *Boece* and other of
Chaucer's works. Compiled in three books, across whose sequence of chapters the initial
letters read 'Margarete of virtw, have merci on thin Usk', the testament takes the form of a
vision (the speaker is 'ravisshed, I can not telle how', I. ii. 3) experienced in 'derke prison,
caitived fro frendshippe and acquaintaunce, and forsaken of al that any word dare speke' (I. i.
15-17), in which the speaker is visited by Love. As Philosophy counsels the Boethian
prisoner, answering his questions about Fortune and her role, so Love responds to Usk's
speaker's complaints about his situation, and specifically about his separation from his lady,
Margaret. Margaret acts as a fluid symbol for several things: a pearl (through the closeness of
her name to the French 'marguerite'); grace; divine wisdom; the church. With much quotation
from the *Consolation* (which Usk probably knew both in Latin and in Chaucer's translation:
Medcalf 1989), the prisoner learns about fortune, properly directed love, the relative values of
earthly and spiritual riches, the coexistence of man's free will and God's providence, and the
nature of true virtue. It is a christianized version of the advice which Philosophy offers to
Boethius's prisoner.

A further level of the work concerns Usk's own apparently intense desire to justify the
course of his perilous political career. He was clerk firstly to John of Northampton, as a

follower of whom he was imprisoned in 1384, to be released only once he had publicly changed allegiance (Bressie 1928; McKisack 1959, 435-36). In his role as a latter-day Boethius, he cloaks his references to some of these events under the cover of discussion of 'mighty senatours', and the 'ruling of citizins' (I. vi. 62, 55), and in his anxiety to exonerate himself has Love commend his behaviour during this period of difficulty. The prison setting of the dialogue (never as explicit as that of, for instance, Ashby's *Reflections*) clearly gains enhanced point in the light of the events of Usk's own life. The more grisly irony is that he was in fact to die after a later period of imprisonment which followed his composition of the *Testament*. Having apparently colluded with his new master Nicholas Brembre on behalf of the court faction against Gloucester and the lords appellant, he was subsequently executed with him (McKisack 1959, 454-59): 'a stern doom', in Skeat's words.

Usk's literary ambitions, whether those of self-justification or of genuine philosophical speculation, could hardly have been fulfilled without recourse to Chaucer's works; his writing seems to have been informed by his reading not only of *Boece*, but also of *The House of Fame* and possibly other poems (Skeat ed. 1897, xxv-xxvii). Above all, the themes and the phrasing of *Troilus and Criseyde* float again and again to the surface, almost as if Usk's acquaintance with Boethius was filtered through the Boethian emphases in this poem.[4] No doubt it was the precedent of *Troilus*, in which earthly love is seen in the context of Boethian and eventually Christian philosophy, which prompted Usk to embed his unique amalgam of philosophical, doctrinal, and autobiographical material in the framework of a secular love-vision.

Such fusing of Boethian philosophy with the image of love's imprisonment most brilliantly informs *The Kingis Quair*, which, in the nature of its response to these themes in Chaucer's writing, draws together many of the points raised so far in this discussion.[5] Probably written by James I of Scotland at some time between 1424 and his murder in 1437, this poem purports to be a recollection, in tranquillity, of the concluding stages of a period of imprisonment suffered by the narrator, and it describes how an amorous glimpse of a beautiful woman from his prison window led subsequently to a dream revelation in which he learned in turn from Venus, Minerva, and Fortune the nature and role of virtuously directed earthly love. On waking he was offered miraculous hope (in the form of a message carried to his prison-window by a bird) and was released into a period of happiness and prosperity.

A crude summary hardly does the poem justice, for much of its appeal and interest lies in ostensibly introductory and transitional passages by which the plot is nudged forward. And once again the facts of an individual biography complicate the issues, for James was captured as a youth by the English in the spring of 1406 as he was being shipped to France in the hope of protection from the threat of Anglo-Scottish hostilities. Like Charles of Orleans, he suffered many years' detainment, both at court and in provincial aristocratic households (diversion was provided by occasional spells of military service in France), and was not released until 1423-

24. The swiftness of his ensuing marriage to Joan Beaufort suggests that negotiations for the union must have begun during his period of imprisonment, and possibly even involved some first glimpse such as that experienced by the prisoner in James's poem.

An eclectic and subtle interplay of individual history, reference to other texts, and moral-philosophical generalization is forged here, and makes fluid use of prison motifs filtered through Chaucerian models. The Boethian context of the poem is made clear at the outset, in the familiar Chaucerian strategy of using bedtime reading as the prelude to a dream. In *The Book of the Duchess* and (less straightforwardly) *The House of Fame* the preliminary reading both prompts or introduces the dreams and is in some way echoed within them. Here, although in the sequence of the finished text the reading prefaces the dream, in the chronology of the narrator's life it is a retrospective gloss on it, for reading the book prompts not a dream but a poem which describes a vision experienced at an earlier point in his life. In bed on a clear winter night, the wakeful narrator takes a book,

> Of quhich the name is clepid properly
> Boece (efter him that was the compiloure),
> Schewing [the] counsele of Philosophye,
> Compilit by that noble senatoure
> Of Rome, (15-19)

and summarizes Boethius's history and written response to its course:

> His flourit pen so fair he set awerk
> Discryving first of his prosperitee,
> And out of that his infelicite;
> And than how he, in his poetly report,
> In philosophy can him to confort. (24-28)

The significant sections of the *Consolation* for this narrator appear at this point to be its early books, those describing Boethius's stoicism, and (as Ashby was to highlight) his faith in individual virtue and his own properly governed youth. What the narrator then does, though, is to show how his own history in effect reverses the pattern of Boethius's: leading from ungoverned youth, through a miserable period of incarceration, to settled happiness. Considering the pattern of his life as against Boethius's leads to an urge to review his personal history — 'how I gat recure / Of my distresse' (67-68) — so strong that the matins bell, coincidentally ringing, appears to instruct him to recount it (Ashby will avoid the apparent egocentricity of personal revelation with a stanza stating that he does not wish to seek 'worldly glory' by writing, but rather to present his history as a warning exemplum). He settles down with writing materials to begin 'sum newe thing': a novel synthesis of individual experience filtered through patterns and forms whose connotations, in prompting recollection of particular literary antecedents, are designed quite naturally to give rise to philosophical generalizations.

The transitional six-stanza section which follows (92-133) exemplifies the fluidity with which these elements are combined. Nine lines on the confused and unstable nature of youth, liable to both good and ill fortune indiscriminately, give way to an extended comparison of this directionless state with a 'schip that sailith stereles / Vppon the rokkis', an ancient image which also surfaces in the *Consolation*:

> O thou, what so evere thou be that knyttest alle boondes of thynges, loke on thise wrecchide erthes. We men, that ben noght a foul partie, but a fair partie of so greet a werk, we ben turmented in this see of fortune. Thow governour, withdraughe and restreyne the ravysschynge flodes, and fastne and ferme thise erthes stable with thilke boond by whiche thou governest the hevene that is so large. (Bo 1.m5, 49-58)

This image the narrator then relates to his own experience: 'I mene this by myself, as in partye'. Although materially well endowed in youth, he lacked the 'ripeness of reason . . . to governe with my will' and (in a striking echo of a passage in Usk's *Testament*, I. iii. 55-68) speaks of his early 'stereles . . . trauaile' on the waves of the world, shortly to be sketched at greater length. From this he leads gracefully into three stanzas invoking the help of the Muses, in which the nautical image is put to a new and more specifically Chaucerian use: the ship becomes the poem, the fierce elements the intellectual and artistic difficulties which threaten its successful completion, in just the configuration used in the proem to Book II of *Troilus*. In his flexible application of the single metaphor, James contrives to recall his personal history (the sea-voyage on which he was captured); to set his situation implicitly alongside that of Boethius (perhaps also that of Troilus); and, with a proper display of modesty, to align himself creatively with Chaucer.

The individual history proper can now begin, and James proceeds to relate the circumstances of his departure from Scotland, at the age of about ten, to take his 'adventure' (significant word) on the sea; his capture by enemies; the misfortune of his eighteen-year imprisonment ' Til Iupiter his merci list aduert, / And send confort in relesche of my smert' (174-75). Despite reminders that this story is to have a happy outcome, the parallels with Boethius's situation are not overlooked. In his 'ward', the narrator laments his living death and asks a whole sequence of rhetorical questions of the kind put by Boethius, and later by Ashby and the 'Lament' author: of what am I guilty? why are animals allowed freedom while men suffer like this? how does fortune operate? why have I been singled out for this bad luck? The weltering motion of the waves of the sea of fortune is kept in mind first by the swings between elation and despair occasioned by the first sight of the lady, and secondly by a few explicit nautical references, as to 'the huge weltering wawis fell / Of lufis rage' (696-97). The

Boethian material however lies dormant for much of the central part of the poem: the narrator's sight of the lady in her spring surroundings, his prayers and laments, his dream-journey to the sphere of Venus.

During and after the interview with Minerva, to whom Venus recommends him, it is effectively reactivated, for here he learns that virtue must direct love (as it must govern every sphere of human activity), and that those who behave virtuously are best equipped to cope with the reversals of fortune: several stanzas are devoted to a synopsis of the arguments about free will and predestination which feature so importantly in the last two books of the *Consolation* (and of course in The Knight's Tale and Book IV of *Troilus*). Furthermore, the interview with Minerva, who perceives that the narrator's love is directed by true virtue, leads to a direct encounter with Fortune in the concluding section of the dream. The 'weltering' of Fortune's slippery wheel takes us back again to the waves of the tempestuous sea, and even the narrator's intimation of his approaching upward course on its circuit cannot quite dispel the uncertainties voiced in the stanza of apostrophe to the human spirit which relates his awakening:

> O besy goste ay flikering to and fro,
> That neuer art in quiet nor in rest
> Till thou cum to that place that thou cam fro
> Quhich is thy first and verray proper nest. (1205-08)

But the illumination offered in the dream, and the love and prosperity which waking life goes on to bring, allow the poem to end in a mood of Boethian 'felicitee' (explicitly recalled at 1281). Here, although the terminology and the moral framework recall the *Consolation*, we must be intended rather to remark the differences between the narrator's situation and that of the imprisoned Boethius. Boethius's consolation is that of philosophy: reasoning which enables him to find within himself resources to equip him with defence against privation. James's consolation, while a reminder of the essence of this philosophy (in an explicitly Christian context: the beneficent workings of the planetary gods are caused 'by the magnificence / Of him that hiest in the hevin sitt', 1368-69), is largely that of an upward turn in his fortune — release from imprisonment — and incorporation into society by means of virtuous love for another. So while the Boethian parallels are a vital part of the texture of the poem, informing its basic structure, its moral and ethical framework, and its imagery, they are in some sense overturned, or realigned, by their incorporation into the model of an individual history different from Boethius's. Like Usk and Ashby and the anonymous 'Lament' author, James constructs his poetic autobiography from Boethian-Chaucerian materials. Perhaps because of his historical good fortune, however, he rebuilds these in unusual ways.

In absorbing his Boethian inspiration into a poem about love, James is of course following the precedent of both The Knight's Tale and *Troilus*, historical romances whose significance is deepened by the incorporation of philosophical speculation in such passages as Theseus's 'first moevere' speech and Troilus's meditations on questions of necessity and free will. And he follows too their exploitation of the correspondence between the Boethian prisoner's initial imprisonment in misfortune and the lover's traditional imprisonment in the chains or snare of love. The pattern of this, as most fully adumbrated in The Knight's Tale, is worth a moment's pause. Palamon and Arcite, taken by Theseus from the ruins of Thebes, are sentenced by him to live out their lives 'in angwissh and in wo' (I.1030) in prison, with no possibility of ransom. One glimpse of Theseus's sister-in-law Emelye, from their prison-window, catapults each in turn into a state of near-terminal love-sickness; not only is she as beautiful as an angel, but in her leisurely May-time garden occupations she represents everything which their incarceration denies them. Even as they vie with each other for a greater claim to her affection they recognize the futility of such strife: 'Heere in this prisoun moote we endure, / And everich of us take his aventure' (I.1185-86), as Arcite says. When quite arbitrarily the intercession of a former friend gains Arcite's release, he realizes that his love exerts a stricter confinement than Theseus's tower: so-called liberty, in which he is exiled from Athens and unable to see Emelye, is hardly to be preferred to Palamon's imprisonment, from which Emelye may still be observed. He defines it categorically as a kind of hell, compared with Palamon's paradise. But to Palamon, of course, this view of things is not evident; left behind, he feels only more acutely the restraints on his liberty, making reference to the 'cage' in which he is confined, and the fetters which restrict him. The first part of the tale (as divided in the Ellesmere manuscript) ends with the insoluble question about which of the two men is better off.

As the story proceeds, and Arcite, secretly returned from exile, encounters Palamon, who has secretly escaped, the metaphor of love's bondage remains active. During his outburst in the grove, Arcite laments that he is still 'caytyf' and 'thral' to love (1552), and even Theseus speaks of his own former confinement in its 'laas' (1817). In other episodes in the poem restrictions of other kinds are apparent. The Theban widows, whom Theseus helps early in the tale, speak of themselves as prisoners of fortune (925); Palamon and Arcite, in their symmetrical outbursts against their situations, imply that their liberty is restricted not just by Theseus's orders, but by the more distant and heartless decrees of their pagan gods; Theseus, although speaking with a desperate optimism at the end of the tale, nonetheless concedes that Arcite is to be envied his departure from 'this foule prisoun of this lyf' (3061). Only the concluding marriage, whose significance of course lies largely outside the confines of the tale, in its imagined future, reinforces the thrust of Theseus's speech with the idea that subjection to an externally imposed contract or plan (here 'the bond / That highte matrimoigne or mariage', 3094-95) can offer a paradoxical sort of liberation.

The narrator of *The Kingis Quair* of course follows exactly the model of Palamon and Arcite in the process of his falling in love. Continuing the account of his past history beyond the sea-voyage on which he was captured, he tells of his subsequent years of imprisonment. As a diversion from troublesome meditation about the justice of his situation, he likes to look from his prison tower into the adjoining 'gardyn fair', with all its harmonious sights and sounds. In May, he hears the nightingales celebrate the coming of summer and the season of love, and speculates on their voluntary subjection to love's 'maistrie'. Perceiving 'the fairest or the freschest yong[e] floure / That euer I sawe' (277-78), walking Emelye-like among the pathways, he too is overcome: 'sudaynly my hert became hir thrall / For euer, of free wyll' (285-86). Uttering a complaint to the lady, he turns again to Chaucer for inspiration: just as Emelye impresses Palamon as a goddess rather than a mortal creature (KnT I.1101), and Criseyde seems a 'hevenyssh perfit creature' sent down to scorn nature's handiwork (Tr 1.103-05) so the lady seems at once divine and worldly. Closer observation, recalled in five stanzas of description, convinces him of her corporeal reality, and he offers a prayer to Venus, yielding to her law and begging for merciful treatment. So intense is his desire for the lady to look up that it seems miraculously to transmit itself to the elements and the natural inhabitants of the garden, the birds, who take up another song to accompany the narrator's prayer to the lady for help. But she leaves as the birds sing their final homage to May, and he is left desolate to utter a complaint (modelled on that of the Black Knight in *The Book of the Duchess*) about the sudden reversal of his hopes.

Where Palamon and Arcite are subjected by love to an intensification of their prison experience, for the narrator in *The Kingis Quair*, paradoxically, subjection becomes a form of liberation. Weeping and lamenting on the evening of his vision of the lady he is granted a dream whose mysterious introduction by means of a beam of light piercing his window suggests some divine inspiration, and which leads him 'furth at the dure in hye' (521) with no opposition. Ascending through the spheres to the 'empire' of Venus he encounters ranks of her servants, mostly those who have loved virtuously and offer her thanks, but including a few who present complaints about their harsh treatment: those forced 'by maistrye' from their chosen lovers, or separated from them by some unfortunate circumstance. Venus, depicted in a 'retrete lytill of compas' rather as she appears in *The Parliament of Fowls*, but without the lasciviousness, hears the narrator's prayer for help and mercy and his vow of perpetual service to her. Her response is that she knew his situation already, and is predisposed to look sympathetically on him, 'Sen of my grace I haue inspirit thee / To knawe my lawe' (733-34); awarding him Good Hope as a companion, she advises him to be patient. But the responsibility for his fate does not lie with Venus alone, as she is at pains to stress; her benevolence is only one part of 'certeyne courses' (755) which operate in interdependence, and the dreamer-narrator must visit Minerva in order to learn more of their workings. Venus's final point is to give the narrator a message for all those on earth who disdain her laws and cause her tears, apparent on earth as the falling rain of spring showers; while they are angry tears they are nonetheless one further manifestation of her beneficence, for they nourish living things and are a part of the natural cycle of seasonal renewal. Only the faithful service of Venus, and celebration of the virtuous pleasures of love, ensure that her 'glad aspectis' will be maintained and that the 'hevinly alliance', in which gods operate in concord, will endure (849-50).

The narrator's lesson about the connection between liberation and correct observance of some kind of divine law continues in his interview with Minerva. She tells him of two courses of action, of which one, the way of 'nyce lust' will be fruitless and end in pain, and the other, that of virtue, 'wil be to thee grete worschip and prise' (894). In what is perhaps a significant semi-nautical metaphor, she makes explicit the Christian obligations of this path of virtue:

> ' Tak him before in all thy gouernance,
> That in his hand the stere has of you all,
> And pray vnto his hye purueyance
> Thy lufe to gye, and on him traist and call
> That corner-stone and ground is of the wall
> That failis noght; and trust (withoutin drede)
> Vnto thy purpose sone he sall thee lede',   (904-10, cf. 960-62, 988-89)

and issues a series of commandments about proper conduct (be true, meek, steadfast) which culminate in a quotation from Ecclesiastes: 'All thing has tyme' (925). The interview is quite stern, and Minerva requires two statements from the narrator about the blamelessness of his intentions, but she is eventually convinced ' That in vertew thy lufe is set with treuth' (1003) and promises that she will henceforth look favourably on him. Her concluding points provide the transition into the next section of the poem, for she extends her hint that Fortune will no longer act against the narrator's wishes, and sketches in for him (condensing into three stanzas the preoccupations of almost two books of the *Consolation*) the relationship between divine providence and necessity, and the operation of man's free will. All that remains is for the beam of light to return the narrator to earth, to a paradisal garden, and for him to encounter Fortune at first hand.

The specific difference between the situation of the narrator of *The Kingis Quair* and Palamon and Arcite (or Troilus) is of course its Christian context. The deities in his cosmos, although encountered in the dream in bodily form, essentially exist in order to effect the operation of the providence of a Christian god, and to ensure that mortals observe his laws. The prisoner's liberation here, from the physical confinement which symbolizes his ignorant and ungoverned subjection to the neutral power of fortune, is brought about because he is enabled through his love for another to perceive the beneficence and harmony of God's creation, and eventually to become a functioning part of it. For Arcite and Palamon, from whom the motives and operations of their gods remain in large part hidden, such a perception is impossible; and certainly at no point do they see their relationship with Emelye as a significant component in any divine plan. Troilus, a prisoner of love whose subjection to his passion inevitably makes of him a prisoner of fortune, comes closer to apprehending the possible role of human love in a divinely-sanctioned order, but as a pagan is denied the final leap of faith which would resolve his difficulties over the problems of free will and conditional necessity, or would illuminate for him the combative force of virtuous conduct.

The passage from solitariness to the acquisition of some social identity is in these terms important in *The Kingis Quair*, and central to its structural and intellectual focus on imprisonment and liberation. As long as the narrator remains 'stereles' and undedicated to a life of altruistic virtue, he appears unanchored and unconnected to others: a solitary prisoner who can only wonder at the community of birds he hears singing outside his tower. The impulse of love for the lady outside enables him to become a part of this community (the birds sing in response to his prayer; he sings to their accompaniment); to leave his prison; to communicate with others (Venus, Minerva, and Fortune), and to recognize the fecundity of creation in the earthly paradise which he glimpses. Eventually, as he discreetly hints at the union which succeeded his release from prison, it allows him to draw in 'lufis yok that esy is and sure' (1346), and to be incorporated in the 'bonds' of love which maintain worldly harmony:

> Eke quho may in this lyfe have more plesance
> Than cum to largesse from thraldom and peyne? —
> And by the mene of Luffis ordinance
> That has so mony in his goldin cheyne,
> Quhich, th[u]s to wyn his hertis souereyne
> Quho suld me wite to write tharof, lat se!
> Now sufficiante is my felicitee. (1275-81)

The emphasis on harmony and concord, suggested in the many musical allusions in the poem, and perhaps too in the numerical patterning which has been detected in it (Miskimin 1977; MacQueen 1977 and 1988) is no doubt a careful reminder of this theme of social interaction. One might even argue that the envoy to the poem extends this network of social reference to the business of its own creation and reception. The readers themselves are requested to take over responsibility for its 'governance' (by reacting in a charitable way to shortcomings, and making good any deficiencies); Chaucer and Gower, for whose souls a prayer is offered, are invoked as necessary co-authors, 'masters' by whom the author was inspired:

Go litill tretise nakid of eloquence,
Causing simplese and pouertee to wit:
And prey the reder to have pacience
Of thy defaute and to supporten it.
Of his gudnese thy brukilnese to knytt,
And his tong for to reule and to stere,
That thy defautis helit may ben here.

Allace, and gif thou cummyst in the presence
Quhare as of blame faynest thou wald be quite,
To here thy rude and crukid eloquens,
Qhuo sal be thare to pray for thy remyt?
No wicht, bot geve hir merci will admytt
Thee for gud will, that is thy gyd and stere,
To qhuam for me thou pitousely requere. (1352-65)

Vnto [th']inpnis of my maisteris dere,
Gowere and Chaucere, that on the steppis satt
Of rethorike quhill thai were lyvand here,
Superlatiue as poetis laureate
In moralitee and eloquence ornate,
I recommend my buk in lynis sevin —
And eke thair saulis vnto the blisse of hevin. (1373-79)

The fact remains that the poem is based on one individual history (whether rooted in historical fact or entirely fictional need not affect the issue), and that in responding to the command of the matins bell, ' Tell on, man, what thee befeel', the narrator is recounting an individual's growing understanding of his place in some universal scheme. This I think is hinted at in the opening stanzas, where the narrator 'in bed allone waking' is at once solitary, and yet at the same time related to 'the hevynnis figure circulere', whose operations, in conjunction with his own will, direct the course of his life. He can also be seen as related to the author of the book he reads, Boethius, whose account of his own history both inspires and informs the creative autobiography which is to follow. It is important, of course, that in the chronology of the poem the narrator of the opening few stanzas has actually benefited from the experiences of imprisonment, love, and dream which he will go on to recount as events in his past. It is the synthesis of this record of individual experience with the forms and themes so wittily but purposefully appropriated from Boethius and Chaucer which in the end gives the poem its status as 'newe thinge'.

For posterity the overlap between certain post-Chaucerian individual lives and compelling textual models is a literary-historical curiosity. In some senses the overlap perhaps created authors of those who would otherwise not have had the inclination to write, for in simple practical terms it may have been only the enforced leisure of imprisonment or detainment which offered the opportunity of literary experiment to those with busy public lives. (The example of Malory's prison undertaking, although of a different literary kind, bears this out.) But the genre of the prison complaint or consolation had nonetheless certain inbuilt attractions for the would-be author. Most obviously, it presented the chance to formulate experience in terms borrowed from Chaucerian models, and so acquire some literary credibility. Furthermore, the prison situation supplied a ready-made authenticating framework in which words of justification or lament from the detainee seem (and indeed in some of the cases I have discussed actually are) plausibly 'real' forms of discourse. In his solitariness, the prisoner can adopt a number of formal modes of address — uttering a complaint, sending out a letter or a testament — which guarantee his communication a quasi-physical existence, sometimes reflected in its title: Usk's 'testament' (a formal legal deposition); James I's 'quair' (small book); Charles of Orleans's 'Livre du prison'. The potential of this genre for connecting texts with life and texts with other texts seems to have been particularly alluring.

Queen Mary and Westfield College
University of London

NOTES

1. See *Jean Froissart: la Prison Amoureuse*, edited by Anthime Fourrier (Paris, 1974), and *Dits et Contes de Baudouin de Condé, et de son fils Jean de Condé*, edited by Auguste Schèler, 3 vols (Brussels, 1866-67), and the discussion of 'Poètes prisonniers du XVe siècle' in Champion ed. 1909, pp. xvi-xxi. From the thirteenth century a rather different 'Prisoner's Prayer' survives in parallel English and French versions: see *English Lyrics of the XIIIth Century*, edited by Carleton Brown (Oxford, 1932), pp. 10-13.

2. Walton's fifteenth-century verse translation of Boethius may have been known to some of the authors discussed here. See *Boethius de Consolatione Philosophiae, translated by John Walton*, edited by M. Science, EETS, OS 170 (1927); see also Johnston 1987.

3. The relationship between the French and English lyrics which have been attributed to Charles of Orleans is complex: for surveys of the scholarship, see Clark 1971 and 1976; Yenal 1984.

4. The debts are documented in Skeat ed. 1897, xxvii. Interestingly, one of the lines from *Troilus* (5.7) quoted by the author of ' The Lament of the Prisoner against Fortune' (62) also appears in the *Testament* (I. vi. 78).

5. For full bibliography to 1978, see Scheps and Looney eds 1986. More recently, see Quinn 1981 and Carretta 1981. The studies I have found most helpful are Ebin 1974; Markland 1957; Preston 1956; Rohrberger 1960; Scheps 1971; Von Hendy 1965.

REFERENCES

Barney, Stephen A., 1972 — Troilus Bound, *Speculum*, 47, pp. 445-58

Bressie, R., 1928 — The Date of Thomas Usk's *Testament of Love*, *MP*, 26, pp. 17-29

Burrow, John, 1988 — The Poet and the Book, in *Genres, Themes and Images in English Literature from the Fourteenth to the Fifteenth Century: the J. A. W. Bennett Memorial Lectures, Perugia, 1986*, ed. Piero Boitani and Anna Torti, Tübingen, pp. 230-45

Carretta, Vincent, 1981 — *The Kingis Quair* and *The Consolation of Philosophy*, *SSL*, 16, pp. 14-28

Champion, P., ed., 1909 — *Le Prisonnier desconforté du château de Loches: poème inédit du XVe siècle*, Paris

Clark, Cecily, 1971 — Charles d'Orléans: Some English Perspectives, *MÆ*, 40, pp. 254-61

———— 1976 — Postscript, *MÆ*, 45, pp. 230-31

Ebin, Lois A., 1974 — Boethius, Chaucer, and *The Kingis Quair*, *PQ*, 53, pp. 321-41

———— 1988 — *Illuminator, Makar, Vates: Visions of Poetry in the Fifteenth Century*, Lincoln and London

Fox, Denton, 1968 — Chaucer's Influence on Fifteenth-Century Poetry, in *Companion to Chaucer Studies*, ed. Beryl Rowland, 1st edn, Toronto, New York, London, pp. 385-407

Fox, John, 1969 — *The Lyric Poetry of Charles d'Orléans*, Oxford

Green, Richard Firth, 1976 — The Authorship of the *Lament of a Prisoner against Fortune*, *Mediaevalia*, 2, pp. 101-09

Hammond, E. P., 1909 — Lament of a Prisoner against Fortune, *Anglia*, 32, pp. 481-90

———— 1927 — *English Verse between Chaucer and Surrey*, Durham, N. C.

Johnston, I. R., 1987 — Walton's Sapient Orpheus, in *The Medieval Boethius: Studies in the Vernacular Translations of De Consolatione Philosophiae*, ed. A. J. Minnis, Woodbridge, pp. 139-68

Kolve, V. A., 1984 — *Chaucer and the Imagery of Narrative: The First Five Canterbury Tales*, London

Leyerle, John, 1974 — The Heart and the Chain, in *The Learned and the Lewed: Studies in Chaucer and Medieval Literature*, ed. Larry D. Benson, Cambridge, Mass., pp. 113-45

McKisack, May, 1959 — *The Fourteenth Century*, Oxford

MacQueen, John, 1977 — The Literature of Fifteenth-Century Scotland, in *Scottish Society in the Fifteenth Century*, ed. Jennifer M. Brown, London, pp. 184-208

———— 1988 — Poetry — James I to Henryson, in *The History of Scottish Literature, I*, ed. R. D. S. Jack, Aberdeen, pp. 55-72

Markland, Murray F., 1957 — The Structure of *The Kingis Quair*, *Research Studies of the State College of Washington*, 25, pp. 273-86

Medcalf, S., 1989 — Transposition: Thomas Usk's *Testament of Love*, in *The Medieval Translator: The Theory and Practice of Translation in the Middle Ages*, ed. Roger Ellis, Cambridge, pp. 181-95

Miskimin, Alice, 1977 — Patterns in *The Kingis Quair* and the *Temple of Glass*, *PLL*, 13, pp. 339-61

Pearsall, D. A., 1966 — The English Chaucerians, in *Chaucer and Chaucerians: Critical Studies in Middle English Literature*, ed. D. S. Brewer, London, pp. 201-39

Preston, John, 1956 — Fortunys Exiltree: A Study of *The Kingis Quair*, *RES*, NS 7, pp. 339-47

Quinn, William, 1981 — Memory and the Matrix of Unity in *The Kingis Quair*, *ChauR*, 15, pp. 332-55

Robbins, Rossell Hope, ed., 1955 — Secular Lyrics of the XIVth and XVth Centuries, 2nd edn, Oxford

Rohrberger, Mary, 1960 — *The Kingis Quair*: An Evaluation, *TSLL*, 2, pp. 292-302

Scheps, Walter, 1971 — Chaucerian Synthesis: The Art of *The Kingis Quair*, *SSL*, 8, pp. 143-65

Scheps, Walter, and J. Anna Looney, eds, 1986 — *Middle Scots Poets: A Reference Guide to James I of Scotland, Robert Henryson, William Dunbar, and Gavin Douglas*, Boston, Mass.

Spearing, A. C., 1985 — *Medieval to Renaissance in English Poetry*, Cambridge

Strohm, Paul, 1982 — Chaucer's Fifteenth-Century Audience and the Narrowing of the 'Chaucer Tradition', *SAC*, 4, 3-32

Von Hendy, Andrew, 1965 — The Free Thrall: A Study of *The Kingis Quair*, *SSL*, 2, pp. 141-51

Yenal, Edith, 1984 — *Charles d'Orléans: A Bibliography of Primary and Secondary Sources*, New York

ON REREADING HENRYSON'S *ORPHEUS AND EURYDICE*

Jane Roberts

An enticingly firm pronouncement on Henryson's *Orpheus and Eurydice* is to be found in the standard history of Scottish literature of a generation ago (Wittig 1958, 44):

> *Orpheus and Eurydice* is one of the very few poems of the Middle Ages that tells a classical tale for its own sake, with no allegorical trappings.

The statement seems extraordinary, given that the narrative, to which it must refer, is complemented by Henryson's *moralitas*, his own reworking of a medieval allegorization of the story of Orpheus. By contrast, more recent critical appraisal of the poem suggests that the significance of the story is plain from the beginning of the narrative.[1] And we have had progressively more and more sophisticated readings of the poem, with one scholar, in his numerological elucidations, presenting Orpheus and Eurydice tropologically as 'allegories of the human soul in two contrasting aspects' (MacQueen 1985, 104).[2] The poem's *moralitas*, with its identification of Orpheus and Eurydice as intellectual and appetitive counters, is now allowed to wag the preceding narrative. In addition, a sudden flurry of learned articles, perhaps the inevitable result of the attraction a good poem exercises on critical ingenuity, suggests that Henryson's *Orpheus and Eurydice* is a coming growth area for debate in scholarly journals. Dangers lie ahead, and I have no wish to anticipate them. Instead I should like to outline a way of reading the poem which I have grown into. And I had better begin by owning up to a sort of creeping rebellion that has caught up with me over the years. I was brought up to term Henryson (Dunbar too for that matter) a Scottish Lydgatian, an outlook that tends to find *The Testament of Cresseid* anomalous among his works. This view has become orthodox, and is to be found, for example, in a recent book called *Anglo-Scottish Relations 1430-1550* (where it is spiced with a certain air of pro-Scottish pride):

> No Scots poet felt obliged to consult Chaucer before taking up his pen. Henryson's *Orpheus and Eurydice* and the *Morall Fabillis*, for example, draw upon a great variety of source materials, little of it English, and only a handful of Dunbar's many poems show any close link with Chaucer's work. (Kratzmann 1980, 22)

We know, from his *Testament of Cresseid*, that Henryson loved and admired Chaucer's poetry. The recognition of Chaucerian echoes in his *Orpheus and Eurydice* does not, however, entail a return to his being described as a Scottish Chaucerian. Henryson is no minor poet, and his writings cannot be pigeonholed dismissively.

The story of Orpheus is so well known as to need no repetition. That Orpheus loved his wife, lost her and sought her in hell remains one of the most popular legacies of the antique world. The Christian world added framing materials, which run as follows in Chaucer's working of the Boethian version:

> Blisful is that man that may seen the clere welle of good! Blisful is he that mai unbynden hym fro the boondes of the hevy erthe! The poete of Trace, Orpheus, that whilome hadde ryght greet sorwe for the deth of his wyf, aftir that he hadde makid by his weeply songes the wodes moevable to renne . . .
> At the laste the lord and juge of soules was moevid to misericordes, and cryede: 'We ben overcomen,' quod he; 'yyve we to Orpheus his wif to beren hym compaignye; he hath wel ybought hire by his faire song and his ditee. But we wolen putten a lawe in this and covenaunt in the yifte; that is to seyn that, til he be out of helle, yif he loke byhynde hym, that his wyf schal comen ageyn unto us.' But what is he that may yeven a lawe to loverys? Love is a grettere lawe and a strengere to hymself thanne any lawe that men mai yyven. Allas! Whanne Orpheus and his wif weren almost at the termes of the nyght (*that is to seyn, at the laste boundes of helle*), Orpheus lokede abakward on Erudyce his wif, and lost hire, and was deed.
> This fable apertinith to yow alle, whosoevere desireth or seketh to lede his thought into the sovereyn day, that is to seyn, to cleernesse of sovereyn good. For whoso that evere be so overcomen that he ficche his eien into the put of helle, that is to seyn, whoso sette his thoughtes in erthly thinges, al that evere he hath drawen of the noble good celestial he lesith it, whanne he looketh the helles, that is to seyn, into lowe thinges of the erthe. (Bo 3.m12)

This passage from Chaucer's *Boece*, into which he has incorporated from Trivet's commentary an explanation of 'the termes of the nyght' by '*that is to seyn, at the laste boundes of helle*', serves to illustrate how the story of Orpheus was generally understood in the Middle Ages. It is also not inappropriate to recall the punch packed by a few plain words when they resonate with the memory of Boethius's account of Orpheus's loss. We have just read the rhetorical question: 'But what is he that may yeven a lawe to loverys?' In The Knight's Tale, the imprisoned cousins Palamon and Arcite, sworn brothers, fall a-squabbling on seeing — a goddess? a woman? Emelye? Arcite argues:

> Wostow nat wel the olde clerkes sawe,
> That 'who shal yeve a lovere any lawe?'
> Love is a gretter lawe, by my pan,
> Than may be yeve to any erthely man. (1163-66)

The dangers of worldly love are quickly brought to mind again in The Knight's Tale when Arcite wins his release from prison through the intercession of Perotheus:

> That felawe was unto duc Theseus . . .
> For in this world he loved no man so,
> And he loved hym als tendrely agayn.
> So wel they lovede, as olde bookes sayn,
> That whan that oon was deed, soothly to telle,
> His felawe wente and soughte hym doun in helle —
> But of that storie list me nat to write. (1192-1201)

The attempt of Perotheus and Theseus to steal Proserpina from the underworld was another of the famous legends of the classical world. Here Chaucer chooses to introduce a story he must have gleaned from *Le Roman de la Rose*. Such was this legendary friendship that Theseus, we are told, sought Perotheus down in hell. The newly skewed account reflects interestingly on the sworn brotherhood of Palamon and Arcite, sincere but so easily forgotten once the two young men have set eyes on Emelye. In the end Emelye marries Palamon. Although Arcite wins her in the lists, a reversal of fortune comes as he rides proudly in triumph through the field, his helmet loosed so as to be seen by all the company. He is looking at Emelye when his horse stumbles, startled by 'a furie infernal' (2684) sent by Pluto. And in his dying speech he observes:

> Allas, myn hertes queene! Allas, my wyf,
> Myn hertes lady, endere of my lyf!
> What is this world? What asketh men to have?
> Now with his love, now in his colde grave
> Allone, withouten any compaignye.
> Fare wel, my sweete foo, myn Emelye! (2775-80)

Paradoxically Arcite, in winning free of what Theseus terms 'this foule prisoun of this lyf' (3061), has achieved 'welfare' (3063), while Palamon lives on 'in alle wele' (3101) in this world. An unstated question, the question that the Boethian resonances prompt, is one not asked often enough of the happy ending of The Knight's Tale: which cousin has won what? We are content with the overtly simple final lines:

> For now is Palamon in alle wele,
> Lyvynge in blisse, in richesse, and in heele,
> And Emelye hym loveth so tendrely,

> And he hire serveth so gentilly,
> That nevere was ther no word hem bitwene
> Of jalousie or any oother teene.
> Thus endeth Palamon and Emelye;
> And God save al this faire compaignye! Amen. (3101-08)

We are content too with the ending of *Sir Orfeo* as it appears in the Auchinleck manuscript (Bliss ed. 1966):

> Lord! þer was grete melody!
> For ioie þai wepe wiþ her eiȝe
> þat hem so sounde y-comen seiȝe.
> Now King Orfeo newe corounnd is,
> & his quen, Dame Heurodis,
> & liued long after-ward,
> & seþþen was king þe steward.
> Harpours in Bretaine after þan
> Herd hou þis meruaile bigan,
> & made her-of a lay of gode likeing,
> & nempned it after þe king.
> þat lay 'Orfeo' is y-hote:
> Gode is þe lay, swete is þe note.
> þus com Sir Orfeo out of his care:
> God graunt ous alle wele to fare! Amen!
> Explicit (590-604)

We are right to be content. For here, it seems, we do indeed have 'a classical tale told for its own sake'. The underworld its Sir Orfeo visits is, however, more like the underworld of Celtic tales than Virgil's or Ovid's, and this Sir Orfeo wins back his Dame Heurodis. The Auchinleck *Sir Orfeo*, the scribal version generally preferred today, is discreet in its commentary, which is probably why we neglect the alternative endings of the other two manuscripts of the Middle English *Sir Orfeo*. In the Ashmolean manuscript the poem ends more abruptly (Bliss ed. 1966):

> Thus endys here 'Orfeo þe Kyng':
> God grante vs all hys blyssing,
> And all þat þys wyll here or rede
> God forgyff þem þer mysded,

To þe blysse of Heuyn þat þei may com,
And euer-mor þer-jn to wonne;
And þat it may so be
Prey we all, for charyté!
Explicet Orfew (596-603)

Even more perfunctory is the ending of the Harleian version (Bliss ed. 1966):

þus cam þey out of care:
God ȝeve vs grace wele to fare,
& all þat have herde þis talkyng
Jn heven-blys be his wonyng!
Amen, Amen, for charyté!
Lord vs graunt þat it so be!
Explicit Orpheo Regis (504-09)

These endings are to us somewhat automatic in their piety, but in the context of the Orpheus story they may prompt uneasy reflection on a less worldly success than the winning of Heurodis from the world of fairies. After all, one urges thoughts of 'þe blysse of Heuyn', and the other asks for 'grace wele to fare'.

The narrative part of Henryson's *Orpheus* ends very differently:

Thus Orpheus, wyth inwart lufe replete,
So blyndit was in grete affection,
Pensif apon his wyf and lady suete,
Remembrit noucht his hard condicion.
Quhat will ye more? In schort conclusion,
He blent bak-ward and Pluto come anone,
And vnto hell agayn with hir is gone.

Allace, it wes grete hertsare for to here
Of Orpheus the weping and the wo,
Quhen that his wyf, quhilk he had bocht so dere,
Bot for a luke sa sone was hynt hym fro.
Flatlyngis he fell and mycht no forthir go,
And lay a quhile in suoun and extasy;
Quhen he our come, thus out on lufe can cry:

'Quhat art thou lufe? How sall I the dyffyne?
Bitter and suete, cruel and merciable;
Plesand to sum, til othir playnt and pyne;
To sum constant, till othir variabil;
Hard is thy law, thi bandis vnbrekable;
Quha seruis the, thouch he be newir sa trewe,
Perchance sum tyme he sall haue cause to rewe.

'Now fynd I wele this prouerbe trew,' quod he,
' "Hert on the hurd, and hand is on the sore;
Quhare lufe gois, on forse turnis the ee."
I am expert, and wo is me thar-fore;
Bot for a luke my lady is forlore.'
Thus chydand on with lufe, our burn and bent,
A wofull wedow hame-wart is he went. (387-414)

Orpheus, like Cresseid, inveighs against Venus. But whereas in the *Testament* Henryson presents an 'vntrew' (602) heroine, in the *Orpheus* his focus is on a hero 'newir sa trewe' (406): a hero who, like Troilus or Arcite, loses his love.

If we look back to Orpheus's reception of the news that Eurydice has been taken to the land of the dead, we see him behave as a courtly lover should:

> the king sichit full sore:
His hert ner birst for werray dule and wo,
Half out of mynd, he maid na tary more,
Bot tuke his harpe and to the wod can go,
Wryngand his handis, walkand to and fro,
Quhill he mycht stand, syne sat dovn on a stone,
And to his harpe thusgate he maid his mone. (127-33)

This is the very icon of a distraught lover. There follow five stately ten-line stanzas of lament, linked by the constant return to the name 'Erudices' at the end of each. The passage has been well described as 'a fine melancholy *aria*' (Gray 1979, 223). It is ornate both in vocabulary and alliterative decoration, yet achieves a sustained lyricism entirely appropriate and satisfying. However, it is not a continuous plaint, but is oddly interrupted. First Orpheus calls upon his harp to 'wepe with me' (137), so that its pegs will be 'with thi teris weit' (140). The trick is one he would have found in the openings both of Boethius's *Consolatio* and of *Troilus and Criseyde*.[3] In his second stanza of lament Orpheus tries a lively tune to cheer himself up:

> Him to reios, ȝit playit he a spryng,
> Quhill all the foulis of the wod can syng,
> And treis dansit with thar leves grene,
> Him to devoid of his gret womenting. (144-47)

This 'spryng', this lively tune, played to cheer himself up, moves the birds of the forest to sing and the trees to dance, equally to cheer him up. What has happened now to the 'weeply songes' that in more traditional tellings of the story 'overcomen alle thinges'? Surprise, a quiet chuckle even, effectively lightens the passage:

> Bot all in wane, thai comfort him no thing,
> His hart was sa apon his lusty quene;
> The bludy teres sprang out of his eyne,
> Thar was na solace mycht his sobbing ces,
> Bot cryit ay, with caris cald and kene,
> 'Quhar art thow gane, my luf Erudices? (148-53)

In the third stanza of this set-piece Orpheus sees himself as casting aside his 'rob ryall' (157) for 'rude russat of gray' (158), setting before us momentarily the image of a wild man of the woods, a role often adopted by unhappy courtly lovers in medieval literature. The final two stanzas of the lament are more purposeful. In them Orpheus calls upon his 'fader Phebus' (164) for 'licht' (171), then on his 'grantschir' (175) Jupiter for 'forse' (177), asking both for help in finding Eurydice:[4]

> 'Ger hir appere, and put my hert in pes!'
> Thus king Orpheus with his harp allone
> Sore wepit for his wyf Erudices. (181-83)

The lyric interlude slips so gently back into the narrative mode that commentators have not always noticed its firm integration into the body of the poem. Friedman, for example (1970, 200), describes these fifty lines as 'a piece which could stand alone as a secular lyric of the day on the theme of Fortune's mutability'. The piece is not separable. Indeed, its achievement is the greater in that it is properly part of a larger whole.

This lament ended, Henryson's Orpheus sets out purposefully to seek for Eurydice:

> Quhen endit was the sangis lamentable,
> He tuke his harp and on his brest can hyng;
> Syne passit to the hevin, as sais the fable,
> To seke his wyf . . . (184-87)

The validating tag 'as sais the fable' almost secures belief, and we are in danger of being lulled easily into accepting the authority of 'the fable'. It is however necessary to question the comprehensive nature of Orpheus's quest, as he descends through the spheres, in turn visiting Saturn (189), 'Iupiter, his grant-sir' (192), Mars (196), 'his fader Phebus' (198) and Venus (204), where:

> Quhen he hir saw, he knelit and said thus:
> 'Wate ye noucht wele I am your avin trewe knycht?
> In lufe nane lelare than sir Orpheus,
> And ye of lufe goddesse, and most of mycht:
> Off my lady help me to get a sicht!'
> 'For suth,' quod scho, 'ye mon seke nethir mare.' (205-10)

So off he goes to Mercury 'but tary' (212), and then to the moon, that sphere of change and inconstancy, where he does not linger. A moment's thought, when Henryson slips in his validating 'as sais the fable', might lead quickly to the realization that Orpheus will not find his love in the heavens. Perhaps there rang in Henryson's mind the search of King James I of Scotland, in *The Kingis Quair,* for another look at the fair unknown he had glimpsed from his prison tower?[5] This new journey of Orpheus is significant. He may not gain the wisdom sought by Scipio, but the knowledge he acquires will serve him well as he continues his quest:

> Thus fra the hevyn he went doun to the erde,
> Yit by the way sum melody he lerde.
>
> In his passage amang the planetis all,
> He herd a hevynly melody and sound,
> Passing all instrumentis musicall,
> Causid be rollyng of the speris round,
> Quhilk armony, throu all this mappamound
> Quhill moving cesse, vnyt perpetuall,
> Quhilk of this warld Plato the saul can call. (217-25)[6]

The heady learned details, two stanzas of them, need not be quoted. It is enough to move on to the narrator's cleverly placed modesty topos that follows them:

> Off sik musik to wryte I do bot dote,
> Thar-for at this mater a stra I lay,
> For in my lyf I coud newir syng a note. (240-42)

The narrative voice rings familiar tones. Henryson has learned from Chaucer how to control a directing voice, of a self-deprecating plain man ready to draw attention to his own shortcomings, a voice that it would be foolish not to listen to very carefully. On earth the search continues 'atour the grauis gray' (244: 'dull woods', but dignified by the choice of the word 'groves', which is specifically poetic in Middle Scots).[7] Although medieval romance heroes are often patterned on Orpheus, paradoxically this Orpheus is no stereotyped hero of romance. He is cold and hungry, and all he has for company is his harp. Twenty days of travelling take him

> Fer and full fer and ferther than I can tell,
> And ay he fand stretis and redy wayis,
> Tyll at the last vnto the yett of hell
> He come . . . (248-51)

Much of the scenery of Hades is familiar enough. First there is 'that vgly hellis hund' Cerberus (255) to be negotiated, and, as is usual in the story, music lulls it asleep: 'And Orpheus atour his wame in stall . . . ' (259). Next comes a river, 'wonder depe' (261). That in itself is hardly a surprising component, for hell is often thought of as bounded by a river. More unusually there is a 'brig' (262), guarded by the three furies. The furies are to be found elsewhere seated before the gates of hell, but they do not sit on a bridge in classical accounts. This 'brig' has slipped in from later presentations of hell. In homilies, for example, it is a common enough motif. The furies turn Ixion's wheel, 'vgly for to see' (265). At a 'ioly spryng' (268) from Orpheus's harp the deadly sisters are asleep and the 'vgly quhele' (270) is motionless: ' Than Ixion out of the quhele can crepe / And stall away . . . ' (272-73). An involuntary thought provoked by this detail is that these furies will have to bestir themselves, when they wake up, to catch Orpheus. Then Orpheus approaches a 'wonder grisely flude' (275) where, after a quick 'clink' (287) on the harp, that 'wonder wofull wicht' (294) Tantalus gets a drink. And the usual vulture flees from the screaming Ticius. Repetition of the intensifier 'wonder', the more so if 'half-mockingly' (Fox ed. 1981, 404), adds to the excitement of the passage.

A dank, murky and slippery (therefore easy?) path leads Orpheus to 'hellis house' (307): 'Quhare Rodomantus and Proserpina / Were king and quene . . . ' (308-09). Rhadamanthus, elsewhere a king of Crete and judge in the underworld, is here a byname for Pluto, which is the king's name elsewhere in the poem.[8] Fourteen people are specifically named among the inhabitants of hell (their histories, one feels, might well have been in the 'celle' of Chaucer's monk): Ector of Troy and Priam, Alexander, Anthiocus, Iulius Cesar, Herode, Nero, Pilot, Cresus, Pharo, Saul, Acab, Iesabell and Nabot (321-35).[9] As well,

> Thare fand he mony pape and cardinall,
> In haly kirk quhilk dois abusion;
> And archbischopis in thair pontificall
> Be symony and wrang intrusioun;
> Abbotis and men of all religion,
> For euill disponying of thair placis rent,
> In flambe of fyre were bitterly turment. (338-44)

It is a passage worth recalling if confronted with the critical view that Henryson is very careful 'to keep out any explicit Christian references' in the narrative part of his Orpheus (Fox ed. 1981, cvii).

'Syne nethir mare' (345) goes Orpheus to the quarters of Pluto and Proserpina, all the time playing his harp. There he recognizes Eurydice:

> Lene and dedelike, pitouse and pale of hewe,
> Rycht warsch and wan and walowit as the wede,
> Hir lily lyre was lyke vnto the lede.
>
> Quod he, 'My lady lele and my delyte,
> Full wa is me to se yow changit thus.
> Quhare is thy rude as rose wyth chekis quhite,
> Thy cristall eyne with blenkis amorouse,
> Thi lippis rede to kis diliciouse?' (349-56)

Orpheus slips quickly into the less formal system of address as he exclaims sadly at Eurydice's pallor. Her only words are expressive of what Pluto terms 'langour' (363): 'Quod scho, "As now I dar noucht tell, perfay, / Bot ye sall wit the cause ane othir day" ' (357-58). The languor which, says Pluto, 'puttis hir in sik ply' (363) is an illusion: 'Were scho at hame in hir contree of Trace, / Scho wald refete full sone in fax and face' (364-65). Pluto's explanation prompts Orpheus to play, and three ornate lines again reveal Henryson's grasp of complex musical terminology, despite the narrator's earlier words of disclaimer. The rest of the narrative is well known. Orpheus may take Euridyce home:[10]

> . . . bot vnderneth this payne:
> Gyf thou turnis, or blenkis behind thy bak,
> We sall hir haue forewir till hell agayn.'
> Thouch this was hard, yit Orpheus was fayn,
> And on thai went, talkand of play and sport,
> Quhill thay almaist come to the vtter port. (381-86)

The lovers talk of 'play and sport' (385), but Orpheus, 'wyth inwart lufe replete' (387) and 'blyndit' with 'grete affection' (388), does not remember the condition imposed upon him. We cannot but reflect upon the blindness of worldly love.

Already it must be evident that this *Tale of Orpheus* is not told entirely 'for its own sake', any more than is *The Testament of Cresseid*. In a way, the 'allegorical trappings' following the *narratio* have been responsible for an unwillingness in modern readers to come to terms with the whole work, and a willingness to neglect the *moralitas*. In one of the best introductions to Henryson we find the *moralitas* described as doing 'its best to drag it [the whole poem] down into the mass of those poems which are simply typical of their age' (Gray 1979, 240). An alternative view is that Henryson, in deciding to equip his *Orpheus* with a *moralitas*, supplies his own double vision of the tale. If so, and if we disregard the *moralitas*, we are in danger of diminishing his achievement. About 1522 Henryson's countryman Gavin Douglas happened to refer to the poem as the 'new orpheus' when noting that like himself Henryson had written 'sum thing' of the nine muses (Smith ed. 1914, xx and 58). Recent criticism has, it seems to me, tended to use his designation 'new orpheus' almost as if it applies only to the narrative part of Henryson's *Orpheus*.

Certainly many readers have wished the *moralitas* away. That it opens by addressing 'worthy folk' (415) can prompt comparison with the final short stanza at the end of *The Testament of Cressseid*, in which 'worthie wemen' (610) are addressed. It is odd therefore to reflect that in one length is deplored and in the other brevity. The *moralitas* begins:

> Lo, worthy folk, Boece, that senature,
> To wryte this feynit fable tuke in cure,
> In his gay buke of consolacion,
> For oure doctryne and gude instruction;
> Quhilk in the self, suppose it fenyeit be,
> And hid vnder the cloke of poesie,
> Yit maister Trewit, doctour Nicholas,
> Quhilk in his tyme a noble theolog was,
> Applyis it to gude moralitee,
> Richt full of frute and seriositee. (415-24)

Here Henryson himself tells us that his preceding Boethian fable was told 'for oure doctryne and gude instruction' and that, even though it is a made up story, a fable, with its matter of substance clothed in 'poesie', Nicholas Trivet (a thirteenth-century Dominican writer who produced a number of commentaries on earlier texts; see Fox ed. 1981, cv-cvi) equipped it with a 'gude moralitee'. Some two hundred heroic couplets rework Trivet's allegorization, a third approximately of the whole poem. Too often modern readers have wished these lines away, perhaps those same readers who lack the patience to read the *moralitates* of *The Morall Fabillis of Esope the Phrygian* . . . (to give them the title of the Bassandyne printed text of 1571). In a way, Henryson's *Orpheus and Eurydice* is like one fable from the beast series, writ large, with narrative and *moralitas* intermeshing in much the same way as in some of the fables. Two further observations must be made at this point. For some unobservant readers all the fables follow a single same pattern. And there is widespread also the assumption that Henryson's *Orpheus* was written long before his *Fables*. Neither assumption need necessarily be true.

Viewed as separate parts of the whole, both the narrative section and the *moralitas* of the *Orpheus and Eurydice* are very different from the other medieval Orpheus poem in English, *Sir Orfeo*. Both are overtly didactic by comparison with the Middle English romance.[11] Yet the *narratio* and *Sir Orfeo* resemble one another because each, first and foremost, tells a story. To a greater or lesser degree these narratives draw strength from the potency of Orpheus as symbol, but they do not carry a second continuous thread of meaning. What lessons they contain are pills well sugared, that is concealed 'vnder the cloke of poesie' (420). By contrast, Henryson's *moralitas* is explicitly allegorical in approach, with its second linear sequence assuming greater importance than the simple tale of Orpheus's loss of Eurydice on which it is structured. It cannot be jettisoned as a mere reworking of Trivet's commentary, as if in some way less valid as poetry because Henryson at the outset states its source. The three earliest texts of the poem all include this *moralitas*, evidence that its earliest readers expected to read both parts. Different they may be, in verse form, content and mode, but are they therefore necessarily separable?

Before any answer to this question is attempted we need to have a clear idea of the shape and overall content of the poem. The three extant early versions all have had their various proponents (Fox 1977 and ed. 1981, cx-cxiv). The version considered earliest (1508) is a quarto from the Edinburgh printers Chepman and Millar, indeed one of the first printed Scottish books. The text in the Asloan manuscript (?1513-1530) is closely related to the Chepman and Millar quarto. The latest of the three, in the Bannatyne manuscript (written in the years approaching and including 1568), provides the fullest text, with perhaps only one line from the *moralitas* missing. Because both early manuscript versions reflect lost printed texts, it is obvious that all three early texts are at some remove from the original. The 1508 text is probably best, even though it has unfortunately lost lines 59-175 and has some other more minor gaps. These three texts, together with the indications of other early lost versions their interrelationship implies, attest the integrity and popularity of Henryson's *Orpheus and Eurydice*.

The sources are essentially Boethius and Trivet. If *Sir Orfeo* was known to Henryson, as it could very easily have been (Mills 1977), he did not draw on it for any major component of his poem (Fox ed. 1981, cv). (The recent discovery of two fragments from a parallel Scots *King Orphius* in a manuscript dated to *c.* 1585 (Stewart 1973) increases the likelihood that

Henryson may have known *Sir Orfeo*, but provides no more evidence that he did.) Striking differences between *Orpheus and Eurydice* and its source materials occur in the narrative section, where clutches of material, all contributing enormously to the poem's aureate decoration and pushing it towards the high style from Henryson's usual use of the mean, flesh out the noble qualities of Orpheus. The opening four stanzas are given over to his ancestry and great virtue, with a further five on the muses immediately following, these nine stanzas leading quite logically to the conclusion:

> No wounder is thocht he was fair and wyse,
> Gentill and full of liberalite,
> His fader god, and his progenitrys
> A goddes, fyndar of all ermonye. (64-67)

The nobility of this courtly lover is fully explained, and it is not at all surprising therefore that Eurydice should wish to marry him. Her forwardness is appropriate: the *moralitas* makes it plain that will seeks out wit.[12] Orpheus's lament (the five long stanzas of lines 134-83) cannot but be lovely, given his nobility and his loss. When setting out to look for his lost love Orpheus turns first towards the heavens, a journey apparently without parallel in his legend. The Boethian text gives but the merest hint for such a development in the phrase *Inmites superos querens*, 'Complaining of inexorable gods above' — '?seeking/finding the gods unyielding' (III. m. 12. 18), and the Trivet commentary little more (see note 5). A hint may have been enough, for fourteenth- and fifteenth-century literature is full of ascents into the heavens. Alternatively, however, it is pleasing to assume that such is Orpheus's love for Eurydice that he turns inevitably to the heavens first as the place to which she might have been taken, despite her serving maid's account: ' "Allace, Euridices ȝour quene, / Is with the fary tane befor myne ene!" ' (118-19). Reason, that is Orpheus, should of course look first to the heavens. His subsequent descent through the spheres (186-218) enables him to acquire knowledge of the music of the spheres, and it allows Henryson to dazzle us with his musical knowledge (226-39 and 368-70). After all, it was commonly assumed (*teste* Macrobius, for example) that the human soul passes through the spheres on its descent to earth, acquiring in each sphere some attributes. From his mother's breast Orpheus had sucked ' The sweit licour of all musike parfyte' (70). Now to his performative gifts he adds the knowledge of theory needed for excellence in artistry (Fox ed. 1981, cvii-cix; Manning 1971). These lengthy passages lend to the poem an air of weightiness. The 'noble fame' of this Orpheus justly gains him a loving wife and true 'accord' (84). This prince is so glorious as to demand, when he loses Eurydice, a reading that looks through the obvious story line to some moral judgement. He has, after all, acted in an undisciplined manner: ' "Bot for a luke my lady is forlore" ' (412). (Curiously, this line is applicable also to Arcite's loss of his lady Emelye as, in triumph, he lets his eye wander from concentration on the victory he had requested to Emelye herself.) We last see Orpheus sorrowful and alone, 'chydand on with lufe' (413), and must wonder where for him 'hame-wart' (414) lies.

The questions implicit within the narrative part of *Orpheus and Eurydice* cry out for discussion. Given the content and organization of the narrative, its sequel, in the form of 'gude moralitee, / Richt full of frute and seriositee' (423-24), opens in an orderly and appropriate manner. The introductory ten lines, addressed as we have seen, to 'worthy folk' (415), indicate Henryson's impeccable sources. Then thirty-four lines are given to explaining Orpheus's loss of Eurydice. Orpheus, the 'part intellectiue' (428), results from the union of Phoebus (the god of sapience) and Calliope (the muse of eloquence). This part of our soul and understanding is 'separate fra sensualitee' (430), whereas Eurydice, 'oure affection' (431), can swing up 'to reson' (433) or down 'to the flesch' (434). And Arestyus, the would-be rapist, 'is noucht bot gude vertewe, / Quhilk besy is ay to kepe oure myndis clene' (436-37). Surely the reader must chuckle when this received identification is trotted out so laconically? The sense of teasing disjunctions is reinforced by the speedy identification of that green May-time meadow, where Arestyus spied Eurydice 'Barfute with schankis quhytar than the snawe' (100), as 'this warldis wayn plesance' (439), a *locus amoenus* in which she 'trampit on a serpent wennomus' (105). The view, put forward in a recent examination of *The Fables* (Powell 1983, 151), that ' . . . those fables which are characterized by a harmonious relationship between their two parts fulfil the purpose of the genre most effectively' is unduly sober. It does not allow for Henryson's sly sense of humour, his evident delight in yoking together unlikely contraries. His best fables do not always show a harmonious relationship between tale and *moralitas*. Keeping the audience on its toes is part of the game.

Once the arguing positions have been stated, it follows that 'dedely sin' (441) has poisoned the soul and that

> parfyte reson wepis wondir sare,
> Seand oure appetite thusgate mys-fare,
> And passis vp to the hevyn belyue,
> Schawand till vs the lyf contemplatyve,
> The parfyte will, and als the feruent lufe
> We suld haue alway to the hevyn abufe. (445-50)

The statement must intrigue those readers of The Knight's Tale who, identifying Palamon as a symbol of contemplative life, assign him a winning role within that poem. After all, Chaucer chose to suppress, when reworking his source for The Knight's Tale, the image of Arcite in the heavens, his eyes cast down to earth. Instead he worked this sequence into his *Troilus and*

Criseyde, where it complements and brings into focus Troilus's perplexed musings on free will.

The greater part of the *moralitas* unfolds the wonders of hell. Sixteen lines go to Cerberus's 'thre hedis' (462), or the possibility of death as child, in 'medill age' or in 'grete elde' (464-67), unless the mind is 'myngit with sapience, / And plais apon the harp of eloquence' (469-70), persuading the will 'fra syn and foule delyte' (473). Ixion gets thirty lines to the forty or so lines each for Tantalus and Ticius, but a lot is packed into his torment. A man 'on lyve brukle and lecherouse' (491), he is spread-eagled on fortune's wheel, which is spun by the furies, that is by 'wickit thoucht, evill word, and frawart dede' (478) — Juno's punishment for the engendering of the Centaurs. When sapience (or Orpheus) plays on the harp of eloquence, persuading fleshly appetite to leave off thinking about worldly delight, Ixion creeps out of the wheel:

> That is to say, the grete sollicitude,
> Quhile vp, quhile doun, to wyn this warldis gud,
> Cessis furthwith, and oure complexion
> Waxis quiete in contemplacion. (515-18)

Tantalus, that splendid 'hostlare' (520) who served the gods with his son well seasoned in a stew,[13] occasions a satirical harangue on avarice. Ticius's crime, identified as attempted usurpation of Apollo's 'craft of diuinacion' (562), leads into an attack on the follies of 'fenʒeid profecy' (586). Elsewhere in his writings Henryson subverts what he terms here the 'superstitioun of astrolegy' (589) less openly.[14] The *moralitas* mode allows him to condemn 'wichcraft, spaying, and sorsery' (588) trenchantly.

From this central panel of the *moralitas* we move on for twenty-eight lines to the 'ferefull strete, / Myrk as the nycht' (303-04) which leads Orpheus into 'hellis hous'. In the fable it led to a

> . . . grondles depe dungeon,
> Furnes of fyre wyth stynk intollerable,
> Pit of dispair wyth-out remission. (310-12)

It is hardly surprising therefore to find it described now as

> . . . nocht ellis bot blinding of the spreit
> With myrk cluddis and myst of ignorance,
> Affetterrit in this warldis vane plesance
> And bissines of temporalite, (601-04)[15]

and hell as 'wan howp . . . And fowll dispair' (608-09).

> Than Orpheus, our ressoun, is full wo
> And twichis on his harp and biddis ho
> Till our desyre and fulich appetyte,
> Bidis leif this warldis full delyte. (610-13)

Accordingly, Pluto must grant reason, or Orpheus, his desire, and Eurydice is won, i.e.:

<table>
<tr><td></td><td>Quhen oure desire wyth reson makis pes,</td></tr>
<tr><td></td><td>And sekis vp to contemplacion,</td></tr>
<tr><td></td><td>Off syn detestand the abusion.</td></tr>
<tr><td></td><td>Bot ilk man suld be war and wisely see</td></tr>
<tr><td>vidit</td><td>That he bakwart cast noucht his myndis ee,</td></tr>
<tr><td></td><td>Gevand consent and dilectation</td></tr>
<tr><td>perdidit</td><td>Off warldly lust for the affection;</td></tr>
<tr><td></td><td>For then gois bakwart to the syn agayn</td></tr>
<tr><td></td><td>Oure appetite, as it before was slayn</td></tr>
<tr><td></td><td>In warldly lust and sensualitee,</td></tr>
<tr><td>occidit</td><td>And makis reson wedow for tobe. (617-27)</td></tr>
</table>

At this point there is almost a sense of *QED*. I find it very satisfying, a sort of poetic double entry, with the 'wofull wedow' of the end of the fable instantly retrievable in 'reson', that is Orpheus. Fable and *moralitas* are balanced.

It remains only for Henryson to close his accounts:

> Now pray we God, sen oure affection
> Is alway prompt and redy to fall doun,
> That he wald vndirput his haly hand
> Of manetemance, and geve vs grace to stand
> In parfyte lufe, as he is glorius.
> And thus endis the tale of Orpheus. (628-33)

The glorious prince Orpheus of the fable (glorious, as the soul or 'part intellectiue' of man), the pattern of a courtly lover for the Middle Ages, looked backward, saw, lost and killed his love. Henryson, in his *Orpheus and Eurydice*, reflects upon the issues that fascinate and bewilder all courtly lovers. Is it fanciful to suggest that a deep knowledge of the implications of The Knight's Tale was a major shaping factor in his composition of this poem? It is pleasing to conjecture that both Chaucer's major narrative poems sparked from Henryson new works of great originality. With *The Testament of Cresseid*, so long accepted as a sixth book of *Troilus and Criseyde*, the evidence is clear. There are, in *Orpheus and Eurydice*, hints indicating that Henryson has absorbed the contents of The Knight's Tale. At the very least it must be recognized that his poem can be read as a commentary on the predicament of courtly lovers. Coincidence it may be, but the central issue of *Orpheus and Eurydice* is well articulated by Arcite:

> Wostow nat wel the olde clerkes sawe,
> That 'who shal yeve a lovere any lawe?'
> Love is a gretter lawe, by my pan,
> Than may be yeve to any erthly man. (1163-66)

King's College London
University of London

NOTES

1. See for example Friedman 1970, 195ff.; Gray 1979, 213ff.; Fox ed. 1981, cv-cxiv and Commentary; MacQueen 1985, 104ff.. Lyall 1981 can find no solid evidence for humanist ideas and influences in Henryson.

2. See also MacQueen 1967, 24-44; 1976. Wright 1971, 46-47 argues, from consideration of sources, against imposing an allegorical reading on the narrative part of the poem.

3. Fox ed. 1981, 398 less appositely compares Job 30. 31.

4. Friedman 1970, 200 notes that these 'petitions have the same ring as those of Palamon and Arcite in the *Knight's Tale* or those of countless other romance heroes'.

5. Mills 1977, 53 suggests that 'the passage through the spheres surely belongs to a set of conventions from the genre of dream vision'. Contrast Powell 1978, 301, who finds the trigger for Orpheus's journey to the heavens in the Aeneid passage cited by Trivet, as does Friedman 1970, 205.

6. Punctuation differs from Fox ed. 1981 in this passage; 'vnyt' is understood as a noun.

7. See Fox ed. 1981, 403. MacQueen 1976, 79 suggests the word ironically carries the connotation 'graves' as well as 'groves'.

8. See Fox ed. 1981, 406 for discussion of the Trivet misreading behind this use of 'Rodomantus'.

9. By coincidence, five of these occur in one section of The Monk's Tale, VII.2463-2766: Nero, Antiochus, Alexander, Julius Caesar and Crassus.

10. Lines 380-83 are assigned to Proserpina by Fox ed. 1981, but could as easily be regarded as continued speech by Pluto.

11. See Friedman 1970, 194-96 for differentiation among Orpheus texts in much these terms.

12. Compare Gray 1979, 221, who suggests that Eurydice is 'charmingly conscious' of her forwardness.

13. Line 526 seems to follow on (as in the three early texts) from line 524 to give this sense. The oddity of Tantalus as innkeeper is often noted.

14. See the ironic conjunction of planets in the opening of *The Testament of Cresseid* and compare The Fox and the Wolf (*Fables* 628-55).

15. Fox ed. 1981, 424 notes that '*Affetterrit* is not paralleled elsewhere'. It is certainly unusual for Middle Scots, but see *OED yfetered* for early use. It may be significant that this word is used by Arcite (KnT I.1229).

REFERENCES

Aitken, Adam J., Matthew P. McDiarmid, and Derik S. Thompson, eds., 1977 — *Bards and Makars*, Glasgow

Bliss, A. J., 1966 — *Sir Orfeo*, 2nd edn, Oxford

Fox, Denton, 1977 — Manuscripts and Prints of Scots Poetry in the Sixteenth Century, in *Bards and Makars*, ed. Aitken *et al.*, pp. 156-71

Friedman, John Block, 1970 — *Orpheus in the Middle Ages*, Cambridge, Mass.

Gray, Douglas, 1979 — *Robert Henryson*, Leiden

Kratzmann, Gregory, 1980 — *Anglo-Scottish Literary Relations 1430-1550*, Cambridge

Lyall, R. J., 1981 — Henryson and Boccaccio: A Problem in the Study of Sources, *Anglia*, 99, pp. 38-59

MacQueen, John, 1967 — *Robert Henryson: A Study of the Major Narrative Poems*, Oxford

———— 1976 — Neoplatonism and Orphism in Fifteenth-Century Scotland, *Scottish Studies*, 20, pp. 69-89

———— 1985 — *Numerology*, Edinburgh

Manning, R. J., 1971 — A Note on Symbolic Identification in Henryson's "Orpheus and Eurydice", *SSL*, 8, pp. 265-71

Mills, Carol, 1977 — Romance Convention and Robert Henryson's *Orpheus and Eurydice*, in *Bards and Makars*, ed. Aitken *et al.*, pp. 52-60

Powell, Marianne, 1978 — Henryson, Boethius and Trevet, in *Actes du 2ᵉ Colloque de Langue et de Littérature écossaises (Moyen Age et Renaissance)*, ed Jean Jacques Blanchot and Claude Graf, Strasbourg, pp. 297-306

———— 1983 — *Fabula Docet: Studies in the Background and Interpretation of Henryson's Morall Fabillis*, Odense University Studies in English, 6

Smith, G. Gregory, ed., 1914 — *The Poems of Robert Henryson*, STS, 1st series, 64

Stewart, Marion, 1973 — King Orphius, *Scottish Studies*, 17, pp. 1-16

Wittig, Kurt, 1958 — *The Scottish Tradition in Literature*, Edinburgh and London

Wright, Dorena Allen, 1971 — Henryson's *Orpheus and Eurydice* and the Tradition of the Muses, *MÆ*, 40, pp. 41-47

THE SIEGE OF THEBES: LYDGATE'S CANTERBURY TALE

Rosamund S. Allen

When Lydgate was born in the Suffolk village from which he took his surname, about 1370 or 1371, Chaucer had probably just completed *The Book of the Duchess*; around 1385, when Lydgate probably became a postulant in the Benedictine house at Bury, Chaucer would have recently begun *Troilus and Criseyde*; Lydgate's ordination as priest in 1397 came just three years before Chaucer's death. Lydgate must have felt that he followed in Chaucer's footsteps, for, just as their lives overlapped, so the later poet, while introducing some new themes, often wrote with self-conscious reference back to Chaucer. As he did so, he amplified Chaucer's idiosyncrasies of metre and syntax and often leaves us more conscious of a muffled echo of the pointed and ironic cadence of his Chaucerian model than of any obvious originality (Pearsall 1970, 52). However, in his *Siege of Thebes* Lydgate does succeed in developing hints in two of Chaucer's major poems to give his own reading of their moral impact.

Lydgate's *Siege of Thebes* is a tale in heroic couplets which he framed as a continuation of Chaucer's already famous Canterbury pilgrimage. It is the only English work which recounts the full story of Thebes (Renoir 1956, 249) and must have been written after the Treaty of Troyes (1420) and probably before Henry V died in 1422. In the Prologue to the *Siege* Lydgate presents a semi-fictional situation in which the narrator, under the poet's name of Lydgate and habited in the black of his own Benedictine order, has gone on pilgrimage to Canterbury after an illness, and has by chance met Chaucer's party of pilgrims about to leave for the return journey to London. When the Host enquires who he is, this persona virtually identifies himself with the poet: 'I answerde my name was Lydgate, / Monk of Bery, ny3 fyfty 3ere of age' (92-93). There is a self-conscious attempt at humour in the passage: the Host advises him to eat suet puddings because he is pinched and thin after illness, and urges him not to refrain from breaking wind if he feels the urge. This seems to be more than clumsy veneration of Chaucer, the master Lydgate eulogizes as 'Floure of Poetes thorghout al breteyne' (40), for Lydgate seeks from the outset to emulate the contents and context of Chaucer's *Canterbury Tales*. If, as seems likely, he did not have a fee-paying patron or client for the *Siege* but was free to select his own subject-matter and framework for the poem then this pilgrimage setting was a personal choice (Pearsall 1970, 151). The Host asks 'Lydgate' to join the pilgrims for supper and to contribute his tale on the route next day. The *Siege* is 'Lydgate's' contribution, begun as they leave the walls of Canterbury.

(i) Lydgate's *Siege of Thebes*: Plot and Significance

Lydgate himself seems to have given the title *The Siege of Thebes* to his account of the fate of Oedipus, of his two misbegotten sons, and of their city of Thebes. It is at first sight an unapt title since the poem gives an account of the history of the city of Thebes from its foundation by Amphion to its final destruction under Theseus, the hero of Chaucer's Knight's Tale.[1] Thebes is assaulted and falls near the end of Lydgate's tale, in Part III of this very unequally divided narrative, in which Part III is longer than the whole of I and II together.

The moral significance of Lydgate's *Siege* is most easily grasped in relation to the plot structure, with its literary echoes and the political warning notes which Lydgate sounds in the narrative. Part I tells of the founding of Thebes, and the tragedy of Oedipus. Part II covers the exile in Argos of his younger son and the embassy and ambushing of Tydeus, a fellow prince. Part III describes the great army which marches on Thebes, and the siege and fall of the city. The narrative focus is on the figure of the king and leader, whether good and successful like Adrastus or self-willed like Oedipus and his sons. The first king presented is Amphion. In one tradition he was the founder of Thebes; just to confuse us with his erudition, Lydgate also mentions the other myth in which Cadmus founded it. Following Boccaccio, Lydgate rationalizes the myth of how Amphion's harp-playing raised the walls of Thebes: 'his song . . . was no thyng but the crafty speche / Of this kyng ycalled Amphioun' (225-27). By his wise words and humility, Amphion persuaded 'the contres envyroun' to come and help him found his city. A good king like Amphion or Adrastus, king of Argos, is a persuasive speaker and is more powerful than a great war-leader (Ebin 1977, 97-100; 1988, 41-43). The *Siege* is, however, rather more a negative exemplum of weak or evil kings, typified in Oedipus and his two sons, Ethiocles (Eteocles) and Polymyte (as Lydgate, like Chaucer, calls Polynices: Renoir 1956, 251-53). Oedipus and his sons are contentious and rude in their speech.

When Amphion died without heirs Labdacus was recalled from banishment to take the throne of Thebes and his son was Laius, father of Oedipus, who, also lacking offspring, petitioned the gods for a son; they sent him Oedipus but devalued the gift by revealing in the stars before his birth that he would kill his father.

Lydgate recounts the familiar myth of how the infant Oedipus was exposed with rivets through his feet, rescued by King Polyboun of Arcadia and brought up as his son. Oedipus is not good princely material; in Lydgate's tale he is an unpleasant youth: aggressive, proud and overbearing, he quarrels with someone who asks in irritation why he is so arrogant when he is not even the son of the king. At his outraged questioning, his adoptive father, Polyboun, another good king, tries to comfort Oedipus by pretending he really is his son and heir, but eventually reveals the truth, and Oedipus consults the oracle of Apollo, where 'the fend . . . With a vois dredful and horrible' (553-54) tells him to go to Thebes where he will hear of his ancestry. Near Thebes Oedipus joins a tournament and there 'cruelly' (581) kills Laius in the fight, and proceeds towards Thebes. He loses his way, and on an inadvertent detour meets the Sphynx. This monster is male, not female as in most traditions. After solving the Sphynx's ridiculously easy riddle, Oedipus proceeds to Thebes and marries Jocasta, his mother. Their sons, in a more savage version of the myth than Sophocles's *Oedipus at Colonus*, are the agents of their father's death. Lydgate softens the detail, probably present in his source, of how Eteocles and Polynices throw Oedipus alive into a pit: in Lydgate's account he dies raving, having torn out his eyes which the sons have trodden underfoot, before they cast him in the pit. The contamination in the ruling house of Thebes has caused one son to kill and two sons to abuse their father already; it will ensure the elimination of that house in the next generation, and the destruction of the entire city. With a warning to 'man and child' whatever their rank, to avoid incest and ' To do honur and due reuerence / To fader and moder' (1022-23) or they will never prosper, a trite and derisory piece of moralizing (Pearsall 1970, 152; Spearing 1984, 354ff.), but with rather different meaning in an age when marriage within eight degrees of consanguinity was forbidden by the Church, Lydgate closes Part I with an injunction to 'make your mirror of Eteocles and Polynices' and the observation that he will continue his tale when the pilgrim cavalcade has descended the hill above Boughton under Blean.

Part II introduces two new characters, Tydeus and Adrastus, and a temporary change of locale, with consequent lightening of tone and moral urgency. Tydeus is the father of Diomede, Criseyde's wooer in *Troilus and Criseyde*, and Tydeus is Lydgate's hero in the *Siege*: he is clearly modelled on Henry V and intended as a compliment to the monarch.[2] In Part II Polymyte, the younger of Oedipus's sons, having challenged his brother's assumed automatic right to the throne, has left Thebes for one year. This is a compromise resolution to their rivalry proposed after discussion by the Theban Council: an important part of leadership in Lydgate's presentation is consultation with those who can advise. At the end of the year, the arrangement is that Polymyte is to rule one year in his turn; inevitably, Ethiocles will break this pact. Polymyte demonstrates his dishonourable nature at the beginning of his exile by refusing to share his shelter in a rainstorm with another exiled prince, Tydeus. Two of Lydgate's explicit themes in the *Siege* are the maintenance of cordial relations among those in positions of power and the mutual co-operation between monarch and populace, with the initiative borne by the monarch. A king and leader must be true (1722, 1742, 1760-73, 1941ff., 2077ff., 2237), humble, kind, and generous (244ff., 2688ff., 2701ff.), for tyranny will alienate his people (258, 2698ff.) leaving him helpless (283ff.; cf. Schirmer 1961, 64).

Tydeus is as exemplary a model of self-control as Polymyte is of irascibility, and replies to Polymyte's surliness 'in ful humble wise' (1312) but, being no coward, eventually joins in a fight. Their illicit fight, with spears, horses and swords, awakens the sleeping King Adrastus, who reconciles them, just as Theseus in Chaucer's Knight's Tale separates the illegal combatants Arcite and Palamon. Lydgate's Adrastus, a wise and practical king who has no sons, resolves to marry his two daughters, Argyve and Deiphyle, to Tydeus and Polymyte, who have now become unshakeable friends. Tydeus, as if typifying courtesy,

> . . . made his brother chese,
> Of gentillesse and of curtesye,
> Which that was most to his fantasye
> Of the sustren for to han to wive. (1642-45)

Typically, the upstart Polymyte chooses the elder and gains the higher status (Ayers 1958, 472).

However, model of self-denial and self-control though he is, Tydeus has had his own family troubles, having accidentally killed his brother, for which he is in exile. Tydeus is also to be cursed in his offspring, for the product of his union with the daughter of Adrastus is the deceitful Diomede. The attempts of Adrastus to cement a friendship between Polymyte and Tydeus by making both of them his sons-in-law are to produce a dual tragedy: both men will die before the end of Lydgate's narrative, and, in the sequel already completed by Chaucer and surely familiar to Lydgate's readers, the son of one will prove unfaithful. Lydgate must have been relying on ironies generated by implicit comparison with Chaucer's *Troilus and Criseyde* to show how human plans can be disrupted by the malevolence of others: Adrastus's apparently ideal matchmaking will fail.

With even greater selflessness, Tydeus undertakes an embassy to Thebes on Polymyte's behalf, to request Ethiocles to relinquish the throne now that his year is up. He arrives 'lich Mars hym-silf, in stiel y-armed bright' (1882) and strides straight through the palace to Ethiocles's throne room, striding out again as majestically after Ethiocles's malevolent and scornful refusal. The climax of this second part of the *Siege* is the ambush of Tydeus by fifty men sent by the treacherous Ethiocles. Tydeus, who rides 'Sool by hym-silf with-oute companye' (2163) catches sight of the moon glinting on shields and plate armour, and valiantly rides straight into them, killing all but one, whom he leaves alive to tell Ethiocles.

Tydeus, discovered in her garden by Lycurgus's daughter, is helped to return to Argos to report the treason of Ethiocles. Meanwhile the survivor of the ambush party arrives to report to Ethiocles, whose reaction is vicious: he accuses the fifty of cowardice and wants to execute the survivor, who remains quietly dignified and courageous in the verbal onslaught, but eventually kills himself in the king's presence in desperation, provoking a near riot. Lydgate leaves him nameless, although Chaucer knew from Statius that he was Hemonydes (Tr 5.1492). Amid the clamour of the dissension in Thebes Lydgate warns that these are the 'kalendys' (only the early days: 2544) of adversity and that the destruction of the king and the entire region results only from the failure to keep a promise. Part II ends with an allusion to the pilgrimage frame in Lydgate's declaration that those who wish will 'hear' more of the narrator's moral teaching. This is almost the last reference to the fictional framework.

Part III is a sombre account of the assembling of Adrastus's forces, their march against Thebes, near death from thirst, and rescue by Ypsypyle, a princess in exile; and of the failure of Jocasta's attempt at mediating between her sons, Ethiocles and Polymyte, which proves as futile as Tydeus's mediation had been. As a truce is being formulated, hostilities are accidentally restarted when a pet tiger belonging to the Theban royal family is killed by Greek soldiers who think it is a wild beast.[3] Like the adder which precipitates the last battle on Salisbury Plain in Malory's *Morte Darthur*, this beast is also the unwitting means of the destruction of a kingdom, its heirs and many neighbouring kings as well. Only Adrastus survives into old age; the rest, including Tydeus and the two brothers, are killed. Even their bones are refused burial by Creon, uncle of the two dead brothers, until the intervention of Theseus. In acknowledgement of Chaucer, Lydgate's narrative at this point is full of reminiscences of Part I of The Knight's Tale. He concludes with the warning which this desolation of all Greece provides for his own time: war pursued in the interests of greed and ambition for power invariably destroys whole realms.[4] He ends with a prayer for peace and forgiveness. There is no concluding reference to a fictitious pilgrim audience; Lydgate has failed, or not tried, to secure a totally framed setting for his 'tale'.

(ii) The 'Historical' Context of Thebes

Lydgate took his material, which he terms 'the story', from a fourteenth- or fifteenth-century prose adaptation of a popular medieval poem, the anonymous twelfth-century *Roman de Thèbes* (c. 1175). We do not know Lydgate's exact source, which must have borne resemblance to the extant *Roman de Edipus* and also to the late fifteenth-century prose narrative, inserted into a French version of Orosius's *History*, entitled *Histoire de Thèbes*; both of these are prose redactions of *Le Roman de Thèbes* (Erdmann and Ekwall ed. 1930; I, vi; Constans ed. 1890, II, clxi; Anderson 1982, 117). This source he amplified, increasing it by about a third (Ayers 1958, 465), by inserting material from such sources as Boccaccio's *Fall of Princes*, *Concerning Famous Women* and *Genealogy of the Gods*. Whereas Chaucer never mentions Boccaccio by name, despite using him as the main source for *Troilus and Criseyde*, for The Knight's Tale and for much of the middle section of *The Parliament of Fowls*, Lydgate drops the name of 'Bochas' (his form of 'Boccaccio') at frequent intervals throughout his *Siege*, giving the false impression that Boccaccio is the source for all 'the story' instead of only the learned accretions. In half a generation Boccaccio has moved up the literary scale in England from total obscurity as the unnamed author of Chaucer's main source for *Troilus*, to the status of an authority flaunted as evidence of a serious text. The distinction lies in the fact that Lydgate cites Boccaccio's Latin works, whereas Chaucer was using his vernacular material, probably through the medium of a French redaction. Lydgate's reticence in naming it shows that he is equally apologetic about his own French vernacular source. In effect, for Lydgate Boccaccio has taken over the role occupied in *Troilus* by the fictitious Lollius.

Le Roman de Thèbes, the first vernacular version of the legend of Thebes, complements the much greater *Roman de Troie* of Benoit de Sainte Maure, which is the distant ancestor of Chaucer's *Troilus and Criseyde*. Benoit's poem appeared in a Latin redaction in 1287, Guido delle Colonne's *Historia Destructionis Troiae*, and Guido's Latin work was the source of Lydgate's *Troy Book*, begun in 1412 under the patronage of Prince Henry (Shakespeare's Prince Hal). Lydgate seems to have completed his *Troy Book* immediately before he embarked on the *Siege* in about 1420.

The story of Troy, with its sequel in Virgil's *Aeneid*, was of intimate concern to all western Europe, for the British, the French and the Italians all imagined that they were descended from the escapees from the sack of Troy. In a poem attributed to Lydgate the kings of Britain are listed, beginning with Brutus (Scattergood 1971, 44-45). The *Gawain* poet celebrates this auspicious origin for the land of Brutus and Arthur at the beginning of *Sir Gawain and the Green Knight*, although perhaps ironically. Chaucer preferred the classical version, Virgil's story of Aeneas, which he recounted twice, in Book I of *The House of Fame* and in *The Legend of Good Women*.

Chaucer followed up his tale of Troy (*Troilus and Criseyde*) by moving back in time with The Knight's Tale, which covers the aftermath of the bitter enmity of Oedipus's sons Eteocles and Polynices of Thebes. Similarly, Lydgate alluded to the Theban legend twice in his *Troy Book* (Pro. 226-44; IV. 3014, 3022-23: Renoir 1967, 112) which he followed with the *Siege*, so moving even further back in time to the founding of Thebes and its corruption by Oedipus's incest.

Chaucer's allusions to Thebes always carry an aura of foreboding from the moral taint associated with all stages of the story of Thebes after Oedipus's sin. This is not at first obvious in the apparently innocuous scene in Book II of *Troilus and Criseyde*, as Criseyde and her ladies sit in their paved parlour reading aloud from 'the geste / Of the siege of Thebes' and are interrupted at the moment when Amphiorax, the 'bisshop', fell through the ground to hell (Tr 2.84, 100-105). This is a moment to which Lydgate was to do full and lurid justice thirty-five years later (*Siege* III. 4019-83). Amphiorax, however, is an ominous figure: he was betrayed into joining the campaign against Thebes by his wife, who was bribed with a fateful brooch, heirloom of the Theban royal house, to reveal where he had hidden, too terrified to join the army voluntarily because he had foretold his own bizarre death in a chasm in the ground. Lydgate observes cynically that he was a fool to tell her (2869ff.; her conscience, not bribery, made her tell: 2852). Alison of Bath knew all this because her husband, Jankin, had read it to her from his book of wicked wives. With a moment's reflection we realize the parallel with

Criseyde, who betrays Troilus with a piece of jewellery he had given her on parting, which she gives to Diomede (Tr 5.1661ff.).[5] There is another more explicitly ominous allusion to Thebes near the close of *Troilus and Criseyde*, when Cassandra reveals the meaning of Troilus's prophetic dream in which he seems to see Criseyde cuddling a wild boar. Cassandra gives a lengthy, and rather boring, resumé of the story of Thebes and concludes it with the brutal and coarse lines: ' This Diomede hire herte hath, and she his . . . This Diomede is inne, and thow art oute' (Tr 5.1517-19). Lydgate's audience came to the first tale in the sequence fully conditioned by Chaucer's handling of the next two sequences of universal history, the legends of Athens and of Troy, in The Knight's Tale and *Troilus*.

Thebes and its fate may seem far less interesting and relevant than Troy's, but the legend of Thebes was well known in the Middle Ages. Chaucer knew the Latin version of the Thebes legend in Statius's *Thebaid* (A.D. 92) (Anderson 1982, 109, 113), and the story of Thebes was popular in the fourteenth and fifteenth centuries, when *Le Roman de Thèbes* was reworked in two or three prose versions and Chaucer used the Thebes legend as a backdrop for his Knight's Tale and *Troilus*.

But Chaucer did not tackle the fate of Thebes directly. It was a topic which required the firmly moralizing stance of a cleric like Lydgate. Thebes was distinct from both Rome and Troy in the medieval imagination: both Troy and Rome were considered ideal cities, the one as the heart of the universal Church, even in the era of the Avignon papacy, the other the founding city of western Europe. But Thebes was the city of evil: from its early days it brought misfortune.[6] This Lydgate stresses in his version of the myth.

The twenty-nine extant manuscripts of the *Siege* (Edwards 1983, 15) show that in the fifteenth century the poem was read in three ways. It was read as a tale of antiquity in association with the story of Troy, and in this context appears in three manuscripts together with Lydgate's *Troy Book*. It was also read as a story in its own right: in some seven manuscripts it stands alone.[7] Finally, it might be read as one of *The Canterbury Tales*: in five manuscripts,[8] and in the early printed editions from Stow's 1561 reprint of Thynne on (Pearsall 1970, 156), it is included with those *Canterbury Tales* which nineteenth-century editors determined were authentically Chaucer's, and from which they and subsequent editors have excluded Lydgate's *Siege*.[9]

(iii) Narrative as Polemic

Like the other two major works (*The Troy Book* and *The Fall of Princes*) the *Siege* is neither an epic (such as the *Thebaid*) nor a romance, as perhaps The Knight's Tale is (Spearing 1984, 353). In his *Troy Book* Lydgate disclaims all pretensions to romance, and in the *Siege* he constantly urges his readers — the fiction of oral tale-telling forgotten — to make a mirror of the characters in the plot, seeing them as examples of good or bad behaviour (Ayers 1958, 469,

473). Lydgate sees narrative as a source of facts, the significance of which he, as historian, interprets in many hortatory passages of advice and warning. His recently completed *Troy Book* had been a *speculum principum* (mirror for princes), offering advice to its patron, King Henry (Benson 1980, 113ff.); the *Siege* can be viewed as a more explicit version of the king's mirror (Ebin 1985, 52, 55). But it has more narrative interest than Lydgate's other two major works and provides a closer focus on individuals in different roles than The Knight's Tale (*pace* Ebin 1985, 56ff.). Although it is a semi-political work,[10] it has several surprisingly romantic episodes. Critics who argue that the *Siege* is a polemic on the dangers of war addressed to those in positions of power ignore these passages of frustrated romance. Perhaps the explanation is that Lydgate was in fact writing for a wider audience than politically prominent males. If the *Siege* is a mirror for princes, it is a mirror for dowager queens, princesses and royal nannies as well.

Two of these romantic episodes are located in gardens, which seem to have been grafted in from dream vision or chivalric romance. In one of these, not found in the *Thebaid* or in the majority of manuscripts of *Le Roman de Thèbes* but present in the derivative French prose redactions, Lycurgus's daughter finds Tydeus lying wounded in her garden, yet Lydgate ignores the perilously romantic implications of this setting, so reminiscent of The Knight's Tale: Tydeus does not fall in love with his royal nurse (although the reader waits with trepidation for it to happen) but remains stolidly loyal to the wife he left at home. Unlike Gawain, Tydeus has proved himself faithful in all points. The other garden episode occurs in an apparent interlude or digression in Part III. Ypsypyle, the royal nurse in Lycurgus's household, rescues Adrastus's army when they are dying of thirst, by showing them a large river (which it seems surprising they had so totally failed to notice themselves) and in doing so neglects for too long her infant charge, the darling son and heir of King Lycurgus. This is no *hortus conclusus*, no enclosed garden of love, but rather a garden of Eden, complete with serpent, which bites the baby, who dies. The episode has in fact been included to allow King Adrastus to plead for Ypsypyle with Lycurgus, who wishes to punish her. Adrastus has already acted a role similar to Theseus's when he reconciles the two fighting princes, who marry his daughters. Here the words Adrastus uses to appease Lycurgus (see section (iv), below) are those Chaucer's Theseus addresses to Palamon, Emelye and the assembled court, to encourage everyone to abandon their mourning for Arcite and, making virtue of necessity, after woe to be merry, 'I rede that we make of sorwes two / O parfit joye, lastynge everemo' (KnT I.3071-72).

This everlasting joy, the union of the Theban Palamon and Emelye in The Knight's Tale, and with them the union of the nobility of the now fallen Thebes with that of Athens, reads like the perfect happy ending we expect from a romance. But the union promoted by Adrastus before the fall of Thebes did not produce 'one perfect joy lasting for ever'. What Lydgate does in the *Siege* is to untie the knots of Chaucer's narrative, where Theseus razes Thebes and 'contains' its evil in the diplomatic union of Palamon and Emelye, by letting loose the corruption and depravity of Thebes so carefully contained and apparently eliminated at the opening of *The Canterbury Tales* in the Knight's tale of joy after woe. And this sense of reversal is ironically reinforced by the fact that Lydgate sets his *Siege* in the sequence of Chaucer's *Canterbury Tales*. It is as if Lydgate is reminding us of what Theseus in that great speech about the First Mover has inexplicably forgotten: that Theseus's own father Egeus has already presented a world-view in which the alternation of 'Joye after wo, and wo after gladnesse' (KnT I.2841) is simply part of the world's 'transmutation'. Lydgate's *Siege* shows the inevitable 'woe after gladness', a situation he actually alludes to in the Prologue to *The Pilgrimage of the Life of Man* (if it is Lydgate's) in the line: 'Wo after Ioye, & after song wepyng' (31). This view of history as an apparently arbitrary alternation of fortunes was to be the motive for Lydgate's *Fall of Princes*, written at Humphrey of Gloucester's request ' To shewe the chaung off worldli variaunce' (Pro. 434).

Although Lydgate sets up the *Siege* as a late tale in the Canterbury sequence, told on the return trip to London, it covers story-matter prior to the events of the first of the tales, the Knight's. Chaucer has shown the resolution of the chaos following the siege of Thebes, as Theseus assists the widows to bury their husbands and enables the now homeless Palamon to become part of his own family. But in this newly-proffered last tale of all, Lydgate shows the evil of Thebes reasserting itself: the myth unfolds again as inevitably as woe succeeds gladness. This sense of reversal, of a mirror-image presentation of Chaucer's *Canterbury Tales*, and notably of its most celebrated opening tale, is strong in the *Siege* and seems to be part of its meaning.

(iv) The Significance of *The Siege of Thebes* in the context of *The Canterbury Tales*

For a Canterbury Tale *The Siege of Thebes* is long: over 4,000 lines. The longest of Chaucer's tales is the Knight's at a mere 2,200; even this seems to have impressed the poet of *The Tale of Beryn* as somewhat taxing on the concentration. For Lydgate, however, 4,000 lines is very short for a major poem, and yet *The Siege of Thebes* has rightly been accepted by critics as one of Lydgate's three major works.

Lydgate conceives his *Siege* as his contribution to the Canterbury story-telling competition begun in Chaucer's General Prologue. In putting forward a story-teller not present among the original 'twenty-nine' in Southwark Lydgate copies Chaucer's own Canon's Yeoman, who bursts into their ranks at Boughton-under-Blean (CYPro VIII.556; Spearing 1984, 337; Hammond 1912, 361). The Monk of Bury 'answers' the Knight's interruption of the tale of Chaucer's Monk, thus left incomplete, by providing a tale which is a companion-piece to Chaucer's Knight's in setting and in its theme of fraternal enmity (Renoir 1967, 114) and which, moreover, has been 'completed' in a way the Knight's is not. Since he places this tale in the same pilgrimage framework, theoretically he has two audiences: one fictitious, the other real. In practice Lydgate almost abandons the fiction of oral story-telling about half-way through his *Siege*; there are only five allusions to the pilgrimage in the tale itself. Lydgate's tale is addressed to a reading audience — whom he actually directs to go away and read Boccaccio and Chaucer in the course of his narrative! Why then did he go to such painful lengths to imitate Chaucer's pilgrimage-setting?

Lydgate does not set his tale in the sequence of Chaucer's tales for the outward journey, but as the first (and last) contribution on the homeward way. In several respects the notion of going back over familiar ground, of treading the same path but in reverse sequence, penetrates the narrative of Lydgate's *Siege* itself. At the same time, Lydgate imparts a finality, a sense of closure and completeness to Chaucer's unfinished poem.

When Chaucer died in 1400 he left *The Canterbury Tales* unfinished: he had not even taken the pilgrims to the gates of Canterbury and several tales were still untold from the outward journey; there are two unfinished tales, the Cook's and Squire's, and patchy mismatches in the assignment of tales to pilgrims. To us the work is irremediably incomplete; to one recent critic this unfinished state is intentional, and part of its meaning (Howard 1976). Since we do not have the four tales from each pilgrim which the Host stipulates in the General Prologue, critics in the last two decades have decided that Chaucer never intended more than one tale each, and never meant to describe the arrival at St Thomas's shrine, but designed the sequence to end apocalyptically with the pilgrims entering the outskirts of an unnamed village as the shadows lengthen and the Parson directs their steps on to the metaphorical good road to soul's rest. Modern editors would never dream of attempting to complete Chaucer's fragmentary masterpiece.

But a prospective medieval reader, placing an order with a bookseller for a copy of the *The Canterbury Tales*, would be less concerned about authenticity than about value for money. He looked for a full text, and booksellers and their scribes tried to meet this demand. Some supplied spurious tales to fill the gaps Chaucer left: *The Tale of Beryn*, discussed in Peter Brown's essay in this volume, is one such.

When, within twenty-two years of Chaucer's death, Lydgate supplied *The Siege of Thebes* as a contribution to *The Canterbury Tales*, he could be sure of gaining a readership. All sixteenth- and seventeenth-century editions of Chaucer from Stow's 1561 edition of *The Canterbury Tales* print *The Siege of Thebes* with Chaucer's tales. These early additions to Chaucer's *Tales* tell us how writers in the immediately succeeding generation reacted to Chaucer, what they thought *The Canterbury Tales* was about, and whether they responded most to the dramatic principle of the pilgrimage framework, as modern critics did until about thirty years ago (Bowers 1985, 32 n. 16) or viewed the work as a collection of varied literary pieces with interconnected themes, as scholars in the 1970s and 1980s tend to do. Did they see Chaucer primarily as an entertainer or an instructor?

The Siege of Thebes shows us that what impressed Lydgate was Chaucer's 'sentence'. This is probably one reason why he chose to write a Canterbury Tale. The Host's competition rules in the General Prologue declare that the winner is to be the one whose four tales are judged to be ' Tales of best sentence and moost solaas' (GP I.798). Lydgate, who was after all a Benedictine monk, could not manage, or perhaps found uninteresting, the humour which a modern reader thinks of as quintessential Chaucer. For Lydgate at least, Chaucer was a poet's poet, a teacher of morals in golden language (Spearing 1984, 338), and it is Chaucer's language as surface texturing which he tries to imitate. He ignores Chaucer's deep tonal complexity, the constant teasing interplay between narrative as characterization of a story-teller and narrative as part of a larger area of meaning unavailable to the limited comprehension of its narrator. One reason for this lack of irony is that Lydgate liked facts. He valued narrative as a sequence of historical facts which were available for constant reinterpretation in terms of moral and practical advice for succeeding ages (Ayers 1958, 463; Bowers 1985, 42), and lacked Chaucer's sympathetic understanding of the autonomy of the pagan past (Spearing 1984, 358). Indeed, he seems to have seen Chaucer primarily as a historian, who presented first a version of the history of Troy in *Troilus and Criseyde* and then the history of one great leader of Athens in The Knight's Tale. *Troilus and Criseyde* and The Knight's Tale are two of the three poems by Chaucer which Lydgate really knows. He does not, we find, know *The Canterbury Tales* as a whole very well!

Lydgate appreciated Chaucer, then, for his excellence of expression. For us today the joy of Chaucer's language is that he can slide with ease down an entire scale from the elaborate opening lines:

> Whan that Aprill with his shoures soote
> The droghte of March hath perced to the roote,
> And bathed every veyne in swich licour
> Of which vertu engendred is the flour;
> Whan Zephirus eek with his sweete breeth
> Inspired hath in every holt and heeth
> The tendre croppes, and the yonge sonne
> Hath in the Ram his half cours yronne,
> And ... That ... (So ...) Thanne ... And ... And ... That ... seeke,
> (GP 1-18; one sentence: ' Thanne' begins the main clause)

through the neutral narrative style:

> Whilom, as olde stories tellen us,
> Ther was a duc that highte Theseus;

> Of Atthenes he was lord and governour,
> And in his tyme swich a conquerour
> That gretter was ther noon under the sonne.
> Ful many a riche contree hadde he wonne;
> What with his wysdom and his chivalrie,
> He conquered al the regne of Femenye,
> That whilom was ycleped Scithia,
> And weddede the queene Ypolita, (KnT I.859-68)

to the colloquialisms of the cynical Theseus:

> She woot namoore of al this hoote fare,
> By God, than woot a cokkow or an hare!
> But all moot ben assayed, hoot and coold;
> A man moot ben a fool, or yong or oold —
> I woot it by myself ful yore agon,
> For in my tyme a servant was I oon. (KnT I.1809-14)

As he claims to have an indelible memory of Chaucer as a poet 'which sothly hadde most of excellence / In rethorike and in eloquence' (*Siege* 41-42) it is obvious that Lydgate thinks of Chaucer as a writer in elaborate style. Fortunately, in the *Siege*, where his memories of Chaucer must have been most inescapable, it is the plain narrative style which dominates:

> And whan he was vnarmed to his sherte,
> She made first wassh his woundes smerte,
> And serche hem wel with dyuers instrumentes,
> And made fette sondry oynementes,
> And leches ek the beste she koude fynde,
> Ful craftely to staunche hem and to bynde. (2391-95)

Yet the *tour de force* of that first, eighteen-line, sentence which opens *The Canterbury Tales* draws Lydgate inexorably. Lydgate's limp-wristed metre, and his syntax, where he is apt to wobble off course and collapse like someone on a monocycle, are not qualifications for an attempt to outdo Chaucer at his own game, but that is exactly how Lydgate tries to begin his Canterbury Tale. From Chaucer's eighteen-line sentence Lydgate has produced sixty-four lines before the editors call a halt and insert a full stop, but in fact this is not a sixty-four line sentence; it is not a sentence at all because Lydgate never manages a main clause (Spearing 1984, 342ff.):

> Whan briȝte phebus passed was þe ram
> Myd of Aprille and in-to bole cam,
> And Satourn old with his frosty face
> In virgyne taken had his place,
> Malencolik and slowgh of mocioun . . .
> And . . . That . . . whan . . . And . . . whan that . . . The tyme . . . whan . . . And
> . . . And . . . Lich as . . . whan . . .Which . . . Which . . . To whom . . . Fro the
> tyme that . . . as . . . Lich as . . .   (1-64)[11]

It sinks away like sugar down a funnel and leaves nothing behind except an after-image of bustling activity: Lygate has taken us from the spring setting, sun, showers, flowers (1-17), through the recapitulation of the varieties of the tales which were told on Chaucer's original pilgrimage (18-38), to a slotted-in allusion to Chaucer, 'Chief Registrer of þis pilgrimage', who 'Al þat was told forȝeting noght at al' (48-49) recorded everything, rejecting only 'the chaff' (39-57), as the tales were told during the entire journey from Southwark under the direction of the Host (58-64).

The all-important missing verb in Lydgate's opening to the *Siege* is an error, and not the only one in these sixty-four lines. In the Prologue to the *Siege* Lydgate is so vague about *The Canterbury Tales* that he attributes to the Pardoner the Summoner's red face and quarrel with the Friar, and the Yeoman's and the Reeve's Miller Symkyn's bald heads, and thinks that the Reeve was drunk like the Miller and Cook (Spearing 1985, 75). Even at the end he alludes to the Knight's tale as if it were recounted at Deptford, which is where the Reeve's is told (Bowers 1985, 40). After this there is unconscious irony when Lydgate assures the reader that Chaucer will 'alwey fressh ben in my memorye' (45).

This opening sequence establishes the strange dual time scheme we have already seen operating between *The Siege of Thebes* and The Knight's Tale. It is spring; if this is the same spring in which Chaucer joined the pilgrimage in the mid 1380s, how is Lydgate in the 1420s able to meet the same people? Yet Chaucer is already an unforgettable memory, Lydgate has declared, and his record of this famous pilgrimage, full and accurate, was made long since. (Lydgate treats *The Canterbury Tales* as factual, and Chaucer as its historian.) Chaucer himself is inexplicably absent from the Canterbury inn: only the Host actually speaks to Lydgate. Chaucer the pilgrim has been replaced by Chaucer the poet, who, in Lydgate's conflation of the real and the fictitious (Ganim 1983, 106), is credited near the end of *The Siege of Thebes* with the authorship of The Knight's Tale, alongside the Knight narrator. Chaucer's place as pilgrim is taken by Lydgate, the next generation's poet, who now takes over the role of both story-teller and historian (Spearing 1984, 338). Lydgate, having stepped back in time, in Wellsian fashion, has not found Chaucer. He, having departed this life in 1400, has left his *Canterbury*

Tales unfinished: an opportunity for Lydgate to enter his tale in the gap left at the end (Spearing 1984, 336, 359; 1985, 68). Perhaps, too, Lydgate regarded this as a chance to remedy an omission at the beginning of The Knight's Tale, namely Chaucer's refusal to recount in detail Theseus's conquests:

> And certes, if it nere to long to heere,
> I wolde have toold yow fully the manere
> How wonnen was the regne of Femenye
> By Theseus, and by his chivalrye. (KnT I.875-78)

There are stylistic echoes of Chaucer's Knight's Tale within the body of the narrative of the *Siege* (cited in Erdmann and Ekwall ed. 1930, notes; see also Spearing 1984). These have the same effect as the imitations of the General Prologue in Lydgate's Prologue; action is translated into a finished poetic structure which is a compound of Chaucer's and Lydgate's poems, instead of a reactivation of an earlier incomplete poem.

Several echoes of The Knight's Tale augment this effect of completion, of a closure of the Canterbury sequence even as it is apparently restarted on its return route. The two chief instances are an allusion to Theseus's final speech, and a passage echoing Arcite's funeral. Allusion to the closing sequence of Chaucer's Knight's Tale, Theseus's great speech on the First Mover, occurs in the speech Adrastus makes to the sorrowing Lycurgus when his baby son has just been killed by a serpent:

> For in this world who so look a-right,
> Is non so gret of power nor of myght,
> Noon so riche shortly nor so bold
> But he mot dey outher ȝong or old.
> And who in ȝouthe passeth þis passage,
> He is eskaped al the woode Rage,
> Al sorowe and trouble of this present lyff . . .
> Wher-for best is, as semeth vnto me,
> No man gruche but, of hegh prudence,
> The sonde of goddis tak in pacience. (3433-44)

The grieving father Lycurgus, as Lydgate reminds us (3522), is the champion who came to Palamon's support in the great tournament in which Arcite was victor but received his fatal injury.

The allusion to Arcite's funeral is even more final. We are not expecting Lydgate to bring Palamon and Arcite into his narrative, and initiate a rerun of *The Canterbury Tales*, like a cycle of regeneration (*pace* Bowers 1985, 48ff.). Any such expectation is dispelled when Lydgate describes the delayed burial of the widows' husbands' bones and imitates Arcite's funeral, reminding us as he does so that Arcite died long ago in this sequence of tales, and we have witnessed his funeral:

> And to the wommen in reles of her care,
> The bonys of her lordys that were slayn
> This worthy duk restoryd hath agayn.
> But what shuld I any lenger dwelle
> The olde Ryytys by and by to telle,
> Nor thobsequies in ordre to devise;
> Nor to declare the manere and the Guyse
> how the bodyes wer to Asshes brent,
> Nor of the gommes in the flaumbe spent . . . (4562-70)

and he continues for nearly forty lines, in imitation of the famous *occultatio* in which Chaucer's Knight declines to describe the funeral obsequies of Arcite.[12] In Lydgate's narrative we should at this point be meeting Palamon and Arcite themselves, lying in the heap of slain outside Thebes, about to be taken prisoner and incarcerated in Athens. The whole sequence of *The Canterbury Tales* seems about to begin again. Indeed Bowers (1985 26-27, 46-50) has said that Lydgate's tale restores the normal circular pattern, of journey out and return home, which one would expect of a pilgrimage; Bowers considers that Lydgate assumed Chaucer's Canterbury pilgrimage was to be a round tour, not the linear and apocalyptic voyage to another world which modern critics read into the unfinished *Canterbury Tales*.

Lydgate's *Siege*, however, works in conjunction with The Knight's Tale to produce a completed sequence. Its plot ends just after the opening of The Knight's Tale, with the first of the two funerals which occur in The Knight's Tale, that of the bones of the widows' husbands. Yet stylistically this funeral, the second we have witnessed in the *Siege*,[13] matches the second funeral (Arcite's) in The Knight's Tale, so completing the tales as a pair, and a pair, moreover, which itself 'frames' *The Canterbury Tales*.

Lydgate must have regarded Chaucer's first tale as an incomplete statement (Spearing 1984, 352). Even the fall of Thebes is not final in Chaucer's Knight's Tale: strangely, after Theseus has dismantled Thebes in Part I 'bothe wall and sparre and rafter' (KnT I.990) we find Palamon and Arcite leaving for ' Thebes with his olde walles wyde' (KnT I.1880) at the end of Part II. Lydgate treats the walls of Thebes emblematically: they were raised initially by the co-operation of neighbouring kings, but have become the exclusive property of Ethiocles, who swears by them in unjustly excluding his brother from the throne (2028ff.). In the *Siege*, walls, with the structures they enclose, become a seminal image of security and domestic peace. Because the walls of Thebes abuse this norm by enclosing corruption, they must be razed. So they have to be forcibly demolished by the loyal Argive wives, who beat them down with pickaxes and mallets (4543ff.). Laius, significantly, is killed outside the gates of a well-walled castle. After his ordeal in the ambush, Tydeus seeks shelter in a garden adjoining the walls of Lycurgus's palace. Outside, in the porch of Adrastus's palace, Polymyte and Tydeus quarrel in the cold and dark: once admitted, they are reconciled, and given warm furs to wear (Spearing 1984, 346ff.). Tydeus and Polymyte and even Ypsypyle are exiles, excluded from the boundaries of their native cities.

So strong is our impression of buildings in the *Siege* that on several occasions we are taken inside down the long perspective of palatial corridors and halls: to the inner sanctum where Adrastus is awakened by the two young men battling outside; or to the council room into which Tydeus strides on his embassy to Ethiocles, and from which he emerges with immense dignity into the danger of the lonely journey home through open country. The impression of enclosure and containment again reinforces the narrative closure of the *Siege* as a conclusion to *The Canterbury Tales*.

If Lydgate's *Siege of Thebes* seems coolly objective in treating story as a means of inculcating morals rather than of arousing emotion or celebrating human achievement (Spearing 1984, 354; Ganim 1983, 120ff.), then at least the morality is not purely directed to a male readership. In this advice for kings, women have an important part to play by tending, rearing and training kings. The structure of the plot, and the presence of the Sphynx with his riddle, to which the solution is the whole life of man from cradle to grave, suggests that the *Siege* is not merely about kings but about the responsibility of all its members for the welfare of any society (Kohl 1979, 123). Like *The Troy Book*, the *Siege* instructs its readers: 'Þat be example þei may be war & lere' (*Troy Book* II. 1890, cited in Benson 1980, 121). Truth is the cement which binds society, and is as essential in a king as in his subjects: Ethiocles's dishonesty and the disaster it causes prove this (*Siege* 1725-84). The treasure of any king is the love of his people, which cannot fail if the people are properly respected and treated generously: 'And the tresour shortly, of a kyng / Stondeth in loue abouen alle thyng' (2719-20). Adrastus, the ideal king, is the 'merour' (mirror) of 'kyngly fredam' (generosity) (2723ff.; cf. 1559).

The moral theme of *The Siege of Thebes* is the responsibility of one individual to another, and the fragility of human security when it is based on such unreliable agents.[14] This is reflected in the structure. Chaucer's Knight's Tale begins with a wedding, a battle and a funeral, and ends with a battle, a funeral and a wedding, suggesting within this structure that individuals serve public causes to which they frequently have to sacrifice their private interests; life goes on even when individuals die. Lydgate's *Siege*, however, is linear rather than circular in structure: it begins with the founding of a city which is destroyed at its close; the birth and death of the city are paralleled by the birth, full vigour, old age and death of individuals, adumbrated in the Sphynx's riddle. But the life-lines are warped: prominence is given to doomed children in Parts I and III, to doomed or brief weddings in I and II, and to the old age of Oedipus and Adrastus in I and III; funerals, the end of all, are described in I and III. Greece remains a desert (4561); Thebes is not rebuilt. Lydgate ends with an Epilogue condemning war (4629-4703).[15]

This is a poem of endings: the downfall of Thebes matches the closure of *The Canterbury Tales* in this last and belated contribution. We do not even hear how the Host receives this last tale: a return to the framework would have suggested continuity. More than Chaucer's Parson, it is Lydgate who has 'knytte up wel a greet mateere' (ParsPro X.28) with his Canterbury Tale.

Queen Mary and Westfield College
University of London

NOTES

I am grateful to colleagues Julia Boffey, Victoria Rothschild and James Simpson for advice in the preparation of this paper.

1. *Le Roman de Thèbes* and its prose redactions, unlike the *Thebaid*, begin with Oedipus's youth (Anderson 1982, 120 n. 22; Constans ed. 1890, II, cxix-cxx and n. 1).

2. Very different is Statius's Tydeus, a warmonger who, in frenzied vengeance, devours the head of Menalippus who had given him his death-blow (*Thebaid* VIII. 761ff.). *Le Roman de Thèbes* omits this incident, but Lydgate obliquely alludes to the context by noting Boccaccio's information that the dying Tydeus was given Menalippus's head; he declines to say more (*Siege* 4235-39).

3. Pearsall (1970, 152) calls this 'a silly episode' but its origin lies in *Thebaid* VII. 564-601: two now tamed tigers from Bacchus's chariot suddenly turn wild and start killing Greek soldiers, whereupon Aconteus wounds them and so precipitates hostilities; in the two French prose redactions, however, they are reduced to a single tame female tiger (Constans ed. 1890, II, cxxvi-vii).

4. Anderson (1982, 133) suggests that Chaucer's references to Thebes in *Troilus* contain a similar warning to the citizens of 'New Troy' (London): 'As Thebes should have been to Troy, so Troy should be to England'.

5. In Anderson's opinion (1982, 127-28) this is the very brooch which Argia (whom he identifies with Criseyde's mother Argyve) used to bribe Amphiarus's (Amphiorax's) wife; on this assumption, it is the brooch which Criseyde gives to Troilus at their first love-making (Tr 3.1370ff.), which he then returns to her as she leaves for the Greek

camp; this does not seem very likely. See also *Fall of Princes* I. 322-23, cited in
Hammond ed. 1927, n. 1, and see also Chaucer's Complaint of Mars, 245-62.

6. Allen and Moritz (1981, 26 and 41 n. 70) suggest that Lydgate, reminding us that
    Thebes, the focus of civil and familial strife, must be dealt with, points to the beginning
    of *The Canterbury Tales* 'rather than its pietistic ending, as the core of its statement'.

7. Copies of the French *Roman de Thèbes* and *Roman de Troie* also often appeared in the
    same manuscripts (Renoir 1960, 16). The *Siege* is found with *The Troy Book* in
    Cambridge, Trinity College MS O.5.2., Oxford, Bodleian Library MS Digby 230, and
    London, British Library MS Royal 18.D.ii. (Pearsall 1970, 158 n. 49). MS Trinity
    O.5.2 was owned by the Knevet family of Norfolk (Pearsall 1970, 77); MS Royal
    18.D.ii was commissioned by Sir William Herbert: the marriage of his daughter Maud to
    Henry Percy (*c*. 1476) is commemorated by his coat of arms at the end of the *Siege*.
    There are thirteen miniatures in this text of the *Siege*, the only extant cycle of
    illuminations for the poem (Pearsall 1970, 77), and all were executed in the sixteenth
    century in a Flemish style, although Herbert seems to have selected the subject-matter for
    the illustrations before he died in 1469 (Lawton 1983, 66-68).

8. The five are: BL Additional MS 5140, Oxford, Christ Church MS 152, BL Egerton MS
    2864, Longleat MS 257, and the Cardigan MS (Austin, University of Texas MS 143)
    (Edwards 1983, 22 n. 33; Bowers 1985, 39 n. 36). MS Longleat 257 positions the
    Siege immediately before Chaucer's Knight's Tale, where Daniel Mosser believes the
    Cardigan MS originally also positioned it (Bowers 1985, 39 n. 36). The list of MSS of
    the *Siege* in Erdmann and Ekwall ed. 1930, II, 36-61 and 211-17 is supplemented by
    that in Hartung, *Manual*, VI, Item 169, p. 2155, which adds a further seven, including
    the mid- to late-fifteenth-century Coventry MS, described in Doyle and Pace 1968, and
    Oxford, St John's College, MS 256, used by de Worde (Bone 1931-32) for the first
    print of the *Siege*, n. d., *c*. 1500 (Hammond 1912, 362).

9. The *Siege*'s affinity with mirrors for princes is seen in its appearance with Hoccleve's *De
    Regimine Principum* in BL Addit. MS 18632 and with Vegetius's *De Re Militari* in Bodl.
    MS Laud misc. 416 (Pearsall 1970, 158-59).

10. 'Perhaps the most overtly political of his longer poems is *The Siege of Thebes*' (Pearsall
    1969, 40). *The Troy Book* also praises peace (II. 1243-70, IV. 960-1134, V. 3399-
    442).

11. This is Lydgate's second imitation of the opening of *The Canterbury Tales*: the first
    occurs in *Troy Book* I. 3907-39; Benson (1980, 99-100) calls this thirty-three-line
    version 'horrendous', 'awkward' and 'intolerable'.

12. Lydgate had already imitated Arcite's funeral from The Knight's Tale (I.2882-2966) in
    Achilles's burial, *Troy Book* IV. 3251-61 (Benson 1980, 112).

13. The first was Laius's, 591-602.

14. Ebin (1977, 77) sees the *Siege* quite differently, as an affirmation of Lydgate's belief in the power of poetry to restore 'concord out of discord, order out of disorder, civilisation out of chaos'. She sees it as a conflict not between individuals but between the word and the sword (1979, 331), yet despite her admission that 'words . . . fail' she claims that Lydgate's *Siege* suggests the power of words to restore 'order and harmony to the world' (1979, 332). The tone and subject-matter of the *Siege* seem to belie this optimistic presentment of Thebes, as Allen and Moritz (1981, 26) note: 'Every civilization faced the temptation to become a Thebes. John Lydgate saw this very clearly, when he inserted his story of Thebes as another, and final, Canterbury Tale'. C. L. McCray also points out that 'both Chaucer and Lydgate expected their audiences to apply the morals of the Troy and Thebes stories to the blunders of their own societies' (unpublished dissertation, University of Nebraska, Item 672 in Peck 1988).

15. As Erdmann shows (ed. 1930, I, vii, echoed by Schirmer 1961, 64 and Scattergood 1971, 100ff.) lines 4690-4703 of the *Siege* echo the words of the Treaty of Troyes, May 1420, the hoped-for peace between France and England. In the French prose redactions Thebes is rebuilt as the medieval city *Estives* (Constans ed. 1890, II, cxxxv), but Lydgate makes the catastrophe complete by omitting this, as does *Le Roman de Thèbes*; Lydgate claims that the women destroyed the walls, as does Boccaccio (*Teseida* 2. 61).

REFERENCES

A complete bibliography up to 1980 for Lydgate's *Siege of Thebes* and critical commentary on it are found in: Alain Renoir and C. David Benson, 'John Lydgate' in *A Manual of the Writings in Middle English 1050-1500, VI*, ed. A. E. Hartung (New Haven, Connecticut, 1980), pp. 2155-58; the *Siege* is described on pp. 1901-04. See also Russell A. Peck, ed., *The Chaucer Bibliography: Chaucer's Romaunt of the Rose and Boece, Treatise on the Astrolabe, Equatorie of the Planets, Lost Works, and Chaucerian Apocrypha: An Annotated Bibliography, 1900-1985* (Toronto 1988). For a select bibliography of Lydgate see below, Ebin 1985, 155-59.

Allen, J. B., and T. A. Moritz, 1981	*A Distinction of Stories*, Ohio
Anderson, David, 1982	Theban History in Chaucer's *Troilus*, *SAC*, 4, pp. 109-133
Ayers, Robert W., 1958	Medieval History, Moral Purpose, and the Structure of Lydgate's *Siege of Thebes*, *PMLA*, 73, pp. 463-74

Benson, C. David, 1980 — *The History of Troy in Middle English Literature*, Woodbridge

Bone, Gavin, 1931-32 — Extant Manuscripts printed from by W. de Worde with notes on the owner, Roger Thorney, *The Library*, 4th Series, 12, pp. 284-306

Bowers, John M., 1985 — *The Tale of Beryn* and *The Siege of Thebes*: Alternative Ideas of *The Canterbury Tales*, SAC, 7, pp. 23-50

Constans, Léopold, ed., 1890 — *Le Roman de Thèbes*, 2 vols, SATF, Paris

Doyle, A. I., and George B. Pace, 1968 — A New Chaucer Manuscript, *PMLA*, 83, pp. 22-34

Ebin, Lois, 1977 — Lydgate's Views on Poetry, *AnM*, 18, pp. 76-105

—— 1979 — Chaucer, Lydgate, and the "Myrie Tale", *ChauR*, 13, pp. 316-36

—— 1985 — *John Lydgate*, Boston

—— 1988 — *Illuminator, Makar, Vates: Visions of Poetry in the Fifteenth Century*, Lincoln and London

Edwards, A. S. G., 1983 — Lydgate Manuscripts: Some Directions for Future Research, in *Manuscripts and Readers*, ed. Pearsall, pp. 15-26

Ganim, John M., 1983 — *Style and Consciousness in Middle English Narrative*, Princeton

Hammond, E. P., 1912 — Lydgate's Prologue to the Story of Thebes, *Anglia*, 36, pp. 360-76

—— ed., 1927 — *English Verse Between Chaucer and Surrey*, Durham, N.C.

Howard, Donald R., 1976 — *The Idea of the Canterbury Tales*, Berkeley and London

Kohl, Stephan, 1979 — *The Kingis Quair* and Lydgate's *Siege of Thebes* as Imitations of Chaucer's *Knight's Tale*, FCS, 2, pp. 119-134

Lawton, Lesley, 1983 — The Illustration of Late Medieval Secular Texts, in *Manuscripts and Readers*, ed. Pearsall, pp. 41-69

Norton-Smith, John, ed., 1966 — *John Lydgate: Poems*, Oxford

Pearsall, Derek, 1969   *Gower and Lydgate*, Writers and Their Work,
                         211, Harlow
———— 1970   *John Lydgate*, London
———— ed., 1983   *Manuscripts and Readers in Fifteenth-Century
                         England: The Literary Implications of Manuscript
                         Study*, Woodbridge
Renoir, Alain, 1956   Chaucerian Character Names in Lydgate's *Siege
                         of Thebes*, *MLN*, 71, pp. 249-56
———— 1960   Thebes, Troy, Criseyde and Pandarus: an
                         instance of Chaucerian irony, *SN*, 32, pp. 14-17
———— 1961   The Immediate Source of Lydgate's *Siege of
                         Thebes*, *SN*, 33, pp. 86-95
———— 1967   *The Poetry of John Lydgate*, London
Scattergood, V. J., 1971 *Politics and Poetry in the Fifteenth Century*,
                         London
Schirmer, Walter F., 1961 *John Lydgate*, trans. Ann E. Keep, London
Spearing, A. C., 1984   Lydgate's Canterbury Tale: *The Siege of Thebes*
                         and Fifteenth-Century Chaucerianism, in
                         Fifteenth-Century Studies: Recent Essays, ed.
                         Robert F. Yeager, Hamden, Conn., pp. 333-64
———— 1985   *Medieval to Renaissance in English Poetry*,
                         Cambridge (similar to preceding; 1984 cited for
                         material common to both or occurring only there,
                         1985 for added matter)

JOURNEY'S END: THE PROLOGUE TO *THE TALE OF BERYN*

Peter Brown

Manuscript 455 (formerly 55) at Alnwick Castle, Northumberland, contains an imperfect version of *The Canterbury Tales*. The order of the tales is eccentric, though perhaps deliberate, and after The Canon's Yeoman's Tale there occurs, on fols 180-235, a unique copy of an apocryphal work generally known as *The Tale of Beryn* (Zupitza 1892, xvi; Bowers 1985, 33-38). It is followed by the end of The Summoner's Tale (III.2159-294).

The entire manuscript is written in the same hand, dated between 1450 and 1470. Dialectal and textual evidence suggest that the scribe or his copytext came from the south-east Midlands. Marks of subsequent ownership locate the manuscript in Devon: it was in the possession of various families at Pilton, Barnstable and Tavistock during the sixteenth century, and by the end of the following century it had travelled to Exeter, where it was owned by a prebendary, Thomas Long. The latter moved to Norwich, and the manuscript was there purchased (evidently then in an unbound state) by the 'Honourable Mrs. Thynn' of Cawston, near Norwich. A member of the Thynn family married a Lord Percy, and the manuscript probably travelled by this route to the Duke of Northumberland's library, where it has been since the early nineteenth century (Urry 1721, k[3]; RCHM 1872, 112b; Spurgeon 1925, I, 325; Manly and Rickert 1940, 387-95; Tamanini 1969, 1-5, 52).

According to some authorities, the first printed version of *Beryn* appeared in John Stow's 1561 edition of Chaucer's works (*IMEV* 1943, item 3926; Bennett 1948, 317), but it is nowhere to be found in that volume, or in other early editions of Chaucer (Thynne ed. 1532). In fact the prologue and tale of *Beryn* did not appear in print until 1721, when they were included in John Urry's posthumous *The Works of Geoffrey Chaucer*. Urry's editor, Timothy Thomas, records that the text of *Beryn* is a transcript made by Urry's amanuensis, a Mr Thomas Ainsworth. Elsewhere he apologizes that, owing to the lack of other copies, *Beryn*'s verse was never 'compleated', as was that of the other contents of the book (Urry 1721, i[3]-k[1], k[4], 7M[2]). *Beryn* therefore escaped the worst excesses of Urry's editorial practices, dedicated to metrical corrections designed 'to restore . . . [Chaucer] to his feet again' (Spurgeon 1925, I, 325) — practices vilified by many subsequent writers (Tyrwhitt 1798, I, x, xiii; Ritson 1802, 20; Chalmers 1810, xiv; Skeat 1900, 143).

Bell reprinted Urry's text of *Beryn* in the sixth volume of his *Poets of Great Britain* (1782, 120-74), as did Anderson for his *Poets of Great Britain* in 1793 (I, 239-73), and Chalmers in 1810 for his *Works of the English Poets* (634-69). Rather more interest was taken by Thomas Wright for his edition of 1851 (191-318). He tried to trace the manuscript used by Urry, but was unsuccessful, and had to content himself with altering 'the more apparent errors', using 'only the corrections that are self-evident'. In the absence of the manuscript it is not entirely clear on what basis Wright made his emendations, but he nevertheless declares cheerfully that 'Urry's faithlessness to his manuscript is quite extraordinary', and 'he not only often misread his original, but he introduced foolish alterations of his own' (Wright 1847, xxiii; 1851, 191 n.). Wright's edition does, however, include some useful annotations.

Beryn has not been happy in its editors. The first edition of *Beryn* as a text independent of *The Canterbury Tales*, one based on a re-examination of the Northumberland manuscript, was that by F. J. Furnivall and W. G. Stone, published for the Chaucer Society in 1876, with ancillary material appearing in 1887. Reissued for the Early English Text Society in 1909, it remains the only generally available complete edition. Unfortunately, the text is marred by extensive editorial intervention, Furnivall having been (in his own words) 'affected for a time with the itch of padding out lines by needless little words in square brackets', on the grounds that 'the MS. is often faulty in metre, and not a correct copy of the original poem' (Furnivall and Stone 1909, xi). Darton published an abbreviated and sanitized translation of *Beryn* in 1904 (pp. 278-365), interpolated with some material from Lydgate's *Siege of Thebes*. In 1930, French and Hale included in their anthology the trial scene from the tale, taken from the Furnivall and Stone edition, lines 2910-3894 (pp. 899-930). Loomis and Willard in 1948 printed lines 1-308 of the prologue in a modernized version (pp. 373-78), at the same time baptizing the Pardoner with the name 'Hugh' (actually a misreading of ME 'huch' = which, at line 176). In 1958 Kaiser included in his revised version of *Medieval English* (pp. 494-96) lines 130-204, 231-50 and 267-99 of the Furnivall and Stone prologue. It was not until 1969 that a full modern edition appeared, based on a rereading of the manuscript (in photographic reproduction) and taking due account of the variants proposed by previous editors. Regrettably, Tamanini's work is relatively inaccessible because it exists only in the form of a doctoral thesis. A modern, readily available, edition of *Beryn* is long overdue, as is a detailed literary analysis of its content. Recently one scholar appeared to believe that after Urry's edition of *Beryn* the manuscript disappeared from view. 'It has not since been located' (Blake 1985, 8).

Since Furnivall and Stone's edition the entire composition has been known as *The Tale of Beryn*. It is a misleading title in that it does not indicate the existence of two connected narratives (in one of which Beryn does not feature), and because it does not follow the usual convention of *The Canterbury Tales* in giving the title to the teller. It is the tale of Beryn insofar as the second half is about Beryn, not by him as narrator. For reasons which will become evident, it is the first part of the composition which is of more interest at present. That is not to say that the story about Beryn, comprising 4024 lines in couplets, does not merit a detailed examination. On the contrary, a lively narrative with considerable emotional appeal, which has been summarized elsewhere, threads through a fascinating range of themes, such as the nurturing of children, the consequences of familial and social misgovernment, gambling and its effects, the different and opposing characteristics of youth and old age, the problems of inheritance after remarriage, the uses and abuses of trade, true and false hospitality, the relative justice of different legal systems, and the deceptiveness of story-telling (Furnivall and Stone 1909, viii-x; French and Hale 1930, 899-900; Winstead 1988, 226-27). Unfortunately, Beryn's tale has suffered neglect because of its association with Chaucer — not merely because the writing is inferior to his, but also because nothing within the tale appears to reflect or shed light on *The Canterbury Tales*. The 731 lines which precede it, however, seem to have been composed out of an infectious enthusiasm for what Chaucer had accomplished, and to provide a commentary on it. They describe the arrival of the pilgrims in Canterbury, their accommodation at a pilgrim inn, their visit to the shrine of St Thomas, and events at the inn on the night before their departure, when the Pardoner's tryst with Kitt the tapster is thwarted (Bowers 1985, 28-33).

The critical reception of *Beryn*, most of which has concentrated on the prologue, falls into two main categories. Some writers, and chiefly those of an earlier period, stress the overpowering influence of Chaucer. More recently, the author has been credited with considerable independence in the exercise of his literary skills. Not unusually, critics maintain an ambivalent attitude, gauging the poet's achievement as at once derivative and innovative. In 1774, Thomas Warton wrote that the prologue to *Beryn* had 'some humour and contrivance' (455). At the turn of the century, Ritson recognized 'a writer of uncommon merit' (1802, 20). Furnivall also responded positively: ' . . . worse than Chaucer's though the hand of the *Beryn*-writer is, a bit, and a good bit, of the Master's humour and life-likeness, the latter verser has in his Prologue. Chaucer's characters are well kept up . . . ' (Furnivall and Stone 1909, vii). In the early part of this century, George Saintsbury condemned the *Beryn* author's handling of metre, but found that he is 'not by any means so un-Chaucerian in matter and temper'. As for the prologue, 'the narrative power is by no means inconsiderable' (Saintsbury 1908, 216).

Double negatives were not for Kittredge, who responded warmly to 'that highly interesting document, the Tale of Beryn', noting that the prologue 'is worth a moment's notice'. He praised the cathedral scene as 'more edifying, and equally vivid' by comparison with events in the hostelry: 'Particularly diverting is the behavior of the Miller and others of his sort'. Kittredge also recognized that, imitator though the *Beryn* author might be, he was also an astute reader of *The Canterbury Tales* who interpreted them remarkably like Kittredge himself (Kittredge 1915, 157-58):

All this is a poor substitute for what Chaucer would have given us, if he had lived to finish his work. But there is some merit in the performance, and it certainly evinces a lively sense of the actuality of Chaucer's Pilgrims. The author of Beryn did not mistake the Canterbury Tales for a volume of disconnected stories. He recognized the work for what it really is — a micro-cosmography, a little image of the great world.

Subsequent writers before mid-century might admire the way in which the *Beryn* writer by and large maintained the consistency of Chaucer's characters (Bashe 1933), but might also be less forthcoming, one finding in 1948 that ' The Prologue has some of Chaucer's realistic vigor but none at all of his sly humor or happy turn of phrase' (Baugh 1948, 292), a remark reiterated in 1967. Tamanini, whose work heralded a reappraisal of the *Beryn* author, nevertheless adopted a familiar position in applauding the way in which he followed *The Canterbury Tales*: 'He hardly achieved a true imitation of Chaucer's work, but . . . he followed more than just the characters and the pilgrimage setting of Chaucer. In the prologue he imitated character and situation with some of the realistic gusto and narrative art of Chaucer' (1969, 39). A year later it was clear that the negative estimate still had a following when one critic wrote that the achievement of Lydgate's *Siege of Thebes* and of *Beryn* 'rests so heavily on a knowledge of the original that they could never stand alone' (Robbins 1970, 234). As late as 1985 another critic was content to maintain the position of a Saintsbury in stating that, although the *Beryn* poet lacks 'his master's gifts as a versifier, he had a fine ear for colloquial dialogue, as well as real talents for inventing and staging comic action.' The writer goes on to praise ingenuity in the narrative structure, an eventfulness superior to that of the General Prologue, and dramatic vitality (Bowers 1985, 27-28, 50).

Thus the received critical image of the *Beryn* author is that of a slavish imitator who enjoyed occasional bursts of confidence. Generally speaking, commentators have been mesmerized by the prologue's associations with *The Canterbury Tales* and unable or unwilling to evaluate it on its own terms. During the past decade, however, *Beryn* has been subjected to some thoughtful rereadings informed by modern critical theory, by an interest in genre, and by an appreciation of Chaucerian aesthetics. As a result, the *Beryn* author has grown in stature to emerge as a writer interesting both in his own right and as a perceptive early reader of *The Canterbury Tales*. In 1983, Kohl read the prologue to *Beryn* (and that to Lydgate's *Siege of Thebes*) as a 'metafiction' which comments on Chaucer's General Prologue to the end of 'pouring ridicule on his moral view of the world'. Kohl's argument might carry more force if he had paid closer attention to the text. He says without irony that 'the Pardoner makes his arrangements in a kind of brothel' (actually a pilgrim inn), that the Wife of Bath and Prioress 'while the afternoon away sitting in the back garden of their inn' (actually the parlour), and he bases a part of his argument on a line composed by Furnivall (line 683) as one of that editor's 'improvements' to the text (Kohl 1983, 226, 229, 234). Two years later, in an article again spoilt by erroneous or misleading references to the narrative of the *Beryn* prologue, Darjes and

Rendall focused on the author's manipulation of the fabliau which occupies the major part of the story. They found that his use of detail is even more sparing than that of traditional fabliau authors, that he does not take advantage of the opportunity to include sexual 'spice', but that in representing everyday speech and character he is considerably more successful (1985, 418-19). In the most sophisticated critical study of prologue and tale yet to appear, Winstead argues that the *Beryn* author's work is finely tuned to Chaucer's modulations of style and technique (1988, 231-32):

> It conveys an understanding of Chaucer's irony, his playful manipulation of generic conventions, his methods of linking components in a work through parallelism and variation, and his juxtaposition of styles, tones, genres and subject matter in order to create meaning. Although none of these devices is unique to Chaucer, Chaucer developed and polished these techniques, and they are today considered hallmarks of his style. Evidently the *Beryn*-writer, already in the fifteenth century, perceived these same features as distinctly Chaucerian.

A fully informed critical debate on the merits of the prologue to *Beryn* cannot avoid the issue of its relationship with *The Canterbury Tales*. Too often, though, that relationship has been seen as derivative when a more constructive approach might have placed the prologue in much the same comparative position as one of Chaucer's tales is often placed in relation to its source material. By this means the distinctive and positive qualities of the poem under discussion become clear. Certainly the critical debate on the *Beryn* author has recently been furthered, and become more interesting, thanks to the efforts of the writers just named. What now follows is an attempt again to enlarge that discussion, but by returning in the first place to questions of authorship, date of composition, and audience. A consideration of such factors affects our understanding of the function of the prologue and that in turn has implications for its critical interpretation.

Although Urry may have believed that *Beryn* was a lost work by Chaucer (Spurgeon 1925, I, 325), Thomas, Urry's editor, was not persuaded of its authenticity (Urry 1721, k[3]):

> It may (perhaps with some shew of reason) be suspected that Chaucer was not the Author of them, but a later Writer, who may have taken the hint from what is suggested in V. 796 of the Prologues, that the Pilgrims were to tell Tales in their Return homewards; but as to that the Reader must be left to his own Judgement.

In Urry's edition, the idea that *Beryn* is of different, or at least doubtful, authorship is sustained by keeping prologue and tale quite separate from *The Canterbury Tales*, towards the end of the volume and in a sequence of miscellaneous works most of which are not by Chaucer.

Warton tested the stylistic evidence for himself and concluded: 'I cannot allow that this Prologue and Tale were written by Chaucer. Yet I believe them to be nearly coeval' (Warton 1774, 456). When *Beryn* and other apocryphal works were subsequently republished, as by Anderson, they appeared with a disclaimer: 'all evidence, internal and external, is against the supposition of their being the production of Chaucer' (Anderson 1793, I, vi). Skeat dealt the death blow, at once appearing to resent Urry's discovery of *Beryn* and acknowledge its usefulness (Skeat 1900, 143):

> . . . it is necessary to say that he added two new pieces to the pile; both of them undoubtedly spurious, though the first is of some importance, and both have a certain interest of their own.

It was hardly necessary of Saintsbury to reiterate: 'Chaucer's own it cannot possibly be' (1908, 216).

The key to the authorship of *Beryn* lies in the colophon (fol. 235):

> Nomen Autoris presentis Cronica Rome
> Et translatoris Filius ecclesie Thome.

> (The name of the author presenting the chronicle of Rome,
> and the translator, is 'son of the church of Thomas'.)

According to one scholar, 'author' and 'translator' are both applicable to the person who fashioned *Beryn* as a chronicle of Rome (where Beryn was born), for he brought to the French tale of Bérinus precision in rendering it into English and a flair for extensive modification (McIntosh 1931, 45-117). But what does 'son of the church of Thomas' mean? For Furnivall it meant 'a Canterbury man — monk, I suppose', and he glossed the colophon: 'A Canterbury monk wrote this Tale' (Furnivall and Stone 1909, vii, 120). McIntosh was more circumspect: ' The identity of the author is as yet unknown. The colophon of the manuscript suggests a man in holy orders . . . but there is no proof that he was a monk of Canterbury, although his familiarity with that city is clearly shown in the prologue' (1931, 1). Manly and Rickert, however, were relatively confident: ' The most natural interpretation of "Filius ecclesie Thome" makes him a monk of Canterbury, and this is confirmed . . . by his intimate knowledge of the town and the doings of the pilgrims' (1940, 392).

If 'son of the church' is indeed fairly clear evidence that the author was in holy orders, there is certainly a difficulty in presuming too hastily that he was a monk of Canterbury. If he had been, then he might have indicated a more obvious connection with one or the other of the two great monastic institutions which the city sustained: Christ Church and St Augustine's abbey. There is, however, another possibility which may be entertained. It is that 'church of

Thomas' refers specifically to the place where the shrine of St Thomas Becket, and associated cults, were accommodated within the cathedral. For the location of the shrine, Trinity Chapel, was 'called almost universally . . . "St. Thomas' Chapel" ' (Knapp 1972, 3). The author of *Beryn* might then be one of the monks charged with custodial duties associated with the shrine and its devotions, such as the articulate John Vyel (fl. 1399-1444) or Edmund Kyngyston (fl. 1401-1428), who were serving as guardians of the shrine in 1428 (Turner 1976).

Internal evidence tends to support the hypothesis that the author was a monk with detailed knowledge of pilgrim practices. Attitudes towards representatives of the church within the prologue suggest his own status. Although the main functions are to indicate the courtesy of the Knight, and to reflect actual practice, the 'prelatis' (presumably the Monk, Friar and Prioress) are twice treated with due deference. At the church door they, together with the Parson and his companions, are allowed to enter first (137),[1] and they are again given special attention before the evening meal (386-88). More revealing, however, is the indulgent representation of monks with minor roles within the prologue, and of the pilgrim Monk himself. The monk who has the task of sprinkling pilgrim visitors with holy water does so (with the author glancing at the General Prologue, line 167) 'with a manly chere' (138). The individual who, at the shrine, names and talks about the holy relics, offering them to be kissed, is a 'goodly monke' (167). Most interesting of all, an episode is devised for the pilgrim Monk which enables references both to a literate member of the Canterbury monastery (such as the author may have been), and to the legendary hospitality to be found there. He invites the Parson and Friar to join him in visiting an acquaintance, 'my brothir in habit and in possessioune' (271) who has been pressing him by letter for three years to make a visit. They are received with memorable generosity:

> For of the best that myght be found, and therwith mery chere
> They had, it is no doubt, for spycys and eke wyne
> Went rounde aboute, the gascoyn and eke the ruyne. (278-80)

On this occasion there is no hint of animosity between Monk and Friar, but elsewhere friars receive short shrift. There is an element of conventional satire, but nevertheless the author is not likely to have belonged to one of their orders (Bashe 1933, 5-6). One incident uses Chaucer's idea of the Friar as a ladies' man sharply to disparage this pilgrim and to illustrate why friars have lost esteem and respect. At the entrance to the church he attempts winsomely ('fetously'), but without success, to gain control of the holy water sprinkler. His motive is not a pious one, it is in order to see the Nun's face. His spirituality, like hers (GP 142, 150) has become misdirected: 'So longid his holy conscience to se the Nonny's fase' (140-44). Other opportunities are taken to associate friars with vicious living. For example, Kitt provokes the sexual affections of the Pardoner 'As thoughe she had lernyd cury fauel of som old frer' (362).

The detail with which he describes pilgrim practices and behaviour supports the idea that the *Beryn* author was a member of the Christ Church community with particular responsibilities at the shrine of Becket. He is familiar, in the first place, with customary matters: the Knight allows the prelates to enter the church door first because he 'knewe righte wele the guyse' (136); the monk with his sprinkler 'did as the manere is' (139); and after the shrine has been visited the pilgrims purchase badges 'as manere and custom is' (171). The stress here and elsewhere on income generated by the shrine is consonant with the responsibilities of the temporal guardian in keeping account of the offerings, undertaking audits, paying the assistant clerks, and making payments of other kinds (Turner 1976, 17). Other procedures followed by the *Beryn* pilgrims are equally authentic. The offerings to be made at the shrine are 'sylvir broch and ryngis' (134), kinds of gift often connected with that place (Robertson 1880, 510-11; Woodruff 1932, 29); the pilgrims kneel at the shrine, tell their beads, praying to St Thomas, and kiss the relics as they are displayed and named by an attendant monk; they then visit 'other placis of holynes' within the church (163-70), presumably other sites associated with Becket, like the Martyrdom, at which the guardians of the shrine and their clerks also performed duties; and buy pilgrim badges (Brent 1880; Robertson 1880, 516-22; Stanley 1912, 217; Foreville 1958, 12-13; Knapp 1972, 3-5; Turner 1976, 19; Fleming 1985, 155-56; Mitchiner 1986, 64-144). Nor does the author ignore the effect of the cathedral on those seeing it for the first time. The stained glass, in particular, still one of the glories of the building, distracts the Pardoner and Miller and others until they are 'half amasid' (158) and have to be ushered forward by the Host, still 'goglyng with hire hedis' (163) (Bashe 1933, 8; Caviness 1977; 1981). That the glass should receive special attention is a further indication of the author's preoccupations: income at the shrine was used for the upkeep of the windows in the shrine precincts (Turner 1976, 21).

Manly and Rickert dated MS Alnwick 455, on palaeographic grounds, to between 1450 and 1470 (1940, 388). Doyle agrees in general, but accepts the possibility of an earlier date: 'it is probably of the third quarter of the 15th century, certainly not earlier than the second' (Tamanini 1969, 1 n. 2). Given that *Beryn* is copied from an unknown exemplar, perhaps from the author's own copy of the work, the date of composition can be set some years earlier than the date of the surviving manuscript. Thus the palaeographic data indicate that the poem must have been composed at the latest by the mid 1460s, and at the earliest by about 1420.

Bennett, on unspecified grounds, dated the composition of *Beryn* to 'after 1400' (1948, 317). It is certainly clear that the author of *Beryn* had access to a reasonably complete version of *The Canterbury Tales*. He was familiar with The General Prologue and the fabliau tales of Fragment I, with The Friar's Tale and Summoner's Tale. He also knew The Canon's Yeoman's Prologue, Pardoner's Tale and Merchant's Tale. Now the earliest surviving collection of *The Canterbury Tales*, that represented by the Hengwrt manuscript (which itself omits The Canon's Yeoman Prologue and Tale), dates from the first years after 1400 (Doyle and Parkes 1979, xx-xxi), so it is reasonable to assume on this evidence that *Beryn* is unlikely to have been composed before about 1410. Pearsall dates *Beryn* to the beginning of the fifteenth century, while Tamanini, after a careful consideration of the evidence, similarly opts for 'early in the fifteenth century' (Pearsall 1977, 298; Tamanini 1969, 76).

As with the question of authorship, some internal evidence needs to be weighed. The Canterbury inn at which the pilgrims stay, the 'Cheker of the hope' (14), was built by Prior Chillenden, specifically for the pilgrim trade, between 1392 and 1395 (Stanley 1912, 213-14; Woodruff 1911, 65, 69). (Its title refers to the inn sign, presumably a square checkerboard enclosed within a hoop of wood or metal.) It remained the most prominent purpose-built accommodation for pilgrims until 1437-38, when The Sun was erected by Christ Church priory, even closer to the cathedral, adjacent to one of the main gates of approach (Tatton-Brown 1987). If the *Beryn* author had been writing after 1438 it is likely that he would have sited the action of the prologue at The Sun by virtue of its closeness to the cathedral and its novelty as a building. That he chose the Cheker of the hope indicates that it was at the time of writing the most suitable setting. The eastern section of the building still stands in Canterbury, at the west corner of Mercery Lane and the High Street. The stone arcades of the ground floor are now occupied by shops.

Again, when the Knight and his companions find time on their hands they go to inspect the defences of the city: the wall and the 'wardes' or defensible gates of Canterbury. The Knight proceeds to deliver an authoritative talk to his son (237-44). There is a degree of topicality in the episode, since the city's defences were extensively rebuilt (under the supervision of Henry Yevele) in the later fourteenth and early fifteenth centuries, in response to the threat of French invasion. Work was under way by 1378 and had been completed by 1409 (Harvey 1944, 61; Turner 1971, 148-54; Frere *et al.* 1982, 21-24; Harvey 1985, 8). It is particularly interesting that the Knight should mention attack by gun — 'the perell and the doubt / For shot of arblast' (241) — and the appropriate form of defence, since provision was made at West Gate, reconstructed by about 1380 at the expense of archbishop Simon Sudbury, for the firing of guns, the gunports for which are still visible (Frere *et al.* 1982, 107-19). Its novelty as a fortification, and indeed the novelty of using guns in siege warfare in the late fourteenth and early fifteenth centuries, provide a plausible context for the Knight's activities and remarks. West Gate is 'the earliest known fortress in this country designed specifically for defence with guns' (Dufty 1962, 369).

The evidence so far presented tends to suggest that the prologue to *Beryn* was composed at the earlier end of the possible period between 1420 and 1460. But what could have prompted a monk of Christ Church, of all people, to compose a bawdy farce about one of Chaucer's pilgrims two decades after Chaucer's death? That it was not unknown for Benedictine monks to compose continuations of *The Canterbury Tales* in the early fifteenth century is clear from the case of John Lydgate, who was familiar with a similar range of Canterbury tales, and whose prologue to *The Siege of Thebes*, as Rosamund Allen recounts elsewhere in this volume, describes the author, in the course of a pilgrimage to Canterbury after a recovery from illness, meeting Chaucer's company at the city inn where they had chosen to stay (Spearing 1984, 337). The following morning the entire company sets off on the return journey, intending to dine at Ospringe. Before they are a bow shot from Canterbury the Host asks the new arrival to tell a tale, and he obliges, passing on the way the village of Boughton (lines 1-176, 1047-60).

Lydgate's composition is generally dated to 1420 or soon after (Parr 1952, 253-56), and in the same year one finds another monk, this time of Christ Church itself, composing a poem in Latin extolling the virtues of a pilgrimage to the shrine of St Thomas. Copies were affixed, much like modern advertisements, at various prominent positions within Canterbury cathedral, and also on the door of St Paul's cathedral in London (Foreville 1958, 134-35). The reason for this literary activity by a Canterbury monk, and perhaps the occasion for Lydgate's prologue, was that 1420 was one of the years of jubilee. Jubilees occurred every fifty years to mark the anniversary of the martyrdom of St Thomas. For this, the fifth jubilee year, more than a normal effort was necessary on the part of the prior and convent. The prior's accounts show a steady decline in takings at the shrine and at other locations during the preceding years. In 1396 the total was £503. 0s. 10d, but by 1410 it had fallen to £265. 18s. 4d (Woodruff 1932, 22). The jubilee year a decade later was promoted and prepared for with unusual care. Financial considerations were one factor. The jubilee also provided an occasion to assert orthodoxy and demonstrate the effectiveness of indulgences against the invective of the Lollards, who had singled out devotion to St Thomas as an example of the false piety of pilgrimage and of idolatry sustained by shrines, images and relics (Davis 1963; Hudson ed. 1978, 153-54; Fleming 1985, 152-54).

Efforts were made well in advance of 1420 to secure from Pope Martin V a plenary indulgence, traditionally all but synonymous with the word 'jubilee' (Foreville, 1958, 21-28, 34). Martin, whose policy was hostile to the incipient autonomy of the English church, withheld his approval. When it was not forthcoming, four doctors in theology examined at Canterbury the indulgence granted by Honorius VI for the first jubilee in 1220, and declared that it was still effective (Foreville 1958, 37-45, 61-66, 115-18; Jacob 1967, 43-46). Such independence of action was accompanied by a propaganda campaign designed to demonstrate the legitimacy of the plenary indulgence to be enjoyed by those attending the celebrations. In addition to the composition of a Latin poem, notices were drafted and affixed to prominent places at St Paul's in London, Christ Church, and Ospringe and, at the turn of the year, a monk — probably Richard Godmersham — composed in the form of a letter a treatise on the fifth jubilee, in effect a chronicle-cum-apologia and anti-Lollard polemic (Foreville 1958, 52-56, 101-13, 129).

In the event the jubilee, which took place in early July, was a great success. Occurring in an atmosphere of international peace and reconciliation (it was the year of the Treaty of Troyes), the fifth jubilee has been called the apogee of Canterbury pilgrimage (Foreville 1958, 17). Such was the crowd of people who packed into the cathedral for Mass on 7 July that the preacher, the Augustinian Thomas Tynwith, had to repeat his homily three times. Significantly, the chosen text, *Annus jubileus est* (Leviticus 25. 10), allowed for a further iteration of how the jubilee enabled remission of the punishment and guilt occasioned by sin. The city bailiffs claimed that 100,000 people came to the city, and were satisfactorily fed and housed, thanks to the co-operation of the local citizens (Foreville 1958, 18, 142-43, 180-81). The jubilee celebrations lasted for fifteen days and, as far as the prior was concerned they were financially satisfactory: his accounts for 1420 show a steep climb in offerings at the shrine and elsewhere, to £644 (Woodruff 1932, 22).

It is not unreasonable to assume that the prologue of *Beryn* was composed as part of the process of promoting the jubilee of 1420, written by a monk of Christ Church, who was probably a guardian of the shrine, to encourage visitors and gifts. Suitably published by being read aloud to appropriate audiences, it would have been capable not only of entertaining, but of creating the pleasing impression among listeners that by visiting Canterbury they would become nothing less than Chaucer's pilgrims incarnate, enacting his fiction, enjoying the jokes and bonhomie, and playing out the appropriate roles. In the course of so doing they would bring *The Canterbury Tales* to fruition by arriving in the city and visiting the shrine where, in the normal course of events, they would make offerings, such as the rings and brooches described by the *Beryn* author, and buy pilgrim badges: 'Ech man set his sylvir in such thing as they likid' (173).

The way in which the prologue is structured provides some sense of the circumstances of its 'publication'. The author adopts a Chaucerian persona, which he uses, as in the opening lines, to establish his values, set the tone of the narrative, thicken the meaning of the story with some sententious statement, or emphasize a particular theme. Subsequently appearing at regular intervals, his interjections of a dozen lines or so would also have indicated to an audience the stage which the narrative had reached and what was to be expected in the way of content. As structural members of the composition they divide the action into segments roughly equivalent to the span of a listener's attention and provide both a breathing space and an opportunity to re-engage interest. Such functions are especially clear in the remarks which conclude the Pardoner's first visit to Kitt, in which the audience is thrice told what it is about to *hear* (119-29).

The nature of the intended audience is indicated by the content of the prologue. It is written on the assumption that its auditors are intelligent, literate, and in particular that they are familiar with *The Canterbury Tales*. The author has studded his composition with references to Chaucer's poetry which operate at various levels of subtlety but which do not work at all if the recipients are ignorant of what Chaucer wrote. The appeal of the prologue is in this respect to a group of initiates, of educated people 'in the know', who carry an awareness of or an affection for *The Canterbury Tales* as part of their cultural outlook. That the author of *Beryn* has chosen a fabliau as the genre on which to base his prologue is a further indication that it is targeted at a bourgeois or would-be aristocratic audience, and one which would not have omitted the likes of the Merchant, who is treated with a certain amount of preference: it has been argued that fabliaux were customarily intended for a mixed audience on the cusp between bourgeois and seigneurial affiliations (Muscatine 1986, 46).

The repeated emphasis on 'curtesy' and 'gentilnes' in a variety of favourable contexts, however much these may be Chaucerian themes, indicates more sharply the outlook of those for whom the prologue was originally intended (Brewer 1968, 298-300). An appeal to such values would have been particularly effective and appropriate, given the extent to which the pilgrimage to Canterbury continued to enjoy royal attention and patronage throughout this period (Stanley 1912, 229-30; Wylie and Waugh 1929, III, 10, 18-19, 21; Foreville 1958, 15-16; Seward 1987, 84-85, 89; Ormrod 1989, 858). The prologue is appealing to and reinforcing the values and ideals of behaviour of those who, if not born to courtly ways, regard themselves as at least capable of adopting and emulating them with reasonable accuracy. There are two approaches to 'curtesy' and 'gentil' behaviour within the prologue. They are taken for granted as desirable qualities, assumed standards which operate among people of certain aspirations; and they are represented as unattainable by others, who become the target of comedy.

Thus, Kitt acts with mock deference to the Pardoner, flattering him by presuming that he is 'gentil' (as in the General Prologue line 669) and 'nobill' (56-57). Later, she lavishes praise on his generosity in paying a groat — an excessive amount — for the hot pie that she has brought him. Again he is a 'gentill sire' and, in order not to offend his 'curtesy' rather than accept the proper payment she puts the entire amount in her purse (88-93). However, when the Pardoner, that evening, stalks into Kitt's bedroom, she reproaches him: 'Yee shuld have coughid when ye com — wher lern ye curtesy?' (323). Here, appeals to 'curtesy' and 'gentilnes' are being used by Kitt as crude instruments of control, as a means of exploiting the Pardoner's vanity so that he becomes vulnerable to her manipulations. The values of behaviour are themselves not denigrated: the satire focuses on the Pardoner, who would imagine that what Kitt implies about his ideals is true. Similarly it is the people, not the ideal, who are the target when the Pardoner and Miller fancy that they can interpret heraldic images in the stained glass of the cathedral, 'Countirfeting gentilmen the armys for to blase' (150).

Meanwhile, other members of the company subscribe to the qualities of 'curtesy' and 'gentilnes' in the knowledge that it is appropriate for them to do so, and as a modus vivendi whereby social relations can be conducted with a minimum of difficulty. The Knight, motivated by 'gentilnes' in the manner of his prototype, acts authoritatively in insisting that 'the prelatis' enter the church before 'the curtesy' (135-37). Subsequently, a word from the Knight is sufficient to smooth over the beginnings of an argument between Friar and Host, one in which the 'curtesy' and 'gentilnes' of each begins to be brought into question: the Friar grants that the Host was courteous in agreeing to feed the company in return for stories, but wonders if he has in practice honoured his commitment, and appeals to the Knight as a witness. For his part, the Host says that the Friar's 'gentilnes' in remembering the agreement ought to be enough (suggesting thereby that it is deficient) and that there is therefore no need to call witnesses. The Knight, as arbiter, sides with the Host and the matter is closed (214-26).

The practice of 'curtesy' and 'gentilnes' by others is widespread and goes beyond similar behaviour in *The Canterbury Tales*. The Monk asks the Parson and Friar 'for curteysy' to join him for his visit to a fellow monk (268); the Prioress assents to the Wife of Bath's invitation to drink wine in the garden of the inn 'as vomman taught of gentil blood and hend' (287); the pilgrims of higher social status, given priority treatment on arrival at the inn (19) and better food 'as curtesy axith', return the compliment by paying for everyone to drink wine — 'Wherfor they did hir gentilness ageyn to al the rout' (403-05); and the Host and Merchant, 'wexen somwhat wroth' at the noise caused by the revellers as they try to compute the accounts, 'preyd him curteysly to rest for to wend' (420-21). For the Host in particular there is a practical use for 'curtesy' in that he may appeal to it for help in running the day-to-day arrangements of the pilgrimage.

The range of social groups among the author's listeners is suggested by some of the interjections by means of which a working relationship with the audience is sustained and developed. He declares that those who value their reputation ('worship') and well-being should avoid the likes of Kitt, her lover and the hosteller: 'no man that lovith his worshipp and hele' (466) should have dealings with them. When it comes to the names which the Pardoner calls Kitt once he has discovered her duplicity the writer stops short for fear of causing offence: such names would not occur to those who (like his audience) are respectable people — either merchants ('men of good'), or men of good reputation ('worship') or high social standing: 'Huch to rech hir wer noon honeste / Among men of good, of worship and degre' (517-18). (This tactic is, of course, only a stimulus for the imaginations of such worthy people to be set racing.)

Women, as forming a distinct group, also feature in the author's understanding of the kind of audience that he is addressing. Once again, a direct reference to the recipients of the narrative is linked with a nice sense of their feelings and general outlook. Commenting on Kitt's success in duping the Pardoner, he uses it as evidence of the success of women in general at deceiving men. But at this he begins to retrace his ground, so leaving the nature of women a matter for debate in case he should offend 'ladies . . . / Or els gentil vomen', who legitimately employ 'daliaunce . . . sportis and . . . goodly chere'. Members of such 'estatis' are not his target but others, lower down the social scale, like Kitt. This is an engaging and adroit passage, designed to tease the audience. It introduces a controversial topic, only to leave it as it were in his listeners' laps while the author decorously disengages himself from any suggestion that he would want to utter words of criticism against any women who might be present (436-46).

If there is some justice in the preceding remarks about the authorship, date and audience of the prologue to *Beryn*, it follows that there are certain consequences for its interpretation as a work of literature. For its main purpose ceases to be that of imitation. Instead, its function becomes that of an occasional piece for which the existence of *The Canterbury Tales*, as a recently composed and well known collection of narratives, was a convenient, but by no means necessary, stimulus. The author's representation of the Pardoner, for example, owes as much to the preoccupations of a Canterbury monk in 1420 as it does to its Chaucerian model.

Superficially, the *Beryn* Pardoner is recognizably the same figure as the one created by Chaucer. The anger which he manifests in response to the Host's attack (PardT VI.956-57) surfaces again on his being rebuffed by Kitt. On that occasion there is also an example of his vindictiveness, such as he sometimes manifests in the pulpit (PardPro VI.421-22), when he calls his would-be mistress 'namys many mo then oon, / Huch to rech hir wer noon honeste' (516-17). The Pardoner's legendary avarice is kept in play in his plan to steal back the money he gives to Kitt (373-76). And his abuse of the authority vested in him as a representative of the church is instanced in his interpretation of Kitt's supposed dream to his own advantage (106-115).

At the same time, the *Beryn* author subjects the Pardoner to a much lengthier and more detailed treatment than any other of Chaucer's characters. He singles out the Pardoner for humiliation, especially by dwelling on his hypocrisy, blasphemy and lechery. That process is best demonstrated by means of an example, one which simultaneously reveals the subtlety of the writer's techniques: the Pardoner's first encounter with Kitt. From the outset, the Pardoner is — unusually for him — unwittingly on the receiving end of a deception (what he would call a 'jape'), while all the time believing that Kitt is his prey and that he is in control of the situation. After the Pardoner has absented himself from the rest of the company, Kitt greets him affectionately, with a 'Welcom, myne owne brother' and 'frendly look, al redy for to kys' (22-23). The Pardoner responds in kind, and is here described with a wry cadence worthy of Chaucer: he is 'ilernyd of such kyndnes' (24), embraces her about the waist and 'made hir gladly chere' as though he had known her for a year (25-26). The Pardoner has fallen for the bait and is now led into a trap. Kitt calls the Pardoner into that part of her tapstry where, affecting an erotically inviting pathos, she says that she lies 'my selff al nyght al nakid / Without mannys company syn my love was ded' (28-29). There follows a virtuoso display of histrionics to demonstrate the depth of her feeling for the 'dead' Jenkyn Harpour (32-39). The Pardoner comes in on cue, proceeding to exploit Kitt's grieving by again laying an affectionate hand around her waist, so offering the sympathy and consolation which might be expected by virtue of his profession, but which he now deploys for his own ulterior motives.

Kitt sneezes, and the Pardoner suggests that this is an indication that her grieving or 'penaunce' (43) is coming to an end. Kitt appears to be keen to accept the Pardoner's suggestions, sprinkling her own response with pious-sounding remarks: 'God forbede it els!' (44). False piety has here become a language for expressing erotic attachment, itself false in the case of Kitt and doomed to failure in the case of the Pardoner. Under its cover, the Pardoner gradually transfers attention from Kitt's 'grief' to his own desire. Blessing the God 'of mendement of hele, and eke of cure' he chucks her erotically under the chin and exclaims 'Allas! that love ys syn!' (46-48), words serving at once to confuse divine and sexual love, and to associate the Pardoner with the libidinous attitudes of the Wife of Bath. If there is a Wife of Bath in this episode it is not the Pardoner but Kitt who, like Dame Alys, has mastered one who would master her. The Pardoner continues: 'For be my trewe conscience yit for yewe I smert, / And shal this month hereaftir, for yeur soden disese' (50-51) — an ambiguous statement, describing at once the Pardoner's professed sympathy for Kitt's bereavement while also conveying quite other emotions. He proceeds to flatter Kitt, putting himself forward as a candidate for her new lover, by taking her grieving as evidence that she is 'trewe' in love, and that therefore the man who might win her love would be fortunate indeed (52-54). Thus the 'death' of Jenkyn Harpour, and her 'soden disese', which is 'green in yeur mynde' (54) become the cause of the Pardoner's own sorrow, ostensibly through legitimate compassion but implicitly because of his unfulfilled desire for her. By the time that the Pardoner concludes 'Ye made me a sory man — I dred ye wold have stervid' (55) the emphasis is predominantly sexual. Thus the lechery of the Pardoner, under cover of priestly authority, is laid bare.

The courting of Kitt is an episode which also demonstrates the extent to which the *Beryn* author's Pardoner is a fundamentally different creature from Chaucer's Pardoner, whose most immediate sexual attachment is to a member of his own sex (Darjes and Rendall 1985, 427-30). Elsewhere, too, the *Beryn* author shifts emphasis: he is at pains to stress the isolation of the Pardoner from the rest of the company, and his unattractiveness, in a way that Chaucer never did (Tupper 1914, 563-65). He is shown as self-seeking, unsharing, separate from the companionship of others, anti-social, gloating inwardly, scheming to himself to another's disadvantage, secretive — and all this to no avail. Thus the first description of him, at the Cheker of the hope, shows him realizing (perhaps resentfully) that the 'statis' are being ordered food first, and that the Host is too busy to pay any attention to him. This he discerns 'al pryvely and asyde swervid' (19-20) to try his luck with the tapster. His devious characteristics are again represented when he remains at the inn while the other pilgrims pursue diversions elsewhere. Then he 'pryvelich when al they were goon / Stalkid into the tapstry' (298-99) and 'stappid into the tapstry wonder pryvely' (309). Having made arrangements with Kitt he keeps his success slyly to himself while others near him are, as they eat, full of 'sportis and of cher'

(390): 'But the Pardonere kept hym close and told nothing of / The myrth and hope that he had, but kept it for himselff' (394-95). Retentive and furtive, a creature of darkness, the Pardoner waits until the merriment has subsided. Each pilgrim goes to rest, 'Save the Pardonere, that drewe apart and wayted hym at rest / For to hyde hymselff till the candill wer out' (424-25).

Such behaviour may lie in the logic of Chaucer's portrait, and be not inconsistent with it, but if so his shaming by the Host has had a devastating effect. He is now a man diminished in confidence, in rhetorical skill, in the success with which he dupes others. He has become a notable failure, rather than the admirable blackguard of the General Prologue (GP 707-14), someone who is pathetic, ineffectual, reduced to a dog-like existence. At Kitt's door he tries to attract her attention, 'And scrapid the dorr welplich and wynyd with his mowith, / Aftir a doggis lyden as ner as he couth' (481-82), at which Kitt's lover shouts 'Away, dogg, with evil deth!' (483). Undeterred, but livid with anger, ' The Pardonere scrapid efft agayne' (507), only to be beaten like a dog when Kitt's lover opens her door. It is altogether fitting, then, that someone behaving 'spitouslich' (520) should spend the night in the litter of a 'spetouse' dog (635-48).

Why should the Pardoner be systematically pilloried and vilified by the *Beryn* author? Certainly the process was initiated by Harry Bailly, but it is continued with inordinate relish and gusto. Chaucer's Host, having been addressed as a man 'envoluped in synne' is invited to 'kisse the relikes everychon, / Ye, for a grote! Unbokele anon thy purs' (PardT VI.942-45). The Pardoner himself receives short shrift, and it is particularly on account of the signs of his false authenticity, his bogus relics — actually animal bones and rags — that the Host launches a virulent attack (Besserman and Storm 1983, 405-06). In rejecting the Pardoner's proposal the Host claims that the Pardoner would make his soiled 'olde breech' into a relic if he could, perhaps implicitly making a contrast with a true relic, the breeches of St Thomas, kept at Canterbury (Knapp 1972, 5-14; Storm 1982b, 815); and, swearing by another true relic, 'the croys which that Seint Eleyne fond', he threatens to cut off the Pardoner's testicles so that ' They shul be shryned in an hogges toord!' (PardT VI.948-55).

In such graphic distinctions between true and false relics, and true and false shrines, lies the clue to the reason for the *Beryn* writer's subsequent attack. For it is the Pardoner's role, both historically and as established in *The Canterbury Tales*, to offer for cash payment access to an indulgence (Jusserand 1925, 312-37; Williams 1965). But this is exactly what a pilgrimage to Canterbury did (if in a less obvious way), the relics of St Thomas providing the conduit through which God's grace was effective — 'pilgrimage' and 'indulgence' being, by this time, virtually interchangeable terms (Zacher 1976, 45-46; Storm 1982a, 440-42). The Pardoner and his kind represented, to those responsible for propagating and sustaining the cult of St Thomas, serious competition (Woodruff 1932, 26-29). That a figure such as the Pardoner would have seemed a *bête noire* from a Canterbury viewpoint is clear from Archbishop Chichele's preoccupation with regulating indulgences by restricting their use and the activities of their purveyors.[2] The subject featured in the English Concordat with the papacy in 1418, the first clause of which criticizes those who diverted money from the parochial clergy 'by reasons of divers indulgences and letters of faculties granted by the apostolic see'. Again, in 1424-25, Chichele's constitution concerned unlicensed pardoners and the collection of money for indulgences (Jacob ed. 1945, 88-98; ed. 1947, 194-96; 1967, 36-37, 41). Hence the Pardoner is a legitimate target for a monastic author charged with the care of an important shrine. The Pardoner as a travelling shrine, a purveyor of false relics and cash absolutions, is a threat to those who might consider themselves to be the guardians of true relics and the means of obtaining legitimate forgiveness for sin, however much the use of similar money-raising agents was at other times condoned by the Canterbury chapter (Jacob ed. 1947, 260-62; Kellogg and Haselmayer 1951, 265; Fleming 1985, 160-64). Even the gifts which Chaucer's Pardoner solicits — 'silver broches, spoones, rynges' (PardT VI.908) — bear a striking resemblance to those which the *Beryn* author anticipates for the shrine of St Thomas.

   Another kind of reform which the archbishop and chapter promoted was directed at heretics. In a series of trials after the Lollard uprising of 1414 they heard evidence, recorded recantations, and inflicted punishments (Jacob 1967, 69-72). To a member of the Christ Church convent sensitized by Lollard trials to the heretics' satire on indulgences and their purveyors, on relics, images, and pilgrimage (particularly to Canterbury), the activities of Chaucer's Pardoner could have read as a similar travesty of the activities in which he and his convent were engaged, especially at the time of jubilee (Knapp 1972, 18-21; Jones 1973; Storm 1982b, 810-13; Owen 1983, 254; Besserman and Storm 1983, 405-06). The *Beryn* prologue, insofar as it denigrates the Pardoner and promotes pilgrimage to St Thomas's relics, might have served as a salvo in the pamphleteering war, consistent with the active suppression of Lollard heresy in which the author and his archbishop and convent were then engaged (Jacob ed. 1945, pt.1; ed. 1947, pt.1; Hudson 1988, 124-25, 164). For Harry Bailly's attack would have warmed the heart of any Canterbury monk hoping to sustain the pilgrim trade. The Host (treated with admiration in the *Beryn* prologue) shames the Pardoner into an angry silence and so saves the day for the shrine of St Thomas. The humiliation and exposure of the Pardoner are, then, processes begun in *The Canterbury Tales* and continued, for his own reasons, by the *Beryn* author, to a point at which the Pardoner and his role became markedly different.

   One further factor helps to explain the extremity of the *Beryn* author's attack. The documents concerning the arrangements for the fifth jubilee indicate that Pope Martin V was not entirely pleased with decisions taken by the archbishop and prior without his consent, particularly in the granting of a plenary indulgence, an act which the pope claimed as his prerogative. Likening Archbishop Chichele and Prior Wodenesburgh to 'damned angels' who were guilty of 'unheard-of presumption and reckless sacrilege', he sent two emissaries to

Canterbury in 1423 for a post-mortem (Woodruff 1932, 23; Foreville 1958, 181-82; Jacob 1967, 47-48). It may be that in attacking Chaucer's Pardoner, who 'streight was comen fro the court of Rome' with his walet 'Bretful of pardoun comen from Rome al hoot' (GP 671, 687) a monk of Christ Church was also expressing the antagonism felt by him, his brothers and his superiors towards papal authority, and their sense of grievance at Pope Martin's reluctance to grant their request.

To credit the *Beryn* author with some independence of motive has the effect of allowing a revaluation of his achievement. That the prologue is derivative goes without saying, but it is far from being slavish imitation. The imaginative life of Chaucer's composition has been internalized to the point where the *Beryn* author can confidently enjoy creative integrity, if not absolute autonomy. His liberties with the Wife of Bath's character, components of which are attributed to the Pardoner, and especially to Kitt, have already been noted in passing, but deserve closer attention because they provide support for the contention that the *Beryn* author is not so much a plagiarizing hack as a sophisticated writer who 'possessed' *The Canterbury Tales* to the point where he could reconstruct its features in his own idiom, according to his own priorities, and with a clear understanding of genre.

Hailed by many a modern reader as one of the most memorable and successful of the personalities whom Chaucer creates, the Wife of Bath is given little prominence by the *Beryn* author. Her one appearance occurs after supper when, 'so wery she had no will to walk', she takes the Prioress by the hand and invites her 'Pryvely' into the garden of the inn to inspect the plants and then share some wine with the innkeeper's wife in her parlour (281-83). The Prioress accepts, and so they enter, 'Passing forth sofftly into the herbery' (289). This muted representation of Dame Alys is consistent with her practice of spending much time with a female 'gossib' (WBProl III.243, 529, 544, 548), and her enjoyment of walking from house to house to hear 'sondry talys' (WBProl III.547), but mention of her other quirks and enthusiasms is omitted. That is because, as suggested earlier, the *Beryn* author has another use for them, for in Kitt the characteristics of the Wife of Bath find a new form (Darjes and Rendall 1985, 423-27). Here is a woman who behaves as Alys did in her youth: she is sexually experienced; anticipates and betters the wiles of an (admittedly bogus) clerk; reaps financial reward from her stratagems; and is master not only of the Pardoner but also of her regular lover, for whom she devises a role in the humiliation of the Pardoner. She even copies one of the Wife of Bath's most successful ploys (WBProl III.575-84) in telling the Pardoner of a presumably invented dream, a ploy that flatters the Pardoner by allowing him to display his 'authority' as an interpreter, and which encourages him to think that she is ripe for sexual approach (99-116).

The 'recycling' of Chaucerian characters occurs also in the case of the Pardoner, whose disappointment in love recalls that of Absolon in The Miller's Tale (Darjes and Rendall 1985,

421-23). Thus the sudden dousing of the Pardoner's expectations at Kitt's door as he demands
the return of his pilgrim's staff, traditionally associated with tumescent male desire (Zacher
1976, 109), is not unlike the deflation of self-image which Absolon undergoes at Alison's
shot-window:

> For who hath love longing, and is of corage hote,
> He hath ful many a myry thought tofore his delyte,
> And right so had the Pardonere, and was in evil plighte;
> For fayling of his purpose he was nothing in ese. (494-97)

Through anger and jealousy he becomes 'almost wood' (501), and when he considers that
another man has enjoyed Kitt's company at his expense his thoughts turn to 'vengaunce' (503),
before he asks for the return of his staff 'spitouslich' (520). Failing in his bid for retribution,
he can only 'curs his angir to aswage, / And was distract of his wit and in grete dispeyr' (628-
29). Absolon, similarly affected by 'love-longynge' (MilT I.3679), suffers the indignity of
kissing Alison's backside and experiences the same emotions as the Pardoner on realizing that
Nicholas has supplanted him: ' . . . on his lippe he gan for anger byte, / And to hymself he
seyde, "I shall thee quyte" ' (MilT I.3745-46). In a frenzied state he rubs his mouth with the
detritus of the ground outside the carpenter's shop, suddenly cured of his erotomania, 'heeled
of his maladie' (MilT I.3757). Absolon, of course, takes quite effective revenge in assaulting
Nicholas with a hot coulter, and to this may be compared the success of the Pardoner in hitting
Kitt's lover on the nose with a ladle.

The migration of detail from its 'original' source in *The Canterbury Tales* to new locations
in the prologue to *Beryn*, the borrowing of descriptions and turns of phrase originally
associated with one character for use with another, may be taken as evidence of artistic failure
on the author's part. Alternatively, it may indicate that literary 'character', as it is generally
understood today, was not, to a medieval writer, inviolate, but more a loose amalgam of
ingredients from various sources, any one of which could be borrowed and recombined
elsewhere. Such a technique of personal delineation is, after all, one that Chaucer himself
used, as Jill Mann has shown (1973). It is a principle of composition which extends beyond
character to the architecture of the narrative itself. Two tales in particular, those of the Miller
and Reeve, are quarries for the *Beryn* author's building materials, as the reappearance of
'Absolon' in the guise of the Pardoner already suggests.

The sparring of Kitt and Pardoner, using wit and words, is in the same vein as the contest
between native wit (or low cunning) and educated intelligence which informs both The Miller's
Tale and The Reeve's Tale. There, clerks are set against ignorant people and (eventually) win.
In the *Beryn* version of this scenario the tables are turned and a supposedly clever clerk is
discredited by the more subtle manoeuvres of his adversary which, ironically, include his being

blinded by flattery along the lines of 'you clerks are so much cleverer than the like of us' (a strategy earlier used, but with less success, by the Miller of The Reeve's Tale, I.4122-26). Turns of phrase echo the source of the *Beryn* author's inspiration. He asks his audience 'who is that a vomain coud nat make his berd'? (436) and the Pardoner later grieves at the 'makeing of his berd' (622) at the hands of a woman. The proverbial expression is amusing applied to the Pardoner, who is notoriously clean-shaven (GP 689-91), but it also recalls Symkyn's comment as he sees through the attempts of John and Aleyn to outwit him: 'Yet kan a millere make a clerkes berd' (RvT I.4096).

Again, the prologue to *Beryn* is an 'argument of herbergage', to use the Cook's phrase (CkProl I.4329), along the lines of that adumbrated in his own fragmentary tale, and explored at length in the preceding two. In this species of tale crucial concerns are who lodges with whom, in which bed, and with which other person. The 'herbergage' topic and its likely outcome are announced at the moment when the Pardoner seeks out Kitt for the second time. 'He wold be loggid with hir, that was his hole entencioun' (301), although in the event 'hym had bette be iloggit al nyght in a myere / Then he was the same nyght' (304-05). The accommodation which the pilgrims find at the Cheker of the hope, termed 'hire herbegage' (379), is satisfactory enough, and the Pardoner, who expects that he will be sharing Kitt's bed, congratulates himself on being 'iloggit . . . best' and at no cost, for he intends to pick her purse (374-76). He is, of course, disappointed in Kitt on both counts, and so prays to St Julian, the patron saint of hospitality, that her own travels be damned, ' That the devill hire shuld spede on watir and on londe, / So to disseyve a traveling man of his herbegage' (626-27). The Pardoner suffers his final ignominy when he is forced to seek his 'logging' in a dog's litter. Even then ' The warrok' will not let him rest (632-48).

Once the nocturnal fracas gets under way the main source of influence shifts to The Reeve's Tale (Darjes and Rendall 1985, 430-31). As in The Reeve's Tale, a dark interior, sleeping figures, and an individual intent on erotic adventure are the prelude to farcical happenings (473-77 and RvT I.4153-98). In pursuit of the Pardoner, Kitt's lover is described as 'Graspyng aftir with the staff' (528) to hit the Pardoner, whom he 'fond' (529), recalling indirectly the way in which John the clerk 'graspeth by the walles to and fro, / To fynde a staf' (RvT I.4293-94). Later, in a more cautious frame of mind, Kitt's lover encourages Jak the innkeeper to go and fetch light because 'thow knowest bette then I / Al the estris of this house' (555-56), a familiarity with an interior shared by the miller's wife in The Reeve's Tale, who is more successful than John in finding a staff because she 'knew the estres bet' (RvT I.4295). Deceptive appearances, caused by the glimmering of the moon as it reflects on Symkyn's bald head, cause the final uproar of The Reeve's Tale (RvT I.4297-301). As if Jak remembers the fate of the Trumpington miller he declines to fetch light 'For by the blysyng of the cole he myght se myne hede' (561). So the action continues in absolute darkness, with the Pardoner finding a ladle when 'he graspid ferthermore to have somwhat in honde' (573) and with the

Host, hurting his shin, obliged 'to grope where to sete' (591) much as, in the pantomime of
The Reeve's Tale, Symkyn's wife 'groped heer and ther' and 'gropeth alwey forther with hir
hond' (RvT I.4217, 4222) in order to find the cradle which signals (or so she thinks) that she
has found her own, adjacent, bed. Fortunately for the Pardoner, and necessarily if the pilgrim
company is to return to London intact, he endures no physical and public defeat — not least
because, by contrast with the moonlit scene at Trumpington, Jak and Kitt's lover cannot find
their quarry (605) and so they take the latter's advice, 'Sith the moon is down, for to go to rest'
(610). When the pilgrims do set out the next morning the Reeve and his tale are not entirely
forgotten: in order to avoid detection the Pardoner hides among his companions 'And evirmore
he held hym amydward the route' (670). The Reeve, for other reasons, rode at the rear, 'And
evere he rood the hyndreste of oure route' (GP 622).

The prologue to *Beryn* is a tale based in contemporary city life in the manner of the
fabliaux of Fragment I of *The Canterbury Tales*. It reveals as much about medieval Canterbury
as The Miller's Tale does about Oxford, The Reeve's Tale does about Cambridge and its
environs, and The Cook's Tale begins to do about London (Rowland 1979, 207-08). Mention
has already been made of the authentic descriptions of Christ Church, its architecture, pilgrim
trade, and monastery; of the city and its defences; and of the functioning of a major pilgrim inn,
the Checker of the hope. Typical of the verisimilitude with which such places are treated is the
author's description of the inn garden or 'herbery' (Crisp 1924, I, 20-23) in which the Wife of
Bath and Prioress walk: there

> . . . many a herbe grewe for sew and surgery,
> And al the aleyis feir and parid and raylid and imakid,
> The sauge and the isope ifrettid and istakid,
> And othir beddis by an by fressh idight,
> For comers to the hoost righte a sportful sight (290-94).

Such topographical detail is entirely in keeping with, say, Chaucer's account of John's house
and its neighbourhood in Oxford, or Symkyn's fenland mill at Trumpington (Bennett 1974,
34-40, 111-12).

In the process of his creative engagement with Chaucer's narratives, the *Beryn* author
maintains a keen sense of what is appropriate to the genre, thereby producing one of the rare
examples of an English fabliau (Winstead 1988, 226; Robbins 1970). The descriptive realism
usually associated with this species of narrative has already been amply demonstrated. But
once the climactic action of the night gets under way the realism slips into another gear. There
are then numerous references to the furnishings, fittings and internal design of the Cheker of
the hope as the three men blunder about in the dark: the candles (425, 473), the opening and
locking mechanism on Kitt's door (477-79), the hosteller's bed (531), the key to the kitchen

(544), the bedchamber of Jak's wife, which is above Kitt's (545), the hall where guests take supper, also on an upper floor, where there is a fireplace (550-52), the pans, water-cans and ladle (565-66, 574, 587), the dog's litter under the stairs (632-33). Now this amount of detail has the effect of making the interior of the inn seem credible and tangible, but in a sense that is a side-effect. The primary purpose is functional: everything mentioned has a use in the unfolding of the action, and is introduced, like a stage property, because it is necessary. Once the usefulness of the object or place has passed, it is forgotten. Such 'disposable realism', if that is an appropriate term, is a familiar feature of the genre (Muscatine 1957, 59-67).

Also characteristic of the fabliau is a strong dramatic element. It finds expression chiefly through dialogue and through episodes of fast action. In addition, the *Beryn* author attends to the expressiveness of movement, posture, gesture and facial expression. This makes the dramatic content of his composition considerably more interesting than it might be in a run-of-the-mill fabliau, and suggests on his part a keen appreciation of the language of the human body. He deploys body language sparingly, using it in the main as a means of communication between the Pardoner and Kitt. As with other forms of language, she is considerably more successful than he is in using it as an instrument of power and control. Thus he signals to her his attitude and intentions in conventional straightforward terms: an embrace (25, 40), a tweak of the chin (47), an amorous look: he 'unlasid his both eyen liddes, / And lokid hire in the visage paramour amyddis' (67-68), a hand on her breast (313). Kitt reads the signs and turns them to her own advantage. But the Pardoner is completely taken in by Kitt's own performance, not least because she is a much better amateur actress. Thus to engage his sympathy for the invented death of Jenkyn Harpour she enacts an impressive range of emotionally charged actions. She weeps, wiping her eyes gently 'with hire napron feir and white iwassh' (33), the very picture of female distress. The tears are superlatively pitiful, and ludicrous to the audience, if not to the Pardoner: 'As grete as eny mylstone upward gon they stert' (35). Weeping and wailing, she wrings her hands 'For love of hir swetyng that sat so nyghe hire hert' (36) and concludes her no doubt well rehearsed business with a display of misery that invites an affectionate gesture: 'She snyffith, sighith and shooke hire hede and made rouful chere' (39).

Beneath the gaiety or 'chaff' of the narrative lies, in Chaucerian manner, a rather more serious content or 'fruit' or, to use the *Beryn* author's own variant of the familiar metaphors, 'yolke' within the 'white' (732). Its notable manifestation concerns the question of fellowship, adopted from *The Canterbury Tales* as an ideal with an alarming propensity to disintegration (Zacher 1976, 87-101). However, the location of the main threat to fellowship is moved away from the quarrelsome relations of the pilgrims themselves and towards an external situation, that of the scheming of Kitt and her accomplices.

At the outset, 'feleshipp' refers to the company of pilgrims (118, 370, 675). It has positive connotations and is actively supported as an improving species of social organization by the Host, who reminds the Miller and Pardoner that they are 'in company of honest men and good' (159). Falling in with the will of the majority and imitating their actions — in this case worshipping at the shrine of St Thomas — will, he suggests, have a beneficial effect, 'For who doith aftir company may lyve the bet in rest' (162). But in spite of the Host's best efforts, rival fellowships, complete with a rival 'covenaunte' (300) of an unsavoury or subversive kind, exist and flourish. If they do not directly threaten the dominant fellowship of pilgrims and their values of honesty, courtesy and good reputation, they at least indicate the potential for social and moral division. Thus Kitt encourages the Pardoner to 'Ete and be mery' and break his fast rather than wait for the 'feleshipp' of the other pilgrims (71-72). False fellowship is particularly associated with the alliance formed by Kitt, her lover and Jak the hosteller, one which prompts even the *Beryn* author to comment sympathetically on what is in store for the Pardoner:

> It was a shrewid company — they had served so many oon
> With such manere of feleshipp, ne kepe I nevir to dele,
> Ne no man that lovith his worship and his hele. (464-66)

Later they are called 'the felisshipp that should nevir thryve' (534), and it is with certain relief that the Pardoner escapes a second drubbing by hiding among the pilgrims, the 'feleshippe' proper (657, 675) or the 'company', as it is here repeatedly described (656, 661, 666). The Pardoner feigns merriment in order to merge better into his surroundings: he 'made lightsom cher' (663) and sings (671). It is as if he has learnt the value (or at least the usefulness) of the true fellowship which this pilgrimage represents and perhaps even of being 'gentil' (658).

The *Beryn* author was one of the earliest poets working in the English tradition to register the 'anxiety of influence', that sense of being indebted to, yet needing to escape from, the work of an earlier English writer. Much of what Spearing says of Lydgate's attempts, in *The Siege of Thebes*, to come to terms with Chaucer's legacy, is also true of the author of the prologue: his perception of a *tessera*, or loose end which forms a link, in the form of the incompleteness of Chaucer's work; his deliberate use of allusions to Chaucer's poetry; his ability to free himself from dependence upon his master; his reliance on an audience well versed in Chaucer's poetry; and his periodic success in achieving irony and an eloquence perfectly appropriate to sense (Spearing 1984). The major difference lies in what the two poets respond to, which in turn has consequences for the kind of writing each produces. Thus Lydgate's *Siege* 'completes' The Knight's Tale with another romance, and in so doing its author affects a high style of latinate language full of formal rhetorical devices. The *Beryn* author, for his part, 'completes' the sequence begun by the fabliau tales which follow The Knight's Tale, choosing for that purpose a demotic style. It is almost as if Lydgate and the *Beryn* author, writing at the same time and both Benedictine monks, were collaborators in a project designed to continue and complete *The Canterbury Tales.*

Whatever the truth of the matter, the *Beryn* prologue deserves to be considered more carefully for the evidence it provides about the reception of *The Canterbury Tales* in the fifteenth century. It has become generally accepted that, following the dispersal, retirement or death of Chaucer's immediate public, the wide range of his writing fell on deaf ears. Early fifteenth-century readers, it is said, set more store by his love lyrics and dream visions than by *Troilus* and *The Canterbury Tales.* That secondary audience, as recently described by Strohm (1982), is said to have existed in the later years of Chaucer's life, then to have enlarged rapidly after his death. Socially, it extended wider and deeper than the knights and esquires of the king's households, lawyers, chancery figures and other civil servants who have been identified as members of the Chaucer circle. Instead, its base was in a literate middle estate of landed gentry and prosperous merchants with a fascination for aristocratic mores, a social order relatively unaffected by the rhythms of professional careers and the vagaries of court patronage. In terms of literary taste, at least on the evidence of anthologies, it was narrowly predisposed towards compositions self-evidently courtly (Pearsall 1977, 212-14; Green 1980, 9-10; Strohm 1982, 18).

Embedded in the prologue to *Beryn*, as we have seen, are courtly aspirations, and so it would appear to appeal to much the same kind of audience. Beneath the surface excitement there is a deep-rooted conservative, orthodox element. Hierarchies are not challenged, genres are not violated. On the other hand, the poetry of the prologue is of a radically different kind from that of other Chaucerian compositions of the early fifteenth century designed for the emergent élite. Unlike those works, it is prepared to embrace, and to respond to, some of Chaucer's most innovative writing, writing which was otherwise unpopular in the fifteenth century (Strohm 1982, 24-25). It may be, then, that the *Beryn* author's audience is in two senses transitional: it spans the period between Chaucer's last years and the 1420s, showing that *The Canterbury Tales* in all their variety enjoyed continuing appeal beyond Chaucer's immediate circle; and it simultaneously accepts the imaginative stimulation of Chaucer's work while wanting to reassert unquestioned, traditional values in a way that was to become more and more the norm (Strohm 1982, 27).

The continuity of appeal from *The Canterbury Tales* through to the prologue to *Beryn* indicates that there was in his larger, secondary audience an element which possessed a keen appreciation of a wide range of his techniques (Winstead 1988, 232). If, on Chaucer's death, there was a 'dispersion' of his literary public, the narrowing of literary taste did not occur until later, in the 1420s rather than the 1400s (Strohm 1982, 8). It is difficult therefore to accept Strohm's conclusion (1982, 15):

Available evidence suggests that Chaucer's public did indeed fail to renew itself, and that by the early years of the fifteenth century it had ceased to exist as a public likely or able to provide a setting encouraging to the creation of literary works.

The evidence available from the prologue to *Beryn* suggests otherwise. Granted that the author was in all probability, like other imitators, on the fringes of court culture, he was nevertheless central in articulating for another, as yet unidentified, section of Chaucer's audience the manifold attractions of *The Canterbury Tales*.

Darwin College
University of Kent

NOTES

1. References are to Furnivall and Stone. I have emended lines from that edition on the basis of photographs of the text of MS Alnwick 455 taken by me in September 1985. For permission to reproduce the MS for the purposes of research I am grateful to Mr Colin Shrimpton of the Northumberland Estates Office.
2. My thanks are due to Pamela King for pointing out the relevance of Chichele's policies.

REFERENCES

Anderson, R., ed., 1793	*A Complete Edition of the Poets of Great Britain*, vol. 1, *The Poetical Works of Geoffrey Chaucer*, Edinburgh
Bashe, E. J., 1933	The Prologue of *The Tale of Beryn*, *PQ*, 12, pp. 1-16
Baugh, A. C., 1948	The Middle English Period (1100-1500), in *A Literary History of England*, ed. Baugh, book 1, part 1, New York; 2nd edn London, 1967
Bell, J., ed., 1782	*The Poets of Great Britain: Complete from Chaucer to Churchill*, vol. 6, Edinburgh
Bennett, H. S., 1948	*Chaucer and the Fifteenth Century* [corrected edn], Oxford History of English Literature, vol. 2, pt 1, Oxford
Bennett, J. A. W., 1974	*Chaucer at Oxford and at Cambridge*, Oxford

Besserman, Lawrence, and Melvin Storm, 1983 — Forum: Chaucer's Pardoner, *PMLA*, 98, pp. 405-06

Blake, N. F., 1985 — *The Textual Tradition of the Canterbury Tales*, London

Bowers, John M., 1985 — *The Tale of Beryn* and *The Siege of Thebes*: Alternative Ideas of *The Canterbury Tales*, *SAC*, 7, pp. 23-50

Brent, Cecil, 1880 — Pilgrims' Signs, *Archaeologia Cantiana*, 13, pp. 111-15

Brewer, D. S., 1968 — Class Distinction in Chaucer, *Speculum*, 43, pp. 290-305

Caviness, Madeline Harrison, 1977 — *The Early Stained Glass of Canterbury Cathedral: Circa 1175-1220*, Princeton

———— 1981 — *The Windows of Christ Church Cathedral, Canterbury*, Corpus Vitrearum Medii Aevi Great Britain, vol. 2, Oxford

[Chalmers, A., ed.], 1810 — *The Works of the English Poets, from Chaucer to Cowper . . .*, vol. 1: *The Works of Geoffrey Chaucer*, London

Crisp, F., 1924 — *Mediaeval Gardens, 'Flowery Medes' and Other Arrangements of Herbs, Flowers and Shrubs Grown in the Middle Ages . . .*, ed. C. C. Paterson, 2 vols, London

Darjes, Bradley, and Thomas Rendall, 1985 — A Fabliau in the *Prologue to the Tale of Beryn*, *MS*, 47, pp. 416-31

Darton, F. J. H., trans., 1904 — *Tales of the Canterbury Pilgrims Retold from Chaucer and Others*, introduction by F. J. Furnivall, illus. by H. Thomson, 2nd edn, London

Davis, J. F., 1963 — Lollards, Reformers and St Thomas of Canterbury, *University of Birmingham Historical Journal*, 9, pp. 1-15

Doyle, A. I., and M. B. Parkes, 1979 — A Palaeographical Introduction, in *The Canterbury Tales: A Facsimile and Transcription of the Hengwrt Manuscript, with Variants from the Ellesmere Manuscript*, ed. Paul G. Ruggiers, Norman, Oklahoma, pp. xix-xlix

Dufty, A. R., 1962 — Review of *Castles and Cannon: A Study in Early Fortification in England*, by B. H. St J. O'Neil, London, 1960, *Arch. J.*, 119, pp. 367-70

Fleming, John V., 1985 — Chaucer and Erasmus on the Pilgrimage to Canterbury: An Iconographical Speculation, in *The Popular Literature of Medieval England*, ed. Thomas J. Heffernan, Tennessee Studies in Literature, vol. 28, Knoxville, pp. 148-66

Foreville, R., 1958 — *Le Jubilé de saint Thomas Becket du XIIIe au XVe siècle (1220-1470): étude et documents*, Bibliothèque Générale de l'Ecole Pratique des Hautes-Etudes, VIe section, Paris

French, W. H., and C. B. Hale, eds, 1930 — *Middle English Metrical Romances*, New York; rpt. in 2 vols, New York 1964

Frere, S. S., S. Stow, and P. Bennett, 1982 — *Excavations on the Roman and Medieval Defences of Canterbury*, The Archaeology of Canterbury, vol. 2, Maidstone

Furnivall, F. J., and W. G. Stone, eds, 1876 — *The Tale of Beryn, with a Prologue of the Merry Adventure of the Pardoner with a Tapster at Canterbury*, Part 1: with a Map of Canterbury in 1588 . . . and Ogilby's Plan of the Road from London to Canterbury in 1675, Chaucer Society, 2nd series, No. 17: Supplementary Canterbury Tales, 1, London

——— 1887 — *The Tale of Beryn* . . . Part 2: Forewords by F. J. Furnivall, Notes by F. Vipan . . . and Glossary by W. G. Stone; with an Essay on Analogs of the Tale, by W. A. Clouston, Chaucer Society, 2nd series, No. 24: Supplementary Canterbury Tales, 2, London

——— 1909 — *The Tale of Beryn* . . . , EETS, ES 105, London

Green, Richard Firth, 1980 — *Poets and Princepleasers: Literature and the English Court in the Late Middle Ages*, Toronto, Buffalo, London

Harvey, John H., 1944 — *Henry Yevele c. 1320 to 1400: The Life of an English Architect*, London

——— 1985 — Henry Yeveley and the Nave of Canterbury Cathedral, *Canterbury Cathedral Chronicle*, No. 79, pp. 20-32

Hudson, Anne, ed., 1978 — *Selections from English Wycliffite Writings*, Cambridge

——— 1988 — *The Premature Reformation: Wycliffite Texts and Lollard History*, Oxford

IMEV, 1943 — *The Index of Middle English Verse*, by Carleton Brown and Rossell Hope Robbins, New York

Jacob, E. F., ed., 1945 — *The Register of Henry Chichele Archbishop of Canterbury 1414-1443*, vol. 3, Oxford

——— ed., 1947 — *The Register of Henry Chichele . . .*, vol. 4, Oxford

——— 1967 — *Archbishop Henry Chichele*, London

Jones, W. R., 1973 — Lollards and Images: The Defense of Religious Art in Later Medieval England, *JHI*, 34, pp. 27-50

Jusserand, J. J., 1925 — *English Wayfaring Life in the Middle Ages (XIVth Century)*, trans. Lucy Toulmin Smith, 3rd edn, London

Kaiser, R., 1958 — *Medieval English: An Old English and Middle English Anthology*, 3rd edn, revised, Berlin

Kellogg, Alfred L., and Louis A. Haselmayer, 1951 — Chaucer's Satire of the Pardoner, *PMLA*, 66, pp. 251-77

Kittredge, G. L., 1915 — *Chaucer and His Poetry*, Cambridge, Mass.

Knapp, Daniel, 1972 — The Relyk of a Seint: A Gloss on Chaucer's Pilgrimage, *ELH*, 39, pp. 1-26

Kohl, S., 1983 — Chaucer's Pilgrims in Fifteenth-Century Literature, *FCS*, 7, pp. 221-36

Loomis, Roger Sherman, and Rudolph Willard, 1948 — *Medieval English Verse and Prose in Modernized Versions*, New York

McIntosh, H. M., 1931 — The Literary Background of The Tale of Beryn, unpublished Ph. D. dissertation, University of Chicago

Manly, John M., and Edith Rickert, eds, 1940 — *The Text of the Canterbury Tales: Studied on the Basis of All Known Manuscripts*, vol. 1: *Descriptions of the Manuscripts*, Chicago and London

Mann, Jill, 1973 — *Chaucer and Medieval Estates Satire: The Literature of Social Classes and the General Prologue to the Canterbury Tales*, Cambridge

Mitchiner, M., 1986 — *Medieval Pilgrim and Secular Badges*, London

Muscatine, Charles, 1957 — *Chaucer and the French Tradition: A Study in Style and Meaning*, Berkeley and Los Angeles

—— 1986 — *The Old French Fabliaux*, New Haven and London. (Ch. 2 is a revised version of his ' The Social Background of the Old French Fabliaux', *Genre*, 9 (1976), 1-19.)

Ormrod, W. M., 1989 — The Personal Religion of Edward III, *Speculum*, 64, pp. 849-77

Owen, Charles A., 1983 — Forum: Chaucer's Pardoner, *PMLA*, 98, p. 254

Parr, Johnstone, 1952 — Astronomical Dating for Some of Lydgate's Poems, *PMLA*, 67, pp. 251-58

Pearsall, Derek, 1977 — *Old English and Middle English Poetry*, The Routledge History of English Poetry, vol. 1, London

RCHM, 1872 — *Third Report of the Royal Commission on Historical Manuscripts* [c. 673], London

Ritson, J., 1802 — *Bibliographia Poetica: A Catalogue of English Poets, of the Twelfth, Thirteenth, Fourteenth, and Sixteenth, Centurys, with a Short Account of Their Works*, London

Robbins, R. H., 1970 — The English Fabliau: Before and After Chaucer, *Moderna Språk*, 64, pp. 231-44

Robertson, W. A. Scott, 1880 — The Crypt of Canterbury Cathedral, Part 2, *Archaeologia Cantiana*, 13, pp. 500-51

Rowland, Beryl, 1979 — What Chaucer Did to the Fabliau, *SN*, 51, pp. 205-13

Saintsbury, G., 1908 — The English Chaucerians, in *The Cambridge History of English Literature*, vol. 2: *The End of the Middle Ages*, pp. 197-222

Seward, D., 1987 — *Henry V as Warlord*, London

Skeat, Walter W., 1900 — *The Chaucer Canon, with a Discussion of the Works Associated with the Name of Geoffrey Chaucer*, Oxford

Spearing, A. C., 1984 — Lydgate's Canterbury Tale: *The Siege of Thebes* and Fifteenth-Century Chaucerianism, in *Fifteenth-Century Studies: Recent Essays*, ed. Robert F. Yeager, Hamden, Conn., pp. 333-64

Spurgeon, Caroline F. E., 1925 — *Five Hundred Years of Chaucer Criticism and Allusion 1357-1900*, 3 vols, Cambridge; rpt. New York, 1960; originally published as Series 48-50, 52-56 of The Chaucer Society publications, London, 1908-17

Stanley, A. P., 1912 — *Historical Memorials of Canterbury*, 11th edn, London

Storm, Melvin, 1982a — 'A Culpa et a Poena': Christ's Pardon and the Pardoner's, *NM*, 83, pp. 439-42

——— 1982b — The Pardoner's Invitation: Quaestor's Bag or Becket's Shrine?, *PMLA*, 97, pp. 810-18

Strohm, Paul, 1982 — Chaucer's Fifteenth-Century Audience and the Narrowing of the 'Chaucer Tradition', *SAC*, 4, pp. 3-32

Tamanini, M. E. M., ed., 1969 — The Tale of Beryn: An Edition with Introduction, Notes, and Glossary, unpublished Ph. D. thesis, New York University

Tatton-Brown, T., 1987 — *Medieval Inns in Canterbury*, Canterbury

Thynne, W., ed., 1532 — Geoffrey Chaucer, *The Works 1532, with Supplementary Material from the Editions of 1542, 1561, 1598 and 1602*, introduction by D. S. Brewer, Menston, 1969

Tupper, Frederick, 1914 — The Pardoner's Tavern, *JEGP*, 13, pp. 553-65

Turner, D. H., 1976 — The Customary of the Shrine of St Thomas Becket, *Canterbury Cathedral Chronicle*, No. 70, pp. 16-22

Turner, Hilary L., 1971 — *Town Defences in England and Wales: An Architectural and Documentary Study A.D. 900-1500*, London

Tyrwhitt, T., ed., 1798 — *The Canterbury Tales of Chaucer, to which are added an essay on his language and versification and an introductory discourse . . . With Memoir and Critical Dissertation by the Rev. George Gilfillan*, 3 vols, rpt. Edinburgh 1860

Urry, J., ed., 1721 — *The Works of Geoffrey Chaucer, Compared with the Former Editions, and Many Valuable MSS. Out of which, Three Tales are Added which were Never Before Printed . . .*, London

Warton, T., 1774 — *The History of English Poetry, from the Close of the Eleventh Century to the Commencement of the Eighteenth Century, to which are prefixed two dissertations . . .*, vol. 1, London

Williams, A., 1965 — Some Documents on English Pardoners, 1350-1400, in *Mediaeval Studies in Honor of Urban Tigner Holmes, Jr.*, ed. J. Mahoney and J. E. Keller, University of North Carolina Studies in the Romance Languages and Literatures, No. 56, Chapel Hill, pp. 197-207

Winstead, Karen A., 1988 — The *Beryn*-Writer as a Reader of Chaucer, *ChauR*, 22, pp. 225-33

Woodruff, C. Eveleigh, 1911 — A Monastic Chronicle Lately Discovered at Christ Church, Canterbury: with Introduction and Notes, *Archaeologia Cantiana*, 29, pp. 47-84

——— 1932 — The Financial Aspect of the Cult of St Thomas of Canterbury as Revealed by a Study of the Monastic Records, *Archaeologia Cantiana*, 44, pp. 13-32

Wright, T., ed., 1847 and 1851 — *The Canterbury Tales of Geoffrey Chaucer: A New Text, with Illustrative Notes*, in *Early English Poetry, Ballads, and Popular Literature of the Middle Ages . . .*, vols. 24, 26, Percy Society, 68, 91

Wylie, James Hamilton, and William Templeton Waugh, 1929 — *The Reign of Henry the Fifth,* vol. 3: *1415-1422*, Cambridge

Zacher, Christian K., 1976 — *Curiosity and Pilgrimage: The Literature of Discovery in Fourteenth-Century England*, Baltimore and London

Zupitza, J., ed., 1892

Specimens of All the Accessible Unprinted Manuscripts of the Canterbury Tales: The Doctor-Pardoner Link, and Pardoner's Prologue and Tale, Chaucer Society, first series, no. 81, London; rpt. New York and London, 1967